Implementing DevOps with Microsoft Azure

Leverage Visual Studio Team Services to automate Microsoft
Azure deployments and incorporate the DevOps culture

Mitesh Soni

BIRMINGHAM - MUMBAI

Implementing DevOps with Microsoft Azure

First published: April 2017

Production reference: 1270417

Published by Packt Publishing Ltd.
Livery Place
35 Livery Street
Birmingham
B3 2PB, UK.

ISBN 978-1-78712-702-9

www.packtpub.com

Credits

Author

Mitesh Soni

Reviewer

Roberto Freato

Commissioning Editor

Pratik Shah

Acquisition Editor

Divya Poojari

Content Development Editor

Monika Sangwan

Technical Editor

Bhagyashree Rai

Copy Editor

Tom Jacob

Project Coordinator

Kinjal Bari

Proofreader

Safis Editing

Indexer

Francy Puthiry

Graphics

Kirk D'Penha

Production Coordinator

Aparna Bhagat

About the Author

Mitesh Soni is an avid learner with 10 years' experience in the IT industry. He is an SCJP, SCWCD, VCP, IBM Urbancode, and IBM Bluemix certified professional. He loves DevOps and cloud computing and also has an interest in programming in Java. He finds design patterns fascinating. He believes "a picture is worth a thousand words."

He occasionally contributes to `http://etutorialsworld.com`. He loves to play with kids, fiddle with his camera, and take photographs at Indroda Park. He is addicted to taking pictures without knowing many technical details. He lives in the capital of Mahatma Gandhi's home state.

Mitesh has authored following books with Packt:

- *DevOps for Web Development*: `https://www.packtpub.com/networking-and-servers/devops-web-development`
- *DevOps for Web Developers [Video]*: `https://www.packtpub.com/web-development/devops-web-developers-video`
- *Jenkins Essentials*: `https://www.packtpub.com/application-development/jenkins-essentials`
- *Learning Chef*: `https://www.packtpub.com/networking-and-servers/learning-chef`

I've missed more than 9,000 shots in my career. I've lost almost 300 games. 26 times, I've been trusted to take the game-winning shot and missed. I've failed over and over and over again in my life. And that is why I succeed.

—Michael Jordan

Acknowledgment

I want to say thanks and share my gratitude for everything I've been blessed with. I would like to thank Jigisha-Nitesh, Dada-Dadi, Hemant-Priyanka, Mihir-Anupama, Nalini, Kirti, Bindiya, Jai Jamba, Nitesh, Munal, Ashish B, Mayur, Rohini, Aakanksha, Rinka, Pampi, Yohan, Chintan, Ruchi, Navrang, Dharmesh, Rohan Chauhan, Krimali, Chitrang, Kanak, Mitul, Jaideep Bapu, Prakash, Ravi, Kirti, Munal, Nitesh, teachers, and Family members.

Gowri and Sharvil, thanks for being there always. Lots of love to Arya.

I am grateful to Bhagyashri, Aishwarya P, Priya, Vijay, Apoorva, Harshal, Avanti, Raksha, Sourabh, Vishakha, Pradnya, Ashita, Viral, Manisha, Aishwarya I, Vaishnavi, Nidhi, Saurabh, and Raghav, who have always helped me, made me smile, and made my life easier in last few months or so. Without you all, I wouldn't have been able to achieve peace of mind. I value your presence in my life!

Special thanks to Sudeep for all his support in bringing the change and for inspiring all of us.

Special thanks to Bhagyashree for helping in verifying content technically.

About the Reviewer

Roberto Freato has been an independent IT consultant since he started to work. He started working for small software factories while he was studying. After his MSc in Computer Science Engineering with a thesis on *Consumer Cloud Computing*, he specialized in the cloud and Azure. Today, he works as a freelance consultant for major companies in Italy, helping clients to design and kick-off their distributed software solutions. He trains the developer community in his free time, speaking at many conferences. He has been a Microsoft MVP since 2010.

www.PacktPub.com

For support files and downloads related to your book, please visit www.PacktPub.com.

Did you know that Packt offers eBook versions of every book published, with PDF and ePub files available? You can upgrade to the eBook version at www.PacktPub.com and as a print book customer, you are entitled to a discount on the eBook copy. Get in touch with us at service@packtpub.com for more details.

At www.PacktPub.com, you can also read a collection of free technical articles, sign up for a range of free newsletters and receive exclusive discounts and offers on Packt books and eBooks.

https://www.packtpub.com/mapt

Get the most in-demand software skills with Mapt. Mapt gives you full access to all Packt books and video courses, as well as industry-leading tools to help you plan your personal development and advance your career.

Why subscribe?

- Fully searchable across every book published by Packt
- Copy and paste, print, and bookmark content
- On demand and accessible via a web browser

Customer Feedback

Thanks for purchasing this Packt book. At Packt, quality is at the heart of our editorial process. To help us improve, please leave us an honest review on this book's Amazon page at `https://www.amazon.com/dp/1787127028`.

If you'd like to join our team of regular reviewers, you can e-mail us at `customerreviews@packtpub.com`. We award our regular reviewers with free eBooks and videos in exchange for their valuable feedback. Help us be relentless in improving our products!

I would like to dedicate this book to lot of people who gave me the ray of hope amidst darkness. I would like to dedicate this book to Shreyansh (Shreyu – my sister (Jigisha)'s baby boy), who showed me the power of innocence and smile; Vinay Kher, for teaching me how to improve always; my parents, who are always there silently and praying for me; Simba (Priyanka Agashe), for supporting and encouraging me all the time and forcing me to believe in myself; Indian Army, and all brave soldiers in uniform for protecting us; and Sheth G.C. Highschool, Pilvai and its teachers who helped me immensely!

Table of Contents

Preface

DevOps is not just a buzzword now – it is a doctrine or a school of thought to improve application life cycle management processes to make applications effective by utilizing disruptive innovations. It has become a part of a serious discussion in organizations. Hence, a change is required. A change in the culture.

Change is no threat to culture. It only improves the culture using disruptive innovations in recent times.

Often, we make mistakes by focusing too much on the technology or tools, but with DevOps this can be a blunder. This book emphasizes not only the technology but also the organization-specific culture that is more important in cultivating the DevOps culture. DevOps is in an early stage. It is changing the existing culture that invites resistance. It is wise to follow what *Socrates* said:

> *"The secret of change is to focus all your energy, not on fighting the old, but on building the new."*

In this book, we will cover all the key components of DevOps, such as continuous integration, cloud computing – PaaS (Azure App Service or Azure Web Apps and Azure SQL Database), continuous delivery, and continuous deployment; how to automate build integration, provision resources in Microsoft cloud environment; deploying web application into Microsoft Azure Web Apps / App Service Environments; application monitoring available in Microsoft Azure; and load testing available in VSTS and Apache JMeter. The main objective is to manage frequent releases effectively. By automating repetitive processes, we standardized the management of the application life cycle and avoided error-prone manual processes. We also provided governance to application life cycle management by providing approval-based application deployment to different environments.

For continuous integration and continuous release (continuous delivery and continuous deployment), we have used Visual Studio Team Services (VSTS). The orchestration of end-to-end automation and approval-based workflows is managed by VSTS too.

Let's begin our *cultural* journey in the land of DevOps using people (development team, QA team, operations team, cloud team, build engineers, and so on), processes (continuous integration, continuous delivery and continuous deployment, continuous testing, and continuous monitoring), and tools (Microsoft stack)!

What this book covers

Chapter 1, *Microsoft Azure – Cloud Platform and Services,* is all about learning the benefits of PaaS in the DevOps culture, and Microsoft Azure – cloud platform and services. It will cover all the PaaS offerings from Microsoft that are required for deploying a web application. This chapter also covers the basic concepts of Microsoft Cloud that are important for creating, using, and managing platform services effectively for deploying applications.

Chapter 2, *Getting Started with Visual Studio Team Services (VSTS),* introduces the VSTS and the sample application structure that is necessary to understand before automating the process of building and deploying an application in a desired environment. It also explains how to use VSTS to manage versions of code and integrate VSTS with Eclipse IDE so the check-in process can be managed directly from the IDE.

Chapter 3, *Continuous Integration with VSTS,* explains how to configure the application code for automated compilation, unit test case execution, and notifying important stakeholders of the status of the build execution in case of failures and success. It also creates a package file and stores it in a shared folder. After this chapter, we will be ready for deployment if the build execution is successful.

Chapter 4, *Continuous Development with Microsoft Azure Web Apps,* covers App Service (Microsoft Azure Web Apps) in detail. Web Apps is used to deploy an application in the process of continuous delivery and continuous development. It covers how we can create different environments that can be used to deploy web applications. It also covers a brief description of database services and providing secure access to all resources using role-based access, which is significant from the security and governance perspective.

Chapter 5, *Azure App Service Environments,* is bit more theoretical, but covers a premium service of Microsoft Azure platform that can be used for specific use cases that Azure Web Apps may not be able to handle effectively. It not only covers creating ASEs but also provides a detailed comparison of Azure Web Apps and ASE to enhance security. Security is one of the most important parts of application life cycle management, and hence this service increases the value in the context of DevOps.

Chapter 6, *Continuous Delivery to Azure Web Apps and ASE Using VSTS,* presents how to deploy an application in Azure Web Apps and App Service Environment using VSTS. It also includes the security and governance aspect while deploying is different environments to ensure that only authorized persons can perform the deployment operation, and the process has to be verified. This chapter will cover end-to-end automation visualization for deploying an application in the PaaS offering of Microsoft Azure.

`Chapter 7`, *Continuous Monitoring in Cloud Platform*, covers another stepping stone in achieving end-to-end automation, and that is continuous monitoring. We cover the importance of it in different ways to monitor and troubleshoot Azure Web Apps and ASE so we can ensure that the application remains issue-free and highly available.

What you need for this book

This book assumes that you are familiar with at least the Java programming language. Knowledge of core Java and JEE is essential if you want to gain better insights from this book. Having a strong understanding of the deployment of a web application in application servers such as Tomcat will help you to understand the flow quickly.

As the application development life cycle will cover a lot of tools in general, it is essential to have some knowledge of repositories, as well as IDE tools such as Eclipse, and build tools such as Ant and Maven. Knowledge of code analysis tools will make your job easier in configuration and integration; however, it is not vital to perform the exercises given in the book. Most of the configuration steps are mentioned clearly.

You will be walked through the steps required to get familiar with VSTS, Microsoft Azure Web Apps, Microsoft Azure App Service Environments, and Microsoft Azure SQL Database.

For Microsoft Azure, you can use a one month trial access. VSTS also comes with a trial account with some restrictions.

Who this book is for

This book is specially aimed at developers, technical leads, testers, and operational professionals, who are the target readers and will want to jump start Microsoft Azure PaaS offerings such as App Services and SQL Database to host applications. Readers are aware of the issues faced by development and operations teams as they are stakeholders in the application life cycle management process. The reasons to jump start Microsoft Azure PaaS and VSTS are to understand the importance of their contribution to continuous integration, automated test case execution, and continuous delivery for effective application life cycle management.

No prior experience with continuous integration, cloud computing, continuous delivery, and continuous deployment is assumed. You may be a novice or be experienced with continuous integration tools such as Jenkins and Atlassian Bamboo.

This book covers continuous integration, cloud computing, continuous delivery, and continuous deployment for a sample Spring-based application. The main objective is to see end-to-end automation and implement it on the Microsoft technology stack that can be extended further based on the understanding gained from this book.

Conventions

In this book, you will find a number of text styles that distinguish between different kinds of information. Here are some examples of these styles and an explanation of their meaning.

Code words in text, database table names, folder names, filenames, file extensions, pathnames, dummy URLs, user input, and Twitter handles are shown as follows: "We can achieve this using the `<ipSecurity>` element."

A block of code is set as follows:

```
<configuration>
  <system.webServer>
    <security>
      <ipSecurity allowUnlisted="true" denyAction="NotFound">
        <add allowed="true" ipAddress="xxx.xxx.xxx.xxx"
          subnetMask="255.xxx.xxx.xxx"/>
      </ipSecurity>
    </security>
  </system.webServer>
</configuration>
```

When we wish to draw your attention to a particular part of a code block, the relevant lines or items are set in bold:

```
<configuration>
  <system.webServer>
    <security>
      <ipSecurity allowUnlisted="true" denyAction="NotFound">
        <add allowed="true" ipAddress="xxx.xxx.xxx.xxx"
          subnetMask="255.xxx.xxx.xxx"/>
      </ipSecurity>
    </security>
  </system.webServer>
</configuration>
```

New terms and **important words** are shown in bold. Words that you see on the screen, for example, in menus or dialog boxes, appear in the text like this: "To create a resource group, click on **Resource groups** in the left-hand sidebar menu."

Warnings or important notes appear in a box like this.

Tips and tricks appear like this.

Reader feedback

Feedback from our readers is always welcome. Let us know what you think about this book—what you liked or disliked. Reader feedback is important for us as it helps us develop titles that you will really get the most out of.

To send us general feedback, simply e-mail feedback@packtpub.com, and mention the book's title in the subject of your message.

If there is a topic that you have expertise in and you are interested in either writing or contributing to a book, see our author guide at www.packtpub.com/authors.

Customer support

Now that you are the proud owner of a Packt book, we have a number of things to help you to get the most from your purchase.

Downloading the example code

You can download the example code files for this book from your account at `http://www.p`
`acktpub.com`. If you purchased this book elsewhere, you can visit `http://www.packtpub.c`
`om/support`and register to have the files e-mailed directly to you.

You can download the code files by following these steps:

1. Log in or register to our website using your e-mail address and password.
2. Hover the mouse pointer on the **SUPPORT** tab at the top.
3. Click on **Code Downloads & Errata**.
4. Enter the name of the book in the **Search** box.
5. Select the book for which you're looking to download the code files.
6. Choose from the drop-down menu where you purchased this book from.
7. Click on **Code Download**.

Once the file is downloaded, please make sure that you unzip or extract the folder using the latest version of:

- WinRAR / 7-Zip for Windows
- Zipeg / iZip / UnRarX for Mac
- 7-Zip / PeaZip for Linux

The code bundle for the book is also hosted on GitHub at `https://github.com/PacktPubl`
`ishing/Implementing-DevOps-with-Microsoft-Azure`. We also have other code bundles
from our rich catalog of books and videos available at `https://github.com/PacktPublish`
`ing/`. Check them out!

Downloading the color images of this book

We also provide you with a PDF file that has color images of the screenshots/diagrams used in this book. The color images will help you better understand the changes in the output. You can download this file from `https://www.packtpub.com/sites/default/files/down`
`loads/ImplementingDevOpswithMicrosoftAzure_ColorImages.pdf`.

Errata

Although we have taken every care to ensure the accuracy of our content, mistakes do happen. If you find a mistake in one of our books-maybe a mistake in the text or the code-we would be grateful if you could report this to us. By doing so, you can save other readers from frustration and help us improve subsequent versions of this book. If you find any errata, please report them by visiting http://www.packtpub.com/submit-errata, selecting your book, clicking on the **Errata Submission Form** link, and entering the details of your errata. Once your errata are verified, your submission will be accepted and the errata will be uploaded to our website or added to any list of existing errata under the Errata section of that title.

To view the previously submitted errata, go to https://www.packtpub.com/books/content/support and enter the name of the book in the search field. The required information will appear under the **Errata** section.

Piracy

Piracy of copyrighted material on the Internet is an ongoing problem across all media. At Packt, we take the protection of our copyright and licenses very seriously. If you come across any illegal copies of our works in any form on the Internet, please provide us with the location address or website name immediately so that we can pursue a remedy.

Please contact us at copyright@packtpub.com with a link to the suspected pirated material.

We appreciate your help in protecting our authors and our ability to bring you valuable content.

Questions

If you have a problem with any aspect of this book, you can contact us at questions@packtpub.com, and we will do our best to address the problem.

1
Microsoft Azure – Cloud Platform and Services

I believe that if you show people the problems and you show them the solutions they will be moved to act.

-Bill Gates

This chapter covers details about the basics of cloud computing, a DevOps overview, the benefits of PaaS in the DevOps culture, and Microsoft Azure – cloud platform and services.

It will cover the required PaaS offering from Microsoft that is necessary for deploying a web application. This chapter also covers basic concepts of Microsoft Cloud that are important to create, use, and manage platform services effectively for deploying applications.
In this chapter, we are going to cover the following topics:

- Overview of PaaS and Application PaaS
- Role and benefits of PaaS and aPaaS in DevOps
- Overview of Microsoft Azure Services
- Overview of concepts related to Microsoft Azure

First, let's see what we will cover in this book and then go ahead with the plan step by step.

What we will cover in this book

The overall vision of the book is to use one sample application and perform the following:

- **Automated build**: Using build tools such as Ant or Maven
- **Continuous Integration (CI)**: CI using **Visual Studio Team Services (VSTS)**:
    - Compilation
    - **Unit test execution**: JUnit test cases
    - **Code analysis**: Using SonarQube
- Cloud platform resources
- **CD using VSTS**: Utility tasks for WAR deployment
- **Continuous deployment using VSTS**: Utility tasks for WAR deployment with governance and an approval workflow for the deployment
- **Continuous monitoring and security**: By configuring notifications in the Azure portal and using role-based access

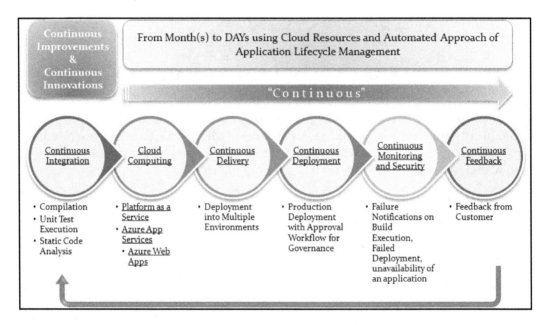

We will integrate Eclipse IDE with the VSTS for repository-related tasks and perform all end-to-end automation operations as described in the preceding diagram. Every chapter is a building block for the next chapter and at the end of the book, we will be able to visualize the technical implementation and high level design in line.

Overview of PaaS and Application PaaS

Evolution is the step-by-step process to reach better alternatives of something that already exists and is adopted. If we observe closely, then evolution is a driving force behind path breaking innovations. And what is the core of any process of evolution? Change! With this background, if we consider evolution in infrastructure in information technology, then cloud computing is the most talked about in recent times and it has opened doors for many path-breaking solutions and innovations.

Charles Darwin was wise enough to say this:

> *It is not the strongest of the species that survives, nor the most intelligent that survives. It is the one that is most adaptable to change.*

This is very apt for cloud computing and its adoption. Let's understand what cloud computing is! There are many good definitions available in the market, but I will discuss here what I understand and what I have experienced.

Cloud computing and its basics

Cloud computing is a type of computing that provides multitenant or dedicated computing resources such as compute, storage, and network to cloud consumers on demand. It comes in different flavors that includes cloud deployment models and cloud service models.

Cloud deployment models describe the way cloud resources are deployed, such as behind the firewall and on-premise exclusively for a specific organization, and this is called the **private cloud**; or cloud resources that are available to all organizations and individuals, and this is called the **public cloud**; or cloud resources that are available to a specific set of organizations that share similar types of interests or similar types of requirements, and this is called the **community cloud**; or cloud resources that combine two or more deployment models, and this is known as the **hybrid cloud**.

Cloud service models describe the way cloud resources are made available to cloud consumers. It can be in the form of a pure infrastructure, where virtual machines are accessible and controlled by a cloud consumer or end user, and this is called **Infrastructure as a Service (IaaS)**; or a platform where runtime environments are provided so installation and configuration of all software needed to run application are already available and managed by a cloud service provider, and this is called **Platform as a Service (PaaS)**; or **Software as a Service (SaaS)**, where a whole application is made available by a cloud service provider with the responsibility of infrastructure and platform remaining with the cloud service provider.

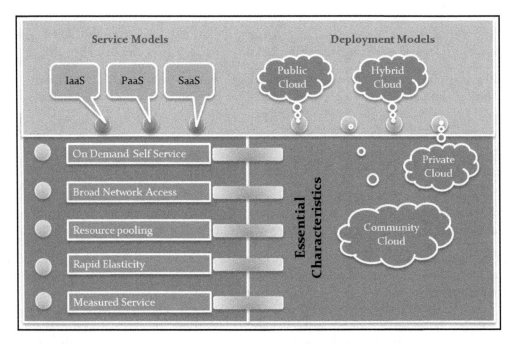

Cloud computing has a few characteristics which are significant such as multitenancy, pay-as-you-use (similar to electricity or gas connection), on-demand self-service, resource pooling for better utilization of compute, storage; network resources, rapid elasticity for scaling up and scaling down resources based on needs in an automated fashion, and measured service for billing.

Over the years, usage of different cloud deployment models has varied based on use cases. Initially, the public cloud was used for applications that were considered non-critical while private cloud was used for critical applications where security was a major concern. Hybrid cloud usage evolved over time with experience and confidence in the services provided by cloud service providers.

In a similar way, there was a usage pattern for cloud service models too. As we usually do in a normal traditional environment, it was easier to adopt IaaS as there is complete control. Over time, organizations realized the cost of managing resources in the cloud as the efforts are the same in managing resources, considering security configurations, and other configurations. Hence, IaaS was becoming difficult day by day with the evolution of PaaS. PaaS has evolved over the years and its approach is much wider, and its services include multiple programming languages such as .NET, Java, PHP, Python, and Ruby.

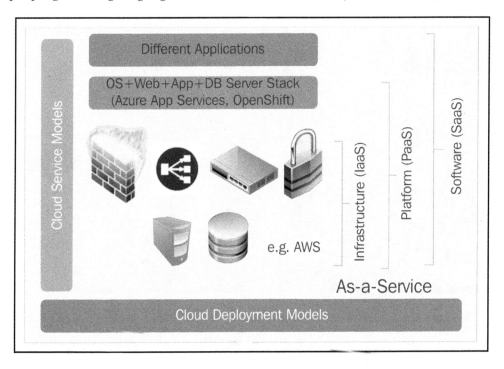

In simple English, PaaS provides infrastructure as well as a runtime environment to deploy an application. The difference is the end user doesn't have control on infrastructure while we can configure a runtime environment and debug an application remotely and troubleshoot issues to some extent. There are PaaS offerings where you can have dedicated infrastructure resources for application deployment, but even in that case, control of infrastructure is in the hands of cloud service providers. In short, we as cloud users need not to worry about downloading different web servers, database servers, and other required software and install them on a machine and maintain them. We don't even need to worry about updating them to newer versions. Cloud service providers are responsible for maintaining availability of the application and its resources. However, as users, we need to follow best practices to configure applications to have a highly available application considering different services provided by the cloud service provider.

Comparison – PaaS and IaaS

Let's visualize how the process workflow is executed in terms of a traditional model or in IaaS, and then we will compare it with PaaS. In a traditional environment, the infrastructure provisioning process takes place in a different manner than the acquisition of a virtual machine in a cloud subscription.

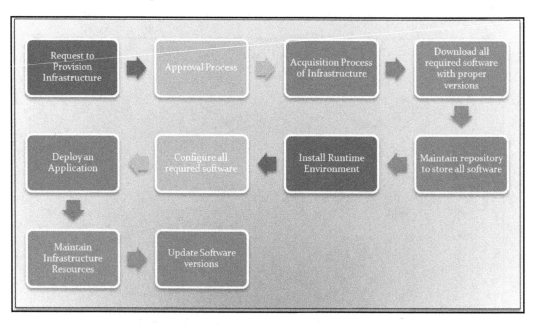

While in the case of PaaS, the flow has less complications than the traditional or IaaS process.

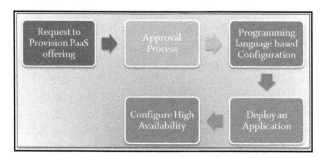

However, the approval process in the cloud environment too has costs associated with it, so organizations keep their own sets of e-mail approval processes to create a virtual machine or to provision any PaaS offering.

Over the years, PaaS has gained its momentum and many organizations have realized that there are less complexities and less management overhead involved in it. Hence, many customers are leaning towards the PaaS offering, as they don't wish to manage virtual machines and apply security policies in the cloud and maintain all of them. In IaaS, as users, we need to configure high availability and scalability, and it is more complicated compared with PaaS.

PaaS offerings manage load balancers and high availability with little configuration and hence save a lot of time, and the architecture is more clear. We need to remember that most of the control is available with cloud service providers and hence we have less things to manage. Cloud service providers have more control and they implement all the best practices and a standard pattern to fulfill the SLAs attached with PaaS offerings. Governance wise, PaaS is less flexible in terms of applying policies as it is a shared environment and is standardized as well. Managing PaaS is also less costly compared with IaaS. In the case of IaaS, we need to manage everything the way we manage on-premise.

In short, those who know better about infrastructures and platforms manage them with efficiency so we have less overhead.

An **Application Platform as a Service (aPaaS)** provides features to design, develop, deploy, and manage an application life cycle, enabling effective resource utilization, agility, and faster time to market. It is getting popular now-a-days as it has less overhead and less complexities of managing resources for the application life cycle management. Usage of thick clients is an old story now and PaaS providers have realized the trend. Developers want offerings all in once place where they can develop, compile, package, and deploy at them. PaaS is accessed through web browsers such as Firefox, Chrome, or Internet Explorer. Most PaaS providers have come up with offerings to support developers within browser IDEs to develop applications. In recent times, DevOps has also gained momentum and PaaS along with the DevOps culture is breaking a lot of barriers in the traditional culture of IT. In the next section, we will discuss DevOps and then we will see benefits of PaaS in DevOps.

Overview of DevOps

DevOps is more about the culture of an organization, processes, and technology to develop communication and collaboration between Development and IT Operations teams so as to manage the application life cycle more effectively than the existing ways of doing it. We often tend to work based on patterns to find reusable solutions from similar kind of problems or challenges.

Over the years, achievements and failed experiments, best practices, automation scripts, configuration management tools, and methodologies became an integral part of the culture. This helps to define practices for ways of designing, developing, testing, setting up resources, managing environments, managing configuration, deploying an application, gathering feedback, performing code improvements, and doing innovations. It helps to train people to think that drive the DevOps culture at every stage.

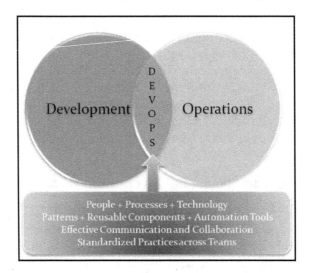

The DevOps culture is considered to be an innovative package to integrate the Dev and Ops teams in an effective manner that includes components, such as continuous build Integration, continuous testing, cloud resource provisioning, CD, continuous deployment, continuous monitoring, continuous feedback, continuous improvement, and continuous innovation, to make application delivery faster as per the demands of the agile methodology.

Considering the way we have been doing things to manage applications over the years, it is a challenge to change the culture. Mr. David Gleicher created the formula for change, and later it was refined by Kathie Dannemiller. This formula is still relevant as it provides a model to assess the relative strengths affecting the success possibilities of organizational change initiatives.

As per the formula, three factors must be available for a meaningful organizational change to take place. I just tried to classify different things in these three factors:

- *D = Dissatisfaction with how things are and how cumbersome they are! (Manual Processes + Repetitive work + Rigidness of processes + No flexibility + Huge CapEx + No visibility)*
- *V = Vision of what is possible and what is the opportunity available with disruptive innovation in recent times (Cost benefits -> Pay as you Use + Automation + Agility + Scalability + Increased efficiency and productivity + Continuous improvements + Continuous innovations)*
- *F = First concrete steps to achieve the vision (Continuous Integration + Continuous Testing + Cloud Provisioning + Configuration Management + Continuous Delivery + Continuous Deployment + Orchestration + Continuous Monitoring + Continuous Feedback);*

If the product of these three factors is greater than *R = Resistance*, then change is possible. If any one factor is absent (zero) or low while *D*, *V*, and *F* are multiplied, then the multiplication will be zero or low and therefore it may not overcome the resistance. Even without numerical values, the outcome of this formula is very much in the favor of *change* considering the values.

To bring an organization-wide change, we must consider the possibility of dissatisfaction in people and try to bring the change in mindsets by sharing industry trends, leadership ideas, best practices, and competitor analysis to identify the necessity for change. Hence, to ensure a successful change, it is the need of the hour to use influence and think strategically to create a vision and identify the basic steps toward it. To change the culture of an organization effectively, we *the people* need to bring in an agile, standardized environment, uniform automation processes orchestration, and DevOps enablers. Essentially, it means the combination of people, processes, and tools to achieve efficiency.

In other words, the DevOps culture is not much different than the organization culture, which has shared values and behavioral aspects. It needs adjustments in mindsets and processes to align with the new technology and tools.

At the end of the day, the ball is in our court and we should remember that we can't make an omelette without breaking a few eggs. To be more precise, the early bird catches the worm.

In the next section, we will describe in detail about the role and benefits of PaaS and aPaaS in DevOps.

Role and benefits of PaaS and aPaaS in DevOps

We saw in the earlier section that PaaS provides flexibility to deploy an application without an overhead of management of resources. As users, we can deploy an application and control its configuration to some extent. Resource management is the responsibility of cloud service providers. Cloud service providers manage servers, operating systems, networks, or storage. They also manage load balancing, scalability, and monitoring of resources. Users only need to configure them properly.

Cloud has a shared responsibility model and that changes based on the cloud service model we use. PaaS is just a perfect mix of flexibility and less overhead.

Now let's understand the difference between using DevOps with IaaS and DevOps with PaaS.

One of the main factor is the speed with which resources are available in PaaS compared with IaaS. Within minutes, we have the environment ready to deploy an application. The reason is simple, we need not to install and configure a runtime environment. It is already available. As a user, we only need to configure it based on the suitability of our application. Consider these examples:

- Programming language
- Web or application server
- Stateless or stateful application
- Application settings as environment variables
- Connection strings as environment variables that can be utilized to facilitate backup
- Virtual directories

Because the deployment environment is available in minutes and we can automate the creation of that environment using commands or scripts, it is very flexible to integrate it in the automation process. Even if the resource provisioning process is not automated, it becomes very easy to integrate the platform into automated deployment scenarios.

The recent trend in the market is **Application Platform as a Service (aPaaS)**. This is a service offering that provides development and deployment environments for application life cycle management.

The aPaaS service model offerings generally provide the following services:

- Agile scrum user stories management
- Code editors in a browser
- Repository as a Service
- Build as a Service
- Testing as a Service
- Release Management as a Service
- Cloud platforms to deploy an application
- Monitoring as a Service
- Security as a Service
- Identity Management as a Service

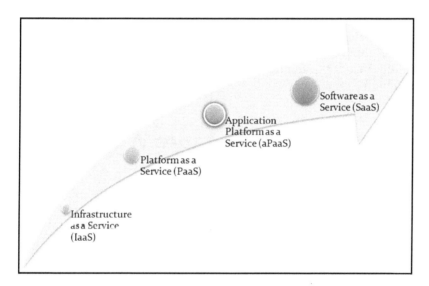

The question is, how are PaaS and aPaaS different from each other?

The following are the important points that bring out the difference and make aPaaS more suitable to manage the application life cycle:

- Agile scrum user stories management
- Code editors in a browser
- Repository as a Service
- Build as a Service
- Testing as a Service

In today's age, aPaaS is driving toward continuous improvements and continuous innovations. It drives for rapid application development and rapid application delivery. The Microsoft Azure application platform services provide application development, repository services, application deployment services, performance testing, security, and governance. The Microsoft Azure App Service is a PaaS used to rapidly build an application that may be web- or mobile-based that can be highly available, scalable, and flexible. Microsoft Azure provides other PaaS offerings—DBMS, App Insights (preview), and so on.

In the next section, we will cover all Microsoft Azure PaaS offerings that we will discuss in this book.

Overview of Microsoft Azure Service

In this book, we will use PaaS offerings of Microsoft Azure such as App Service, database services, and storage services. We will also utilize other services such as Azure Active Directory, App Insights, and Traffic Manager. We will use all these services for managing the application life cycle for tasks such as application deployment, databases authentication, monitoring, and high availability.

App Service – Microsoft Azure Web Apps

App Service is one of the most popular offering from Microsoft Azure. It is a PaaS. There are four kinds of applications that are created in App Service:

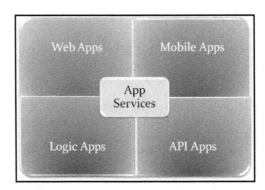

In this book, our focus is on Web Apps. Web Apps are a PaaS offering that have computing resources and runtime environments managed by Microsoft Azure while the user is only responsible for the application and configurations related to Web Apps and high availability.

The following are some quick points about Azure Web Apps:

- Web Apps runs on virtual machines – virtual machines are managed by Microsoft Azure
- Five pricing tiers are available – Free, Shared, Basic, Standard, and Premium
- Web Apps support applications written in Java, ASP.NET, PHP, Node.js, and Python
- We can integrate Web Apps with Visual Studio or GitHub
- We can create Web Apps from the Azure portal and also from the command line using PowerShell commands; thus it is easier to automate the creation process
- We can set CI and CD or deployment using Build and Release of VSTS
- We can configure autoscaling and make it available across the regions; we can set high availability as well

Let's see some basic difference between Azure Virtual Machines and Azure Web Apps:

	Microsoft Azure virtual machines	**Microsoft Azure Web Apps**
Offering	IaaS	PaaS
Support	Support for Linux, Windows Server, SQL Server, Oracle, IBM, and SAP	Linux (in preview), Windows
Categories	General purpose Compute optimized Memory optimized GPU High performance compute	Free Share Basic Standard Premium
Cost	Per-minute billing	Per-minute billing
Virtual infrastructure responsibility	User	Microsoft Azure
Out-of-the-Box support for VSTS	No	Yes
Management overhead	Yes	No

Installation and configuration are required	Yes, the customer is responsible for managing the resources	Web Apps come with a platform that supports different programming languages; we only need to configure the application settings

To have a quick hands on, follow these steps:

1. Go to `https://tryappservice.azure.com`. Select **Web App**:

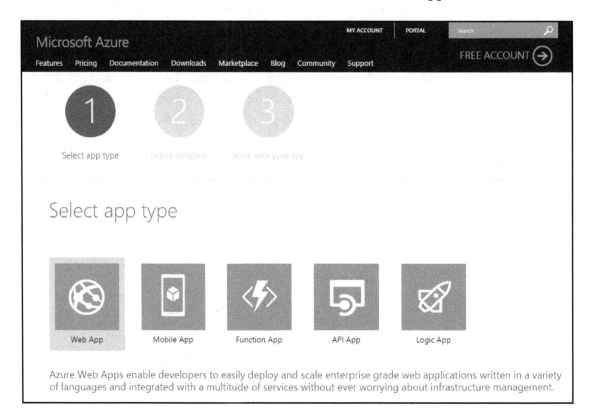

2. Select a template, in our case it is a Java template. Click on **Create**:

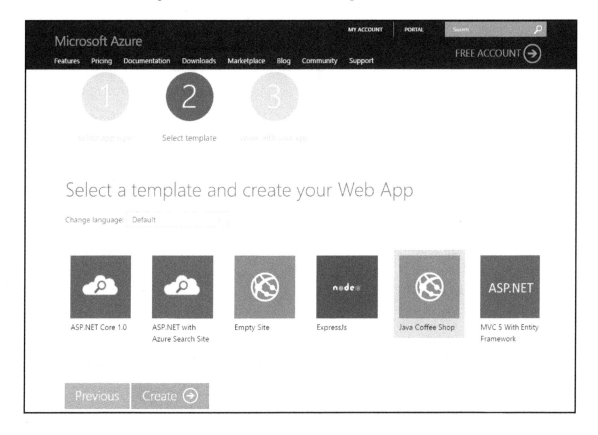

3. The web app is ready. Note the URL given to access it:

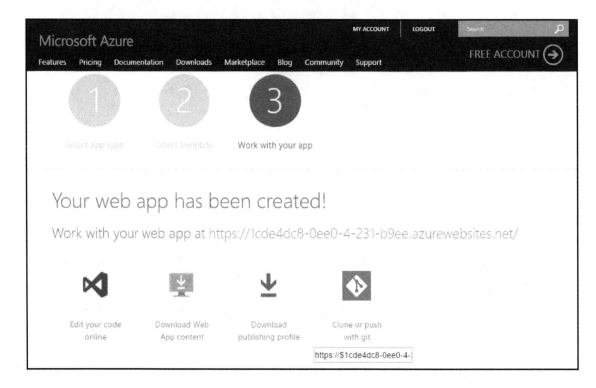

4. Visit the web app at a given URL:

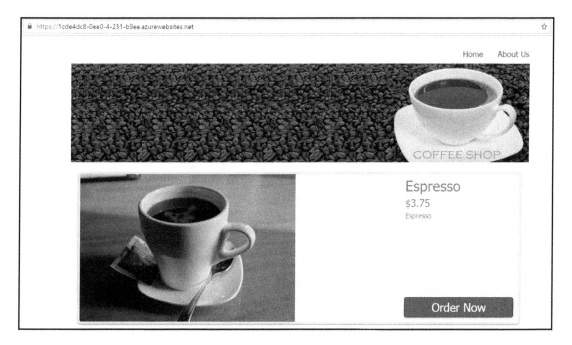

This is how we can create a sample Azure web app.

Data and storage

The Microsoft Azure SQL Database is a RDBMS in the cloud. It supports the SQL Server engine and hence we can use existing SQL Server tools, libraries, and APIs to manage the SQL Database in the cloud. It comes in different pricing tiers such as Basic, Standard, and Premium service tiers that have different capacities for different workloads.

Microsoft Azure Storage is a cloud storage offering that is highly available, scalable, and durable. Microsoft Azure Storage services provide Blob storage, Table storage, Queue storage, and File storage:

- **Blob storage** (Object storage): This is used to store unstructured object data such as documents, media files, and binary data
- **Table storage**: This is used to store structured data such as NoSQL key-attribute data
- **Queue storage**: This is for reliable messaging
- **File storage**: This is used to store file data that can be used by Azure virtual machines and cloud services

Azure Active Directory (**Azure AD**) is a cloud-based, multitenanted, and highly available identity management service from Microsoft. It can manage users, groups, and multi-factor authentication; add an application organization that is developing for authentication; add an application from the gallery for authentication; add a custom domain; add role-based access control; and so on.

To access Azure AD from the Azure portal, go to `https://portal.azure.com` and click on **Azure Active Directory**.

Verify the **Overview** details with **Users and groups**, **App registrations**, and **Azure AD Connect**.

The application Gallery supports 2,771 applications for Azure AD integration at the time of writing this chapter. Categories include Business Management, Collaboration, Construction, Content management, CRM, Data Services, Developer Services, E-commerce, Education, ERP, Finance, Health, Human resources, IT infrastructure, Mail, Marketing, Media, Mobile Device Management, Productivity, Project Management, Security, Social, Supply Management, Telecommunications, Travel, and Web Design and Hosting.

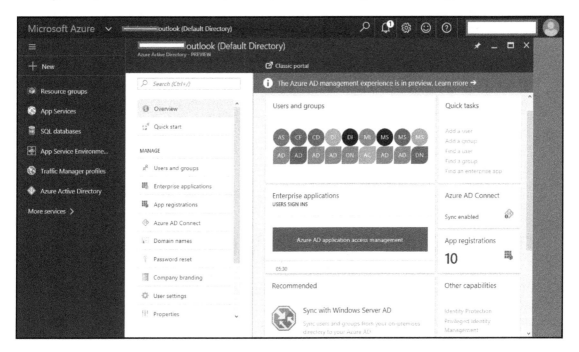

Major applications supported are Office365, Salesforce, ServiceNow, Google Apps, and so on.

Go to `https://manage.windowsazure.com` to access Azure AD from the classic portal:

One of the biggest benefits that we will utilize in this book is the way we can provide authentication to access Azure Web Apps. We can configure Azure Web Apps with Directory so only specific users can access the application hosted on Azure Web Apps.

Application Insights

Visual Studio Application Insights is a flexible analytics service. It helps us to get the insights of performance and usage of an application. It can be used for .NET- or J2EE-based applications that are hosted on-premise or in the cloud. We will cover only a few important features that come with this service in this book.

Create a sample application and go to its **MONITORING** section. Click on **Application Insights**. Select **Create new** and click on **OK**:

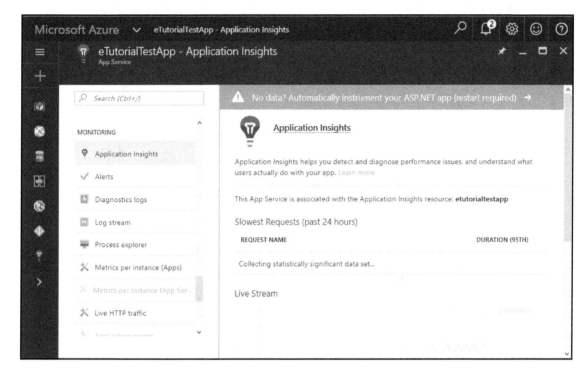

We can create a web test for testing the availability of applications from multiple regions. We can select a ping test or multi-step test to check the availability. The alert criteria can also be configured.

Performance testing is also a very interesting feature available in App Insights. It is more of a load testing based on the number of users for a specific duration.

We will see the *how to* of both in this book where we intend to cover monitoring.

Traffic Manager

Microsoft Azure Traffic Manager provides a feature to distribute user traffic to different endpoints. These endpoints can be Azure App Service (Azure Web Apps), cloud services, Azure Virtual Machines, and external endpoints. It is a DNS-based traffic routing. Azure Traffic Manager supports three traffic routing methods to decide how traffic can be routed to different endpoints. In simple terms, it is a way to decide which endpoint should serve the DNS request.

There are two different deployment models in Microsoft Azure—the classic deployment and Resource Manager deployment models. Microsoft Azure Traffic Manager uses different terminology for traffic routing methods (known as the load-balancing method in the classic deployment model):

- **Priority method** (Failover method): Select the Priority or Failover method for traffic routing when you need resources in a specific region to serve all the traffic and only use other endpoints if the main endpoint is unavailable.

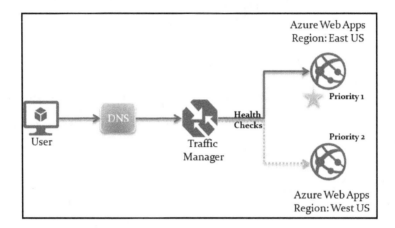

Often this method is cost-optimized and the usage of the application is very well known and specific to a region.

- **Weighted method** (Round-robin method): Select the Weighted or Round-robin method for traffic routing when you need resources to serve in a different region or across a set of different endpoints.

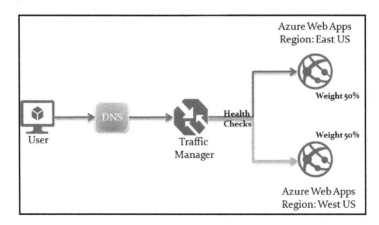

Let's say we know that our application hosted in Azure Web Apps is going to be equal or in a specific ratio, then the Weighted method can be more appropriate.

- **Performance method**: Select Performance for the traffic routing method when we want to provide equal performance to the user of the resources hosted in Azure.

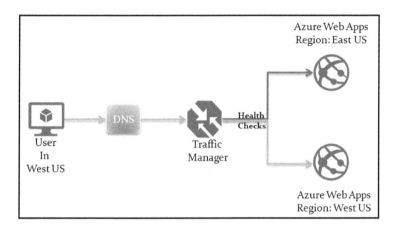

So, in simple terms, users will be redirected to the nearest endpoint to serve the response. Some benefits of Microsoft Azure Traffic Manager are as follows:

- Easy to use and configure
- Easy learning curve
- Configuration is available from Azure Portal as well as Azure PowerShell
- DNS level traffic routing
- Helps in high availability of the business critical application
- Provides automatic failover
- Supports multiple endpoints: Microsoft Azure and external endpoints
- Helps to support the scenario of planned maintenance
- We can combine hybrid applications as it supports multiple endpoints

Overview of concepts related to Microsoft Azure

Microsoft Azure comes up with some core concepts that are important to understand before we go ahead and work with it. These core concepts help to manage resources and help to understand the pricing structure as well.

Regions

Microsoft Azure services are available in 34 regions around the globe and more regions are continuously planned to be supported. The more regions, the more it allows customers to achieve better performance with cost optimization. It also helps in scenarios where data location is legally restricted.

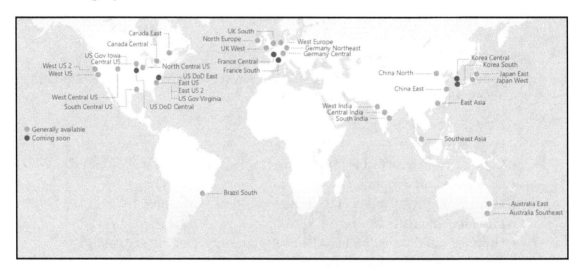

To get the latest details on Microsoft Azure regions, visit `https://azure.microsoft.com/en-in/regions/`.

To verify **WEB + MOBILE** products available by region go to `https://azure.microsoft.com/en-in/regions/services/` and check the **WEB + MOBILE** section:

Azure is generally available in 34 regions and 12 geos around the globe. It has already announced plans for six additional regions and two additional geos. For customers, it is extremely important to have legal compliance in the context of a storage location of their data. There are two different possibilities/authorities in this scenario:

- The customer may copy, move, or access data from any location

- Microsoft may replicate data in other regions of the same geo for high availability:

 To get more details, go to `http://azuredatacentermap.azurewebsites.net/`.

Resource groups

Resource groups in Microsoft Azure is nothing but a logical container. It can be used to group all different resources such as App Service, SQL Databases, and Storage Accounts, available in Microsoft Azure. We are going to consider services that we will use in this chapter for most of the examples. Resource groups provide a simple way to manage resources together. One of the biggest advantages is to manage the role-based access on the resources in an easy manner.

For example, we need to create resources such as Azure Web Apps, SQL Database, and Storage Account in the West US and provide access to all of them to some users. It is painful to assign a user to individual resources. Rather, it is more manageable if we can provide group access to all resources. This way resources can be managed in a better way.

To create a resource group, click on **Resource groups** in the left-hand sidebar menu. Click on the **+Add** button to create a resource group. Provide the **Resource group name**, select **Subscription**, select **Resource group location**, and click on **Create**:

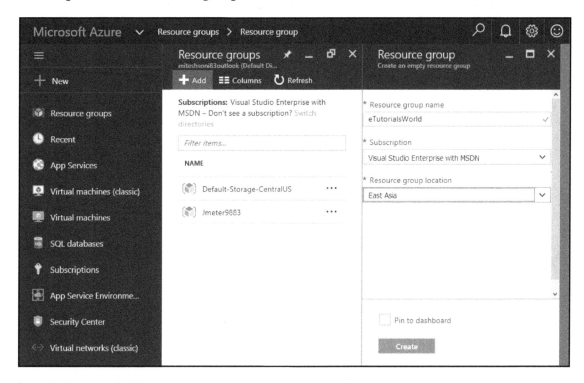

Wait until the resource group is created.

Once the `eTutorialsWorld` resource group is created, click on it and verify the **Overview** section.

As of now, there are no resources in the resource group; hence there are **No deployments** in the **Overview** section—**No resources to display**:

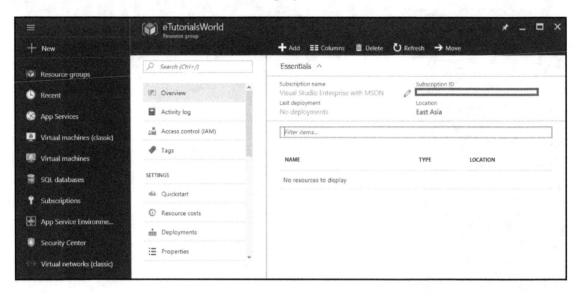

As there are no resources, there is no cost available in the **Resource costs** section of the `eTutorialsWorld` resource group:

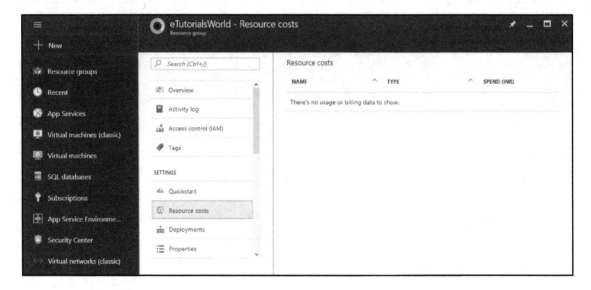

We will use this resource group in the coming chapters as a logical container for different resources such as Azure Web Apps and Azure SQL Database.

App Service plans

An **App Service Plan** (**ASP**) is a set of capacities (the instance size and instance count on which the application is hosted) and features. Capacity is directly linked to cost and hence it is similar to choosing a pricing tier. There are different capabilities and limits within ASPs.

There are five pricing tiers, namely Free, Shared, Basic, Standard, and Premium. Each ASP can be used for different purposes and they are different in providing features too. SLAs for Basic, Standard, and Premium are 99.95 percent. Autoscale, geo-distributed deployment, VPN hybrid connectivity, deployment slots, and automated backups are available only in the Standard and Premium tiers. In the Standard tier, five deployment slots are available, while in the Premium tier, 20 slots are available. Another major difference is the maximum instances, as they are directly associated with scaling. Hence, it is important to pick the proper tier or ASP to gain the desired performance. The Basic, Standard, and Premium tiers allow up to 3, 10, and 50 instances respectively.

The App Service or Azure Web Apps is a main or Production slot. In Standard and Premium tiers, we can create other deployment slots other than the main slot where we deploy an application. We can use deployment slots for different environments before deploying an application into the Production slot. Slots are not different from a live web app. They have their own set of content, configurations, and hostnames. We can swap slots to roll back failures too.

The following are some important points regarding ASPs:

- ASPs can be shared by multiple applications
- Deployment slots are usually deployed on the same ASP
- Azure Web Apps configured with an ASP are changed and these changes affect all applications hosted on the ASP
- By default, an ASP comes with a single instance. If we increase the instance count, then applications hosted on a single instance will be hosted on other instances too
- The number of instances in an ASP is directly associated with the price of the Azure Web Apps

Let's consider the Azure calculator and understand how the pricing works. Go to `https://azure.microsoft.com/en-in/pricing/calculator/`. Click on **+Add items** and click on **App Service** in the **Featured** category:

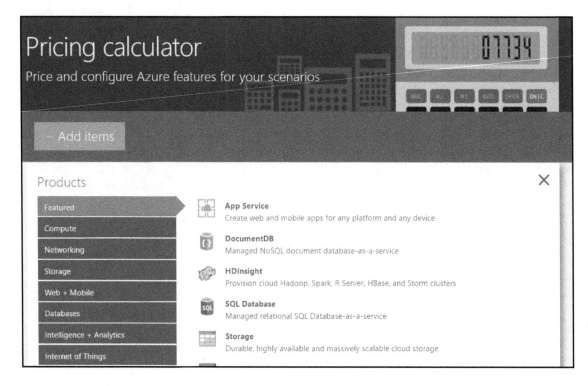

Select **REGION, TIER, INSTANCE SIZE**; by default, the instance size is 1 and the hours are 744. Verify the cost estimate:

Now change the instance count and verify the cost:

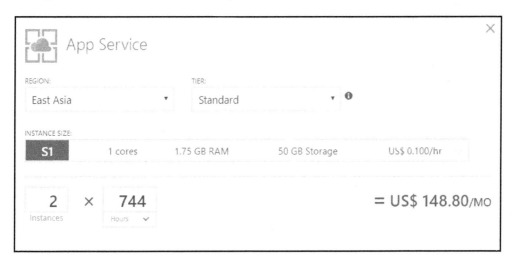

As the instance count directly affects pricing, let's see from where we can change the instance size as we need to be careful while doing it.

Let's create an ASP and verify the instance count. Go to the left-hand side menu bar, find **App Service plans**, and click on **+Add**.

Select the `eTutorialsWorld` resource group we created; select **Operating System**, **Location**, and **Pricing tier**. Click on **Create**:

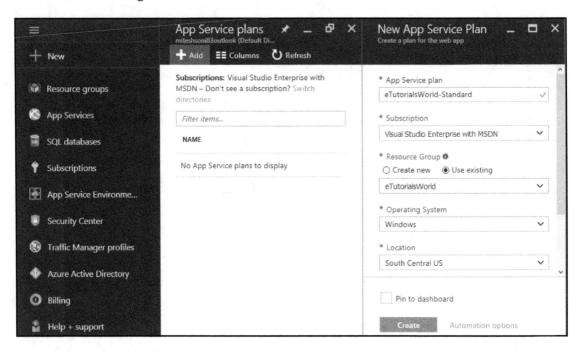

Once the ASP is created, verify its **Overview** section. Verify the **Apps / Slots** count. It is **0 / 0** as no app or the slot is using the ASP:

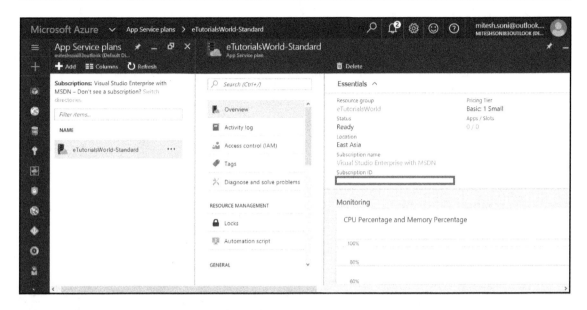

Go to the **Scale out (App Service plan)** section in **APP SERVICE PLAN**, and verify the default number of instances. As we kept the Basic pricing tier, it allows us to scale up to three instances only:

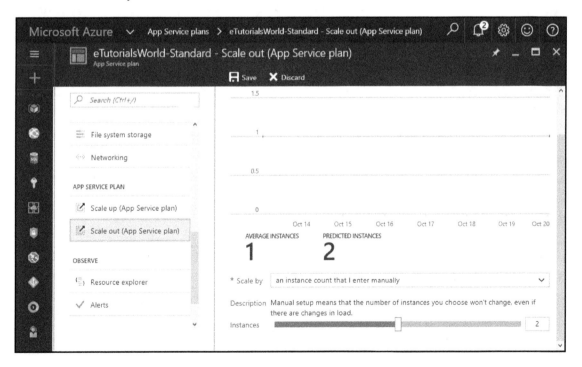

If we want to cancel the changes, click on **Discard**.

 This pricing and features information is latest on the day this chapter was written. For the latest information visit `https://azure.microsoft.com/en-in/pricing/details/app-service/plans/`.

Autoscaling

Scaling resources is a significant part of making an application highly available and having good performance. There are two types of scaling:

- **Vertical Scaling** (scale up and scale out): We can increase or decrease the size of the instance by choosing different pricing tiers. We can do it manually:

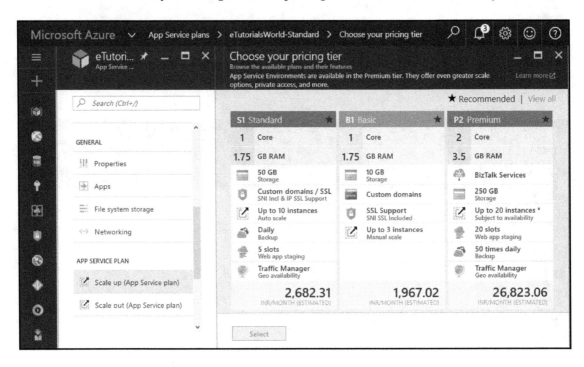

- **Horizontal Scaling** (scale in and scale Out): We can increase or decrease the number of instances that are used to host web applications.

  Horizontal scaling is the most commonly used as we can schedule it also. It is important to understand what will impact on the performance and availability of an application and accordingly we can decide the scaling part:

  - Gather the data the load application faces in the existing condition; find the peak load data and date
  - Note the existing capacity of Azure Web Apps and database that are used for the web application
  - Make sure the architecture of the application supports stateless
  - Use any load testing tool and find out how many concurrent requests it can manage before crashing
  - Increase the database capacity to manage concurrent requests
  - Schedule autoscaling for Azure App Service instances based on different conditions
  - Understand the usability of an application from the number of regions

There are three types of scaling out supported in Azure Web Apps:

- Scale instances manually
- Scale instances by the CPU percentage
- Scale instances by schedule and the performance rule

Scale instances manually

We can configure a number of instances manually based on the existing patterns and usage and these will serve the application hosting. We cannot change this dynamically. We need to change the setting in the ASP:

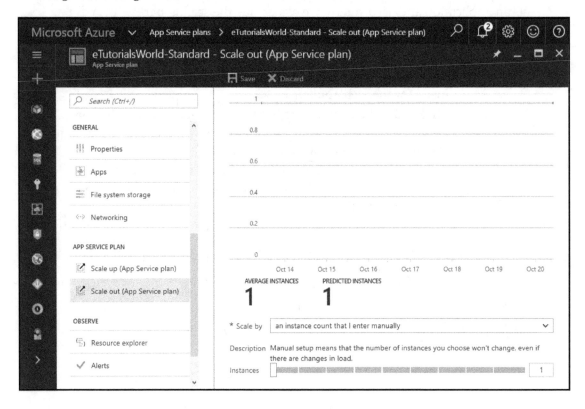

Scale instances by CPU percentage

We can automatically or dynamically scale up or down instances based on the performance of the CPU we have configured. We can also configure the number of instances too.

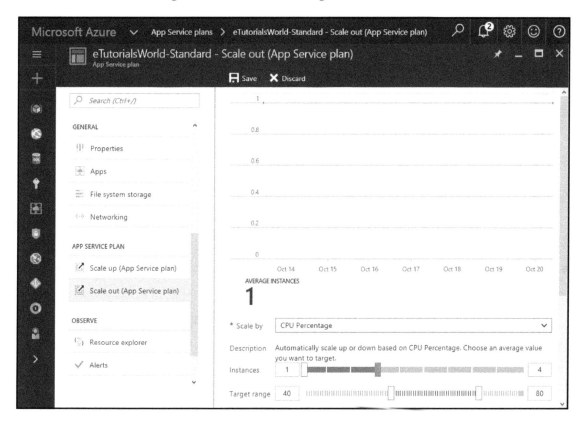

Scale instances by schedule and performance rule

Based on multiple rules, we can increase or decrease the number of instances used in an ASP. This is the most flexible and widely used scale out option out of the three:

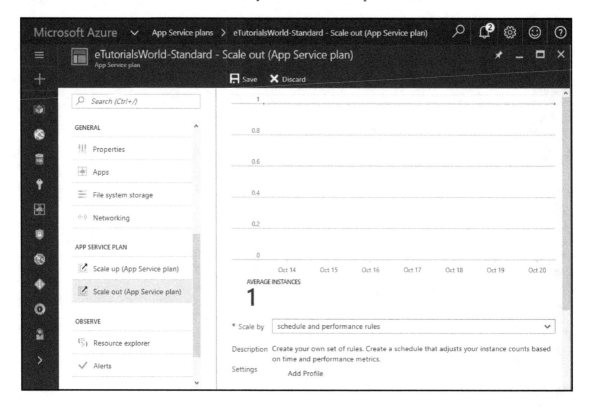

Summary

In this first chapter, you learned the basics of cloud computing, its service models, and deployment models. We covered PaaS in depth and also provided details of the new trend of the modern day and that is aPaaS.

We discussed the role and benefits of PaaS and aPaaS in DevOps by explaining the services that each one provides and what is the difference between both of them. The next step is to know about tools or services that we are going to use in end-to-end automation for the application life cycle management. We covered brief details on App Service: Microsoft Azure Web Apps, Azure SQL Database, Storage Services, Azure Active Directory, App Insights, and Traffic Manager with its routing methods.

It is also important to understand the basic concepts related to Microsoft Azure Cloud so we can easily create and manage resources in Microsoft Azure Cloud. The basic concepts have covered topics such as regions, resource groups, ASPs, and autoscaling.

In the last section, we covered the overall vision of the book. We provided glimpses of the high-level design that we want to implement in the coming chapters.

In the next chapter, we will cover VSTS and how to check in code into VSTS using Eclipse.

2
Getting Started with Visual Studio Team Services (VSTS)

Technology is just a tool. In terms of getting the kids working together and motivating them, the teacher is the most important.

—*Bill Gates*

In this chapter, we will introduce **Visual Studio Team Services** (**VSTS**) and the sample application structure that is necessary to understand before automating the process of building and deploying the application in a desired environment. We will cover the basics of the agile process framework supported in VSTS. This chapter also explains how to use VSTS to manage code and integrate VSTS with the Eclipse IDE so the check in process can be managed directly from IDE.

The following topics are covered:

- Introduction to VSTS
- Creating a free account in VSTS
- Configuration and user management in VSTS
- Overview of agile in VSTS
- Overview of a sample JEE application
- Eclipse integration with TFS online in VSTS

Introduction to VSTS

In a nutshell, DevOps is all about cultivating the culture of effective communication and collaboration between the development and operations teams to make processes efficient. The DevOps culture involves implementation of source control systems, build tools, CI, cloud computing (service models such as IaaS, PaaS, and SaaS; deployment models such as the public cloud, private cloud, hybrid cloud, and community cloud), containers, configuration management, **Continuous Delivery** (**CD**), continuous deployment, continuous feedback, security, governance, and so on.

Microsoft Toolsets provides an easy way to deploy applications having a platform such as Java, .NET, Android, and iOS. The intent of VSTS and Microsoft Azure Cloud Services is to provide agility, scalability, faster time to market, and automation for end-to-end application life cycle management.

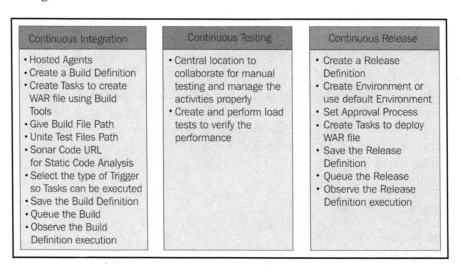

VSTS is a cloud-based service offering from Microsoft that provides the **Team Foundation Server** (**TFS**) like version control system. As we have already discussed the different components for developing the DevOps culture, source control systems are an important and integral part of the end-to-end automation process. They are at the core of the DevOps culture.

VSTS supports **Team Foundation Version Control** (**TFVC**) and the Git repository. VSTS provides hosted agents to execute builds, and in this book, we are going to use the same approach and not private agents, where we can install the required artifacts and manage agents on our own in a preferred environment.

In VSTS, we can manage CI, continuous testing, or unit testing, and static code analysis in the **Build** section; performance testing is managed in the **Test** section; and CD and continuous deployment are managed in the **Release** section. We can also provide security and governance while configuring release operations of deployment based on the approval system. For example, we can only deploy to the development environment if approval from Mr. A (configured in the release definitions) is available. In this book, you will learn about the different functionalities provided by VSTS and how we can configure and utilize them for end-to-end automation.

Creating a free account on VSTS

To create a free account and your first project on VSTS follow these steps:

1. Go to https://www.visualstudio.com/team-services/.
2. Click on the **Free Account** button on the main page:

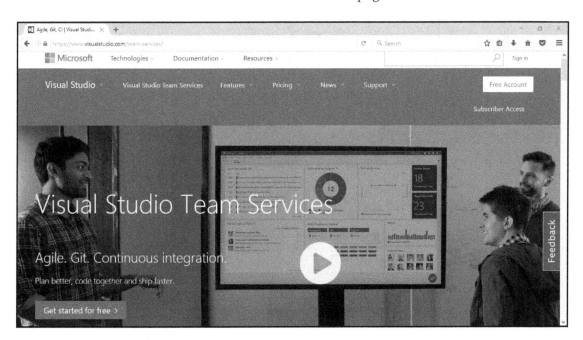

Make sure to create or have a live Microsoft Outlook ID before going further.

In our case, we have a Microsoft account already, so we will use the same ID to create a free account with VSTS.

3. Enter the e-mail ID and click on **Continue**:

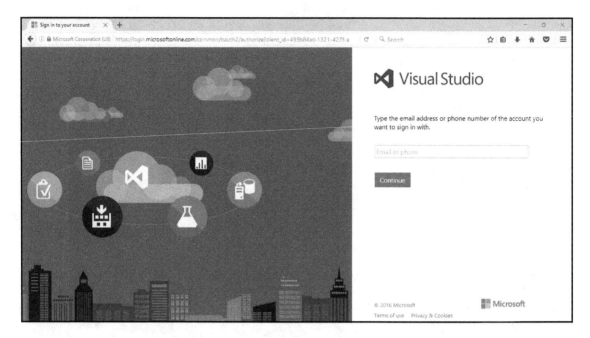

4. If the username exists, then it will ask for the password. Enter the password and click on **Sign in**:

5. You will be presented with the **Visual Studio Team Services Accounts** page. In our case, we already have two accounts. For this book, we will create another account:

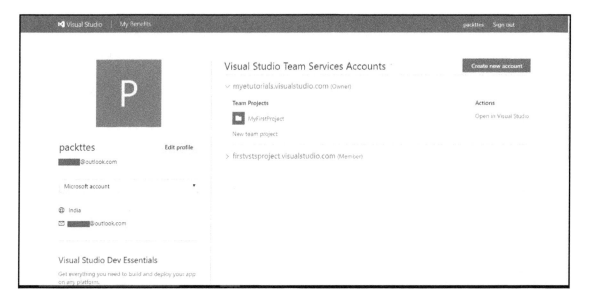

6. Click on **Create new account** and a dialog box will be opened:

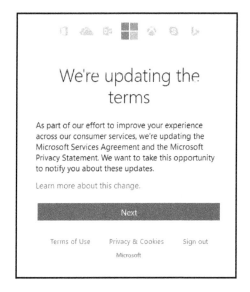

7. Enter the name of the account and select the repository with which we will manage the code. In our case, we will select **Team Foundation Version Control**. This selection is per project and not account specific.

Once the project is ready, we can add code. We will create a new project.

8. Once the account is created, you can see the available list of accounts on the main page after logging into VSTS. Open the newly created account. We have `MyFirstProject` available:

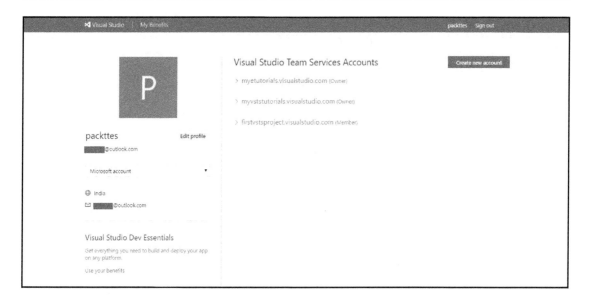

9. Click on the settings icon, and it will bring us to the **Projects** page. Click on the ... icon and delete the existing project:

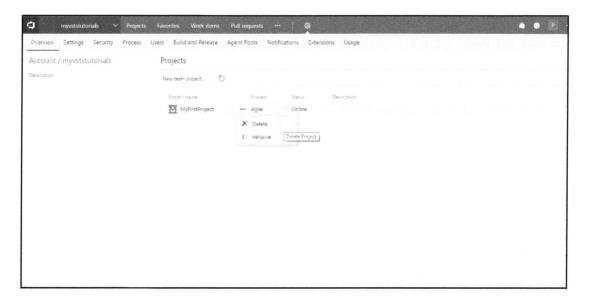

10. This will open a dialog box; enter the name of the project and click on **Delete Project**:

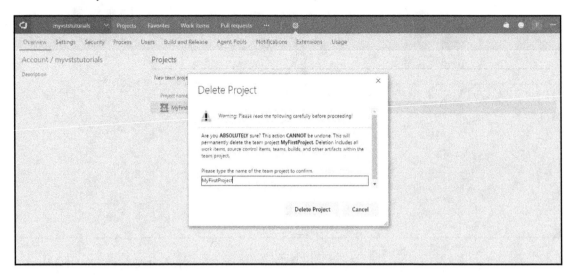

11. Close the dialog box:

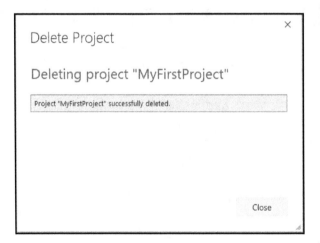

12. Go to the **Projects** page of the account and it will ask for creating a project. Provide **Project name**, select **Work item process**, and select **Version control** for the team project. Click on **Create**:

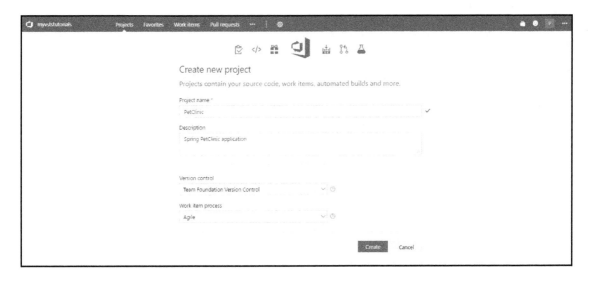

13. Once successful, it will ask you to manage code or add code:

14. Now click on the settings icon, and check whether the recently created project is available or not:

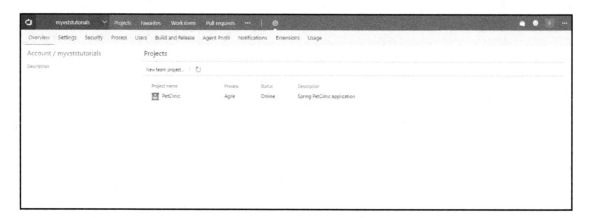

We have successfully created a new project in VSTS. In the next section, let's configure the team to manage users.

Configuration and user management in VSTS

For configuration and user management follow these steps:

1. Open the newly created project `PetClinic` and click on the settings icon. On the **Project profile** page, the team information is available. Click on **PetClinic Team**:

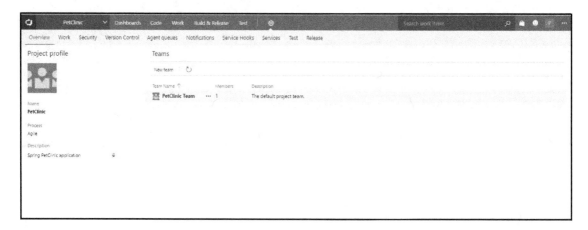

2. By default, the admin account is already available as a team member. Click on **+Add** to add a new team member for collaboration:

3. Use sign-in addresses or group aliases and click on **Save changes**:

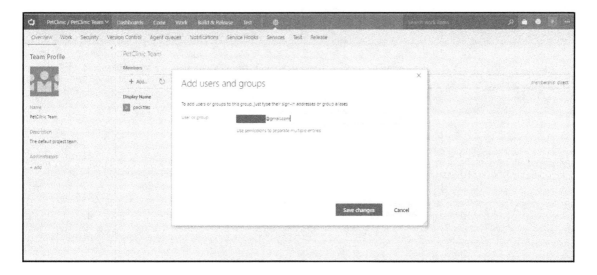

4. Verify the team members of **PetClinic Team** in the dashboard:

5. Go to **Dashboards** of the team project and verify the **Team Members** section as well:

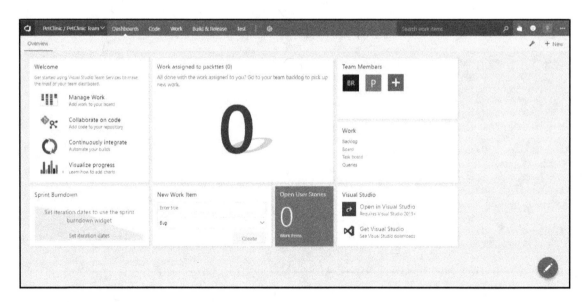

We have successfully added a team member to the main team of the project. This is how we can create a project and manage a team. In the next section, we will discuss how agile can be managed in VSTS.

Overview of agile in VSTS

Agile principles have changed the game in recent times. Because of the feature-wise implementation and short sprints, delivery of the application becomes extremely faster. An end-to-end discussion on agile is out of the scope of this book; however, we will try to give a brief summary.

There are different phases in SDLC, and traditionally, all those phases are managed or executed in a sequential manner—the waterfall model. The problem with this model is that it is in sequence and a one-time activity; each phase takes a lot of time and changes are not easy. Feedback from the customer take so long that at the end of all the phases, we as developers are not sure whether we have implemented the same product that was intended and communicated by the customer or there was a communication gap. The ideal way to deal with this is to provide frequent delivery to the customer for a few features and receive frequent feedback to fix things or innovate. The visible benefit is this: "The faster we realize the failure or potential failure or a bug, the faster we can fix it. Agile is the answer for all the problematic questions surfaced because of the waterfall approach.

Let's draw some parallels between DevOps and agile. Let's also remember that both are not the same. Agile complements DevOps as it comes with short release cycles, so it requires frequent delivery of the application, and hence we need automation to remove the manual errors in the application life cycle management. Let's come back to drawing a parallel, and there is some similarity between the definitions of DevOps and agile. Agile is not a methodology, and similarly, DevOps is not a methodology or a framework or a combination of tools. Agile is a movement and DevOps is also a movement or a culture and hence it is bit similar in the way it is defined.

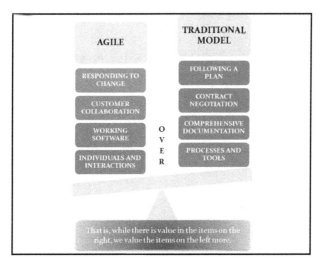

The **Agile Manifesto** is a published declaration that includes recommendations to develop applications in an efficient manner.

According to `agilemanifesto.org`, the following principles are based on the Agile Manifesto:

Scrum is a methodology or framework for effective application development. VSTS supports common agile and scrum-based projects. In this section, we will cover the basic agile process template in our project:

1. Open the `PetClinic` team project and click on the **Work** link available on the top bar.

   Remember, we selected the **Agile** process template while creating this team project.

2. Once the user stories are available, the next task is to plan the first sprint and other sprints too based on them:

3. To add the user stories into sprint 1 or **Iteration 1**, just drag the **User Story** on the specific iteration. After dragging the user stories, verify the iteration path:

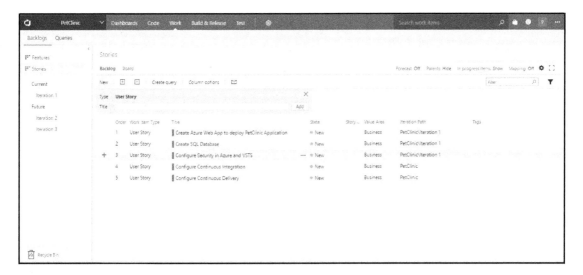

4. Once the user stories are moved to **Iteration 1**, click on **Iteration 1** and the next suggestion will be to create multiple tasks for a specific **User Story**.

5. Click on the plus sign for the specific **User Story**. Click on **Task**:

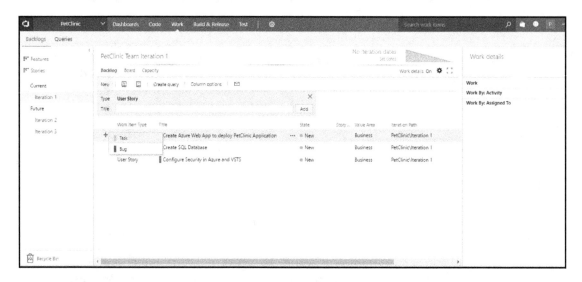

6. Give a name to the **New Task**. Select the team member to assign the task to. Add **Description**, **Activity**, and **Priority**:

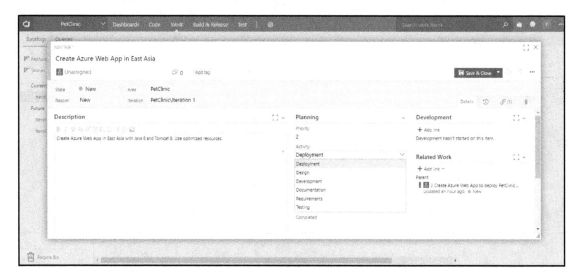

7. Assign the remaining user stories to other iterations and verify the iteration path of each story:

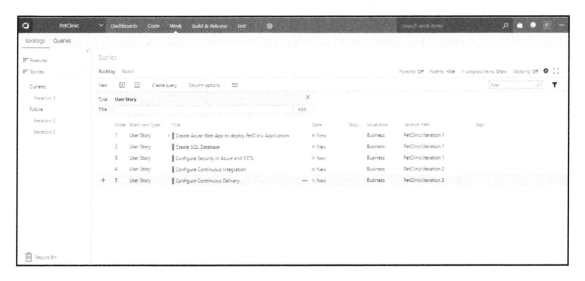

8. Go to **Iteration 1** and create tasks for each **User Story**:

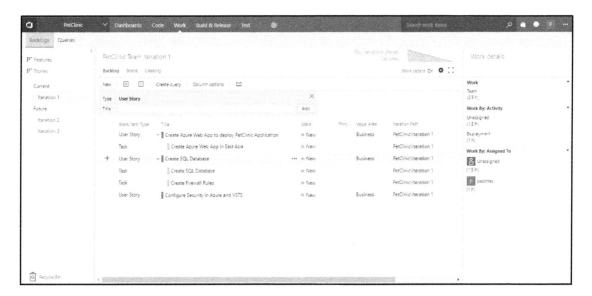

9. Based on the activities performed on the tasks, the team members will update the time taken to finish the task, and they can change the state of the task too. We can verify the existing status of tasks from the board.

    New, **Active**, **Resolved**, and **Closed** are the four main stages as per the following board. We can also drag and drop based on the status of the task:

10. Go to the **Dashboards** page of the team project and here we can see the **Work assigned to** section, which gives details on what task is assigned, to whom it is assigned, and what is the state of that task:

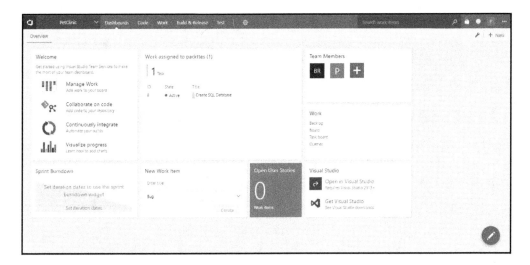

11. Click on **Iteration 1** at the bottom left and we will get the burndown chart for the activities we performed in this iteration or sprint:

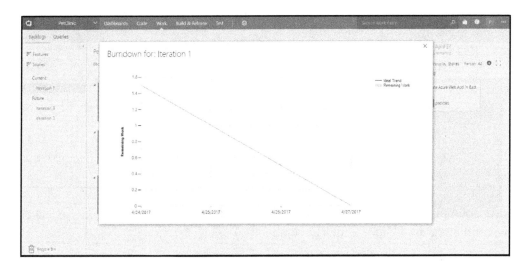

In this book we will focus on the basics of agile and scrum. For more details, refer to following VSTS references/links:

- http://agilemethodology.org/
- https://www.agilealliance.org/agile101/
- https://www.scrumalliance.org/why-scrum
- http://etutorialsworld.com/agile-scrum/

In the next section, we will introduce the sample Spring-based application available on GitHub that we will use throughout the book to demonstrate the capabilities and features of VSTS.

Overview of a sample JEE application

For this book, we will use a sample Spring-based application available at `https://github.com/spring-projects/spring-petclinic`. You can also download this application from `https://github.com/mitesh51/spring-petclinic`.

Just download the `PetClinic` application and then we will use it in our next section where we will integrate Eclipse with TFS online.

Eclipse integration with TFS online in VSTS

In this section, we will integrate Eclipse with TFS online so we can check in any changes we do in the code to VSTS / TFS online.

First, we will download Eclipse from `http://www.eclipse.org/downloads/packages/ecl ipse-ide-java-ee-developers/marsr`:

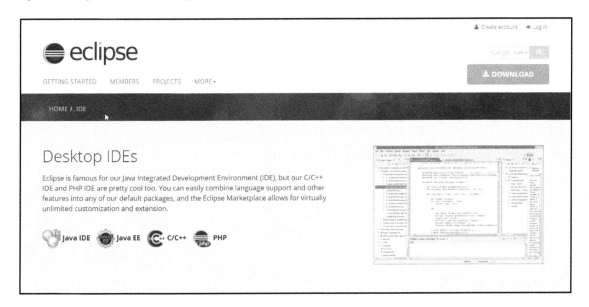

Click on **Java EE** and from Eclipse IDE for Java EE developers, download the appropriate version of Eclipse:

Extract the files from the compressed Eclipse installation file. Now, click on `eclipse.exe`:

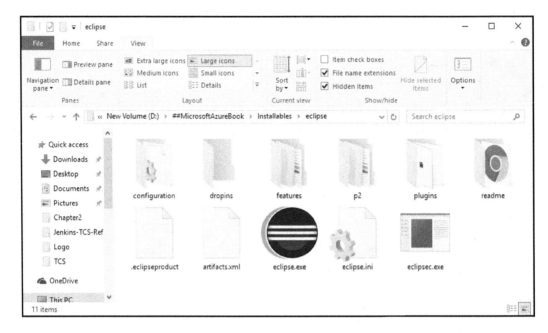

Our task is to install the TFS plugin, so we can connect TFS from Eclipse, check in code, or make any changes to the code, and save it to the TFS repository.

Click on the **Help** menu and select **Install New Software...**:

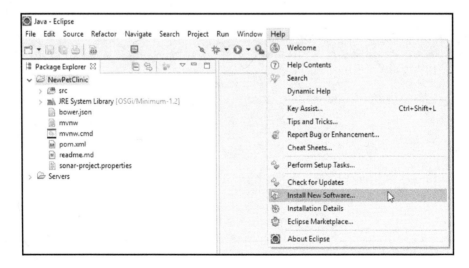

Click on the **Add...** button to add a site:

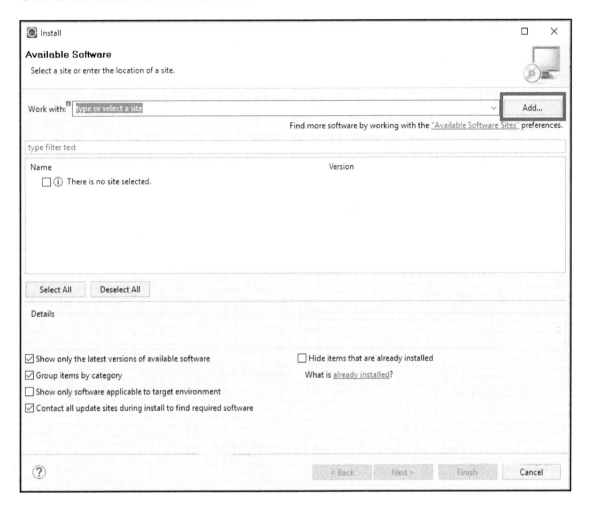

It will open an **Add Repository** dialog box. Provide the **Name** and the site of the repository. In **Location**, enter `http://dl.microsoft.com/eclipse`. Click on **OK**:

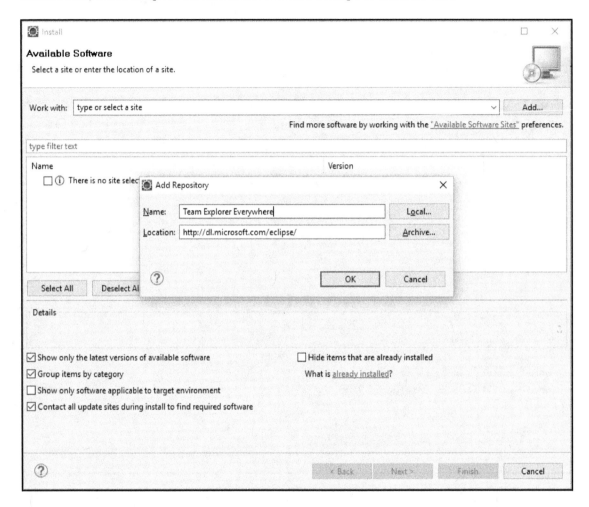

In the **Available Software** list, select **Azure Toolkit for Java** and **Team Explorer Everywhere**:

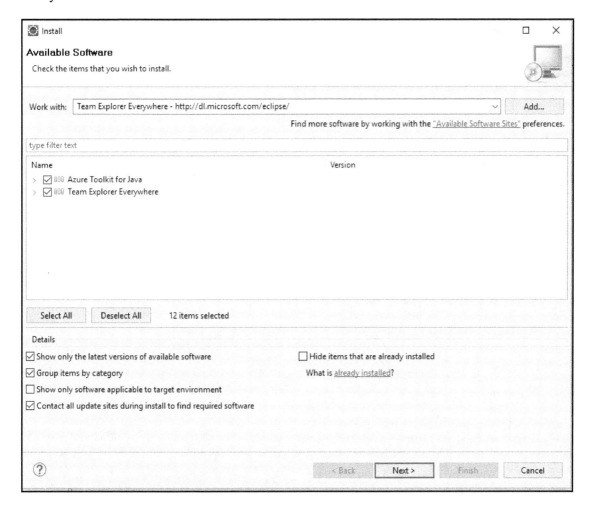

Expand both the list items to verify the list of items that will be installed. Click on **Next**:

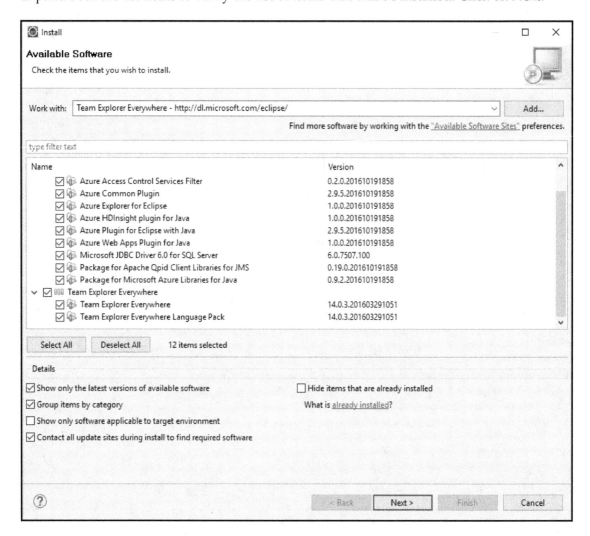

Verify **Install Details**. Click on **Next**:

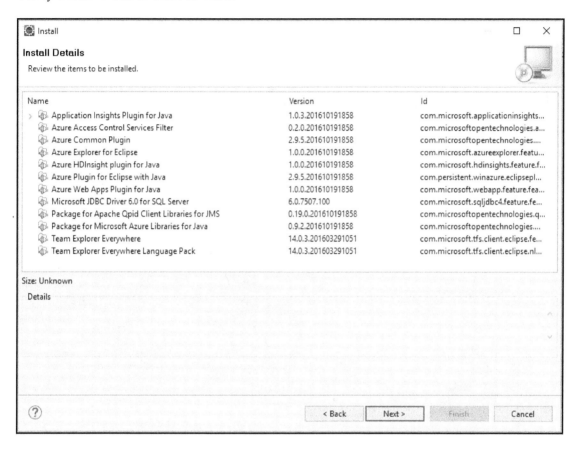

In the **Review Licenses**, select **I accept the terms of the license agreements**. Click on **Finish**:

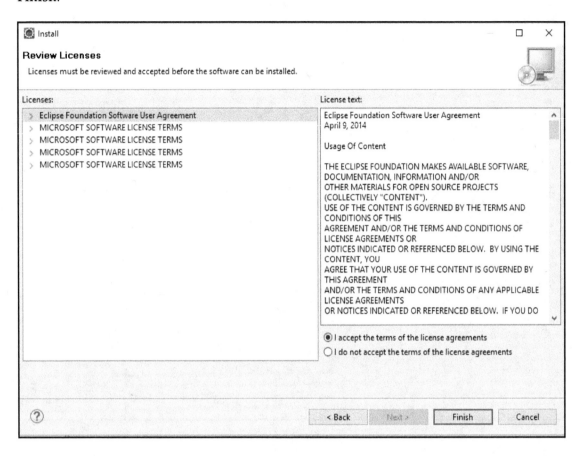

Now, all the packages required to install plugins in Eclipse will be installed and it will take some time. We can run this activity in the background also.

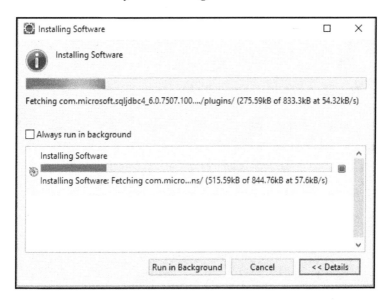

Once the installation is successful, it will ask if you want to restart Eclipse. Click on **Yes**:

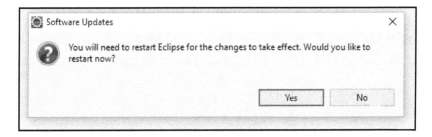

After the restart, it will ask if you want to accept the **License Agreement**. Click on **Finish**:

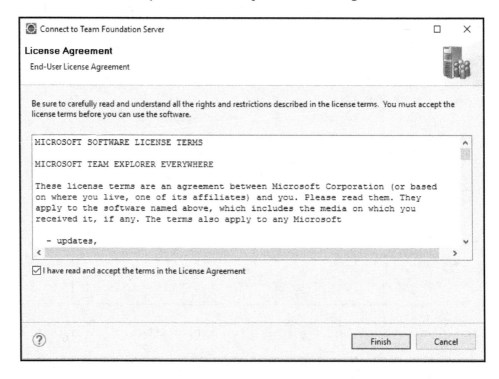

For the dialog box for Azure Toolkit, select **Yes** or **No** based on your preference:

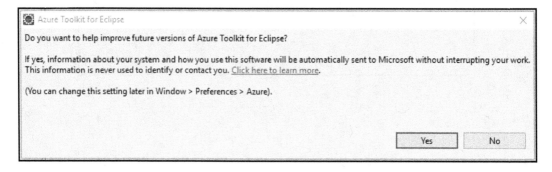

Let's verify what items have been installed in Eclipse. Go to the **Help** menu and select **Installation Details** to verify this:

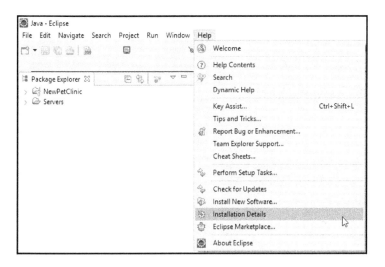

A list of items and their versions will be displayed in a dialog box:

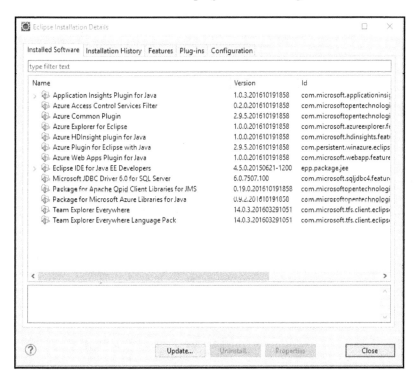

Close the dialog box, and we are now ready to go ahead with the connectivity to TFS from Eclipse.

First, we need to open **Perspective**. Click on the **Window** menu and select **Open Perspective** from **Perspective**:

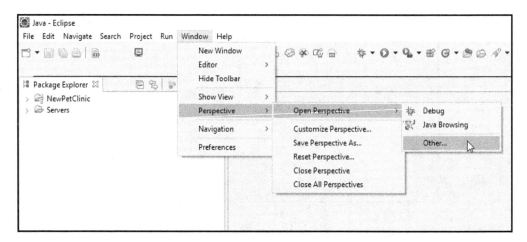

Select **Team Foundation Server Exploring** and click on **OK**:

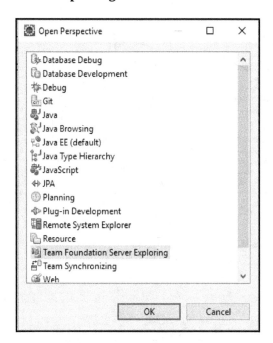

Import the `PetClinic` project into Eclipse. Once the project is imported, we can see a screen similar to the following one. As of now, TFS connectivity is not done. Click on **Connect to Team Services or a Team Foundation Server**:

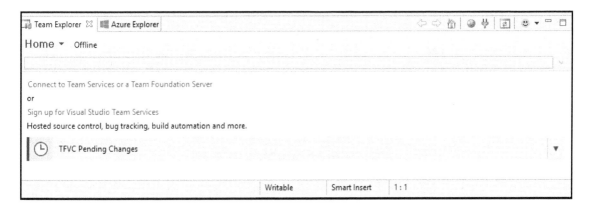

Click on **Add...**, in the **Team Foundation Server list**. Enter the URL of TFS. We created a VSTS account earlier in this chapter. Click on **OK**:

It will try to fetch the project information by connecting to the TFS URL. It will prompt for the Visual Studio login. Enter the username:

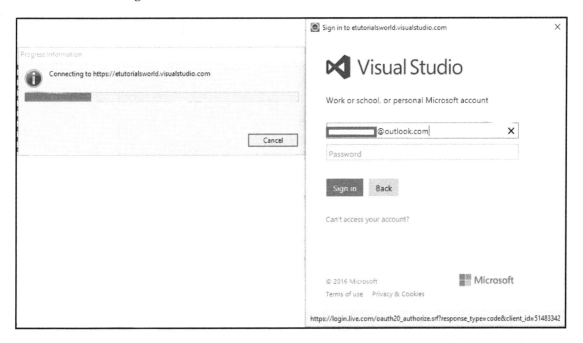

The username will be verified and the password will be requested. Enter the password and click on **Sign in**:

Once the connection is successful, TFS is added to the list of servers. Click on **Next**:

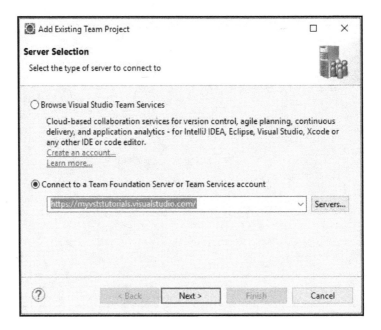

Add the existing team project available from TFS, and click on **Finish**:

Let's check whether the team project has any code or not. It is still not showing the code:

Go to Eclipse and verify the **Team Explorer** window. It is now connected:

Select the Eclipse project that we want to check in and right click on **Project**, select **Team**, and click on **Share Project**...:

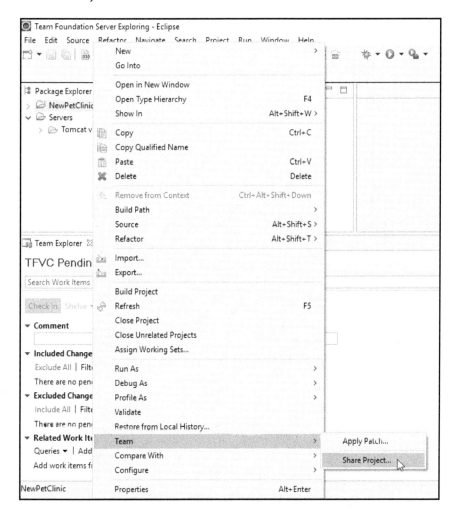

Select the repository type. Click on **Next**:

Select a team project from TFS:

Select a server location to share to:

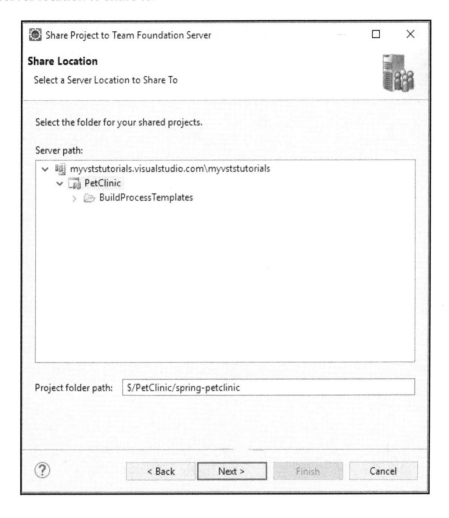

Review the share configuration, and click on **Finish**:

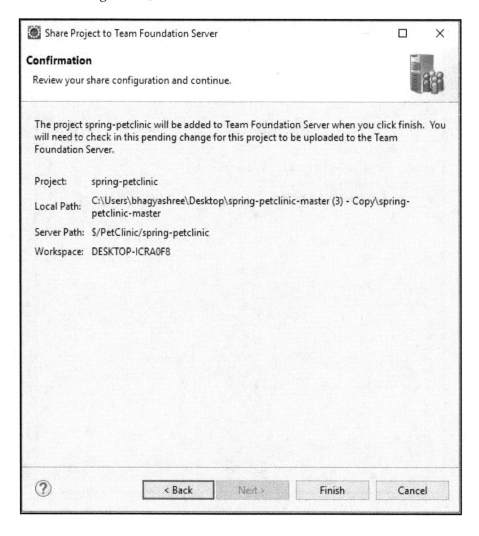

Go to **Team Explorer**. Verify the included changes and enter the comment for **Check In**:

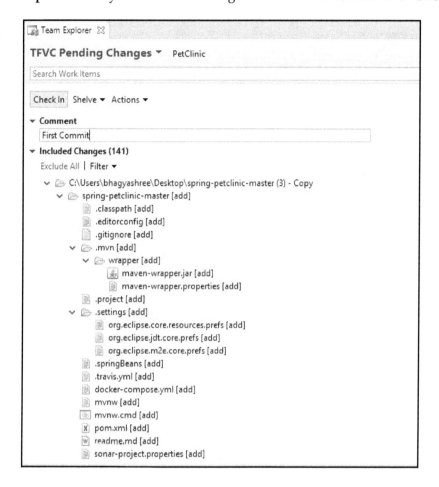

Click on **Check In**. Confirm the check in and click on **Yes**:

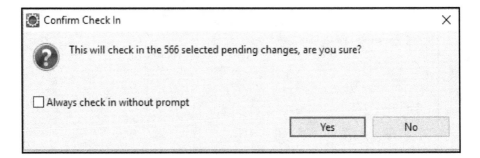

Check the **Progress Information** while the code is checked-in:

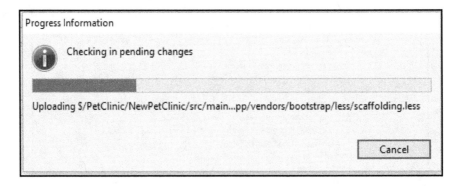

Once the check-in process is successful, look for the small yellow icons for each file and folder in **Package Explorer**:

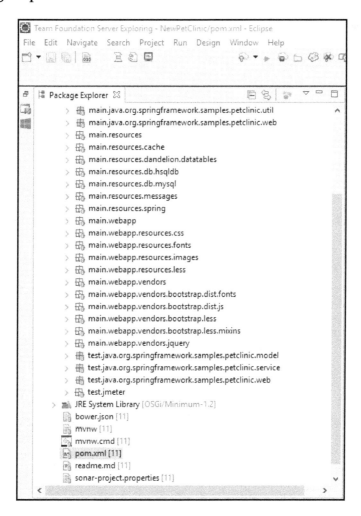

Go to VSTS accounts and refresh the page. Now we can see that the source code is available in the VSTS account under **Code**:

Until now, we successfully created a team project in VSTS, configured Eclipse with TFS connectivity, and checked-in the code into Team Services.

Summary

In this chapter, we covered an overview of VSTS, created a free account in VSTS, performed user management in VSTS, did an overview of the agile process template in VSTS and an overview of a sample JEE application, and performed Eclipse integration with TFS online in VSTS.

As we have set up the base, we will go ahead with CI and CD. In the next chapter, we will setup CI by using VSTS.

3
Continuous Integration with VSTS

As we look ahead into the next century, leaders will be those who empower others.

--Bill Gates

In the previous chapter, we covered details on **Visual Studio Team Services** (**VSTS**). In this chapter, we will see how to utilize VSTS for continuous integration. We will use a sample Spring application available on GitHub and try to integrate it with VSTS.

We already saw in `Chapter 2`, *Getting Started with Visual Studio Team Services (VSTS),* how to use TFVC; in this chapter, we will also see how to create a project where code is managed in Git.

This chapter shows how to configure application code for automated compilation, unit test case execution, and notify important stakeholders on the status of the build execution in case of failures and success. In this chapter, we are going to cover the following topics:

- Overview of continuous integration
- Creating a build definition for VSTS Project
- Configuration of continuous build integration in VSTS
- Unit test execution for automated testing
- Continuous feedback on build execution
- Git project in VSTS

After this chapter, we will be ready for deployment of the package file (the WAR file, in the case of the sample application) once build execution is successful.

Overview of continuous integration

Let's understand what continuous integration means in simple English.

Continuous Integration (**CI**) is a fundamental or base *DevOps practice* to commit code to a shared repository such as Git or SVN based on the bug fixes or feature completion. This change is verified against automated build using tools such as Ant or Maven, static code analysis tools such as SonarQube, and unit test execution with tools such as JUnit for Java.

Understanding of the CI differs based on what you have in practice while implementing it, but the core remains the same. Essentially, it is an application development practice. Team members share the code in the shared code repository and that results in integration. In the DevOps culture, we focus on collaboration and communication a lot. At first glance, it seems in place, but in practice, it is very difficult to get that culture into the mindset of developers, testers, and the operations team.

The obvious question here is, why are we including testing and operation teams while talking about the code repository?

In recent times, the practice is to store almost everything into a shared repository. All the testing related files need to be stored in the repository as well. It not only allows sharing of testing resources but also tracking of those resources which are extremely essential in the application life cycle management.

The next question is, it is understandable for code, but how about infrastructure? The moment we discuss infrastructure, we also need to consider about configuration management or the runtime environment management as well. **Infrastructure as Code** (**IAC**) can be achieved with one of the most disruptive innovations in recent times and that is cloud computing. Infrastructure can be set up using commands, API, and configuration management tools plugins (script or commands), and then it can be stored in a repository for sharing and tracking.

Configuration management tools, in case of IaaS, have cookbooks, runbooks, or other scripts that can be used to install a runtime environment on virtual machines available in the cloud environment. All such scripts are managed by configuration management tools at a central location. For example, in case of Chef, cookbooks are stored in the Chef server that might be available on-premise or can be hosted. In short, everything that can be stored in the repository, including code, test files, configuration scripts, infrastructure related commands, library files, and dependencies, should be stored in a shared repository, for better collaboration among the team and sharing of those resources.

Once we have the source code and relevant dependencies in the repository, we can easily integrate it with the CI server. It can be an open source or a commercial tool. In our case, we will use VSTS for CI and CD.

The code is compiled, verified against unit test cases, and static code analysis is performed. Such repeated integration in automated fashion helps to detect issues at early stages. The benefit of this practice is that issues or bugs are found at early stages and coding standards can be maintained.

 It is important to remember that the earlier we detect issues, the less complex it is to fix the issue. The more time it takes to detect the issue, the more complex it becomes to fix the issue because over the time, dependencies increase and it becomes a complex task to fix such issues.

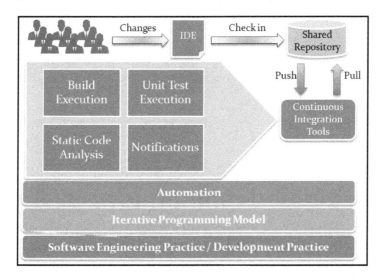

Let's understand how the CI practice can be followed:

- Developers develop a new feature or make changes in the existing code to fix the bug using IDE such as Eclipse or Visual Studio
- Once the feature is developed or the bug is fixed, the developer checks in the code into a shared repository

- The CI tools are configured in such a way that any change in the code repository will trigger a build execution

 The important thing to note here is the timing of build integration. It can be manual or trigger-based. It can be scheduled based on time and it can be based on the modification in the source code repository.

- Normally, build execution contains a series of steps or tasks, as follows:
    1. Compilation of the source code.
    2. Execution of unit test files (JUnit in the case of Java web application).
    3. Static code analysis using tools such as SonarQube.
    4. E-mail notification to stakeholders. Notifications are a very important part of CI as stakeholders need to be informed regarding the status of build in terms of success or failures.

In case of the CI tool, we need to have build scripts available so that the CI tool can execute build files to compile, execute the unit test, and create the package file (the WAR file in case of the Java web application).

In the next section, we will discuss build definition for VSTS project. Yes, it is our first step into the world of CI.

Creating a build definition for VSTS project

The objective of this section is to configure a code repository with VSTS in such a way that every time a developer checks in the code into the repository, it should automatically trigger the build script to execute and thus complete compilation, unit test execution, and SonarQube analysis (static code analysis), and notify different stakeholders based on the outcome of the CI process.

We should always remember that a process is always the same irrespective of the tools we use, be it open-source tools or commercial tools. We need build scripts; in case of a Java-based project, we need `build.xml` for Ant or `pom.xml` for Maven to execute the build. We need unit test cases written in JUnit or any other supported language.

Before explaining the steps for CI, we need to understand and remind ourselves that the DevOps is a culture and combination of people, processes, and tools. It is not only about automation. It is also about mindset change, change in existing inefficient processes and standardized tools as well as approaches to make things better and more effective than in the existing situation.

It is very straightforward to configure CI in VSTS. VSTS provides templates for configuring it. The important thing is to keep innovative ways in place to make developers responsible for implementing new features or fixing bugs and check in into the repository. Nowadays, e-mails, SMS, tweets, and other different ways can be implemented to notify specific stakeholders on the outcome of the CI activity.

In VSTS, we need to create a build definition to configure CI. From 10,000 feet, the following steps can be performed:

1. Create a new build definition from the predefined templates available in VSTS.
2. Select a repository.
3. Specify the default/hosted agent for execution.
4. Add the build step (configure the build tool specific XML file, JUnit test results, and code coverage).
5. Save the build.
6. Queue the new build (execute the build definition).
7. Configure build alerts using build templates for successful and failed builds.

Default/hosted agent is an important term here. It is important because it provides an environment so we can execute the build definition. It provides a machine where common tools are installed already and it can be used to execute the build definition.

To verify the existing hosted agent, go to the VSTS account, click on the **Settings**, select **Agent Pools**, click on **Hosted**, select **Hosted Agent**, and click on the **Capabilities** link. It will show the list of tools available in the preconfigured virtual machine or hosted agent.

The list is divided into two categories:

- **USER CAPABILITIES**: This shows information about user-defined capabilities supported by this host
- **SYSTEM CAPABILITIES**: This shows information about the capabilities provided by this host

The following table provides available packages already installed. It shows what the hosted agent contains:

Packages	Description
Agent.Name	Hosted Agent
Agent.Version	2.110.0
AndroidSDK	C:javaandroidsdkandroid-sdk
ant	C:javaantapache-ant-1.9.4
AzurePS	1.0.0
bower	C:NPMModulesbower.cmd
Cmd	C:Windowssystem32cmd.exe
curl	C:Program Files (x86)Gitbincurl.exe
DotNetFramework	C:WindowsMicrosoft.NETFramework64v4.0.30319
grunt	C:NPMModulesgrunt.cmd
gulp	C:NPMModulesgulp.cmd
java	C:Program FilesJavajre1.8.0_40
JDK	C:Program FilesJavajdk1.8.0_40
maven	C:javamavenapache-maven-3.2.2
MSBuild	C:Program Files (x86)MSBuild14.0bin
node.js	C:Program Filesnodejsnode.exe
npm	C:Program Filesnodejsnpm.cmd
SqlPackage	C:Program Files (x86)Microsoft Visual Studio 14.0Common7IDEExtensionsMicrosoftSQLDBDAC120sqlpackage.exe
VisualStudio	C:Program Files (x86)Microsoft Visual Studio 14.0
VSTest	C:Program Files (x86)Microsoft Visual Studio 14.0Common7IDECommonExtensionsMicrosoftTestWindow
Xamarin.Android	5.1.4.16

Let's start configuring the build definition for our sample Java/Spring project.

Go to the main page of the project we have created in the VSTS. We will create a build definition for the `PetClinic` project. Click on the `PetClinic` project in the **Recent** section:

Here, we are on the **Dashboards** page of the `PetClinic` project, and we can see the top bar with different menu items such as **Code**, **Work**, **Build & Release**, and **Test**.

In `Chapter 2`, *Getting Started with Visual Studio Team Services (VSTS)*, we already worked in the **Code** and **Work** section. To revise quickly, the **Code** section contains all the files that are checked in the repository. In our case, we are using TFVC as the repository.

In the **Work** section, we can manage scrum backlog, user stories, tasks, task assignment, task status, and so on:

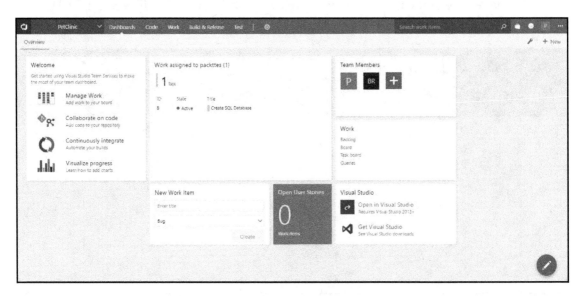

Click on **Build & Release** on the top bar. We will get different sections such as **Builds**, **Releases**, **Task Groups**, and **Explorer**.

Click on **Builds**. As this is a new account created by us, there are no build definitions available here. Build definition in VSTS is nothing but a group of tasks to be performed for continuous build execution or CI.

Click on **+New Definition**:

In the **Create new build definition** dialog box, we will get multiple options to select such as **Maven**, **Jenkins**, and **Visual Studio**. We can queue a Jenkins build job and download its artifacts; we can use templates available for Visual Studio, Ant-based Java project, and so on.

The build system has a capability to build the following types of applications:

- Build, test Java/JEE-based application
    - Build with Apache Ant
    - Build with Apache Maven
- .NET-based applications
    - Build, test, and publish using .NET core command line
    - Build with MSBuild
    - Build with MSBuild and set the Visual Studio version property
- Android
    - Build an Android application using Gradle and optionally start the emulator for unit tests
    - Sign and align Android APK files
    - Build using a Gradle wrapper script

- iOS
  - Build an iOS app with Xamarin on macOS
  - Build an Xcode workspace on macOS
  - Generate an `.ipa` file from Xcode build output
- Cross platform applications
  - Build with the CMake cross-platform build system
- JavaScript
  - The JavaScript task runner
- Gulp
  - Node.js streaming task-based build system
- Others
  - Index your source code and publish symbols to a file share
  - Queue a job on a Jenkins server
  - We can also add our own tasks

We have a Maven-based Java/Spring project. It has `pom.xml`, hence let's select **Maven** task. Click on **Next**:

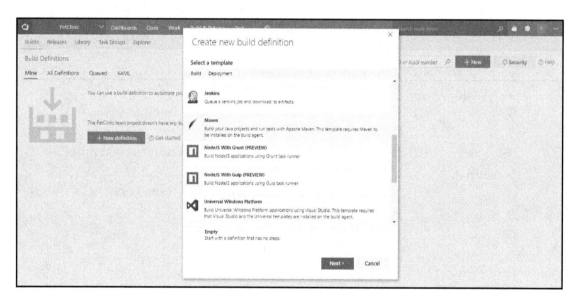

In the next dialog box, we need to select **Repository**. There are four options available for **Repository Source**:

- **PetClinic Team Project** (TFVC)
- **GitHub**
- **Remote Git Repository**
- **Subversion**

For this build definition, we will select the TFVC repository for the source as we have created the project using TFVC repository. In the last section of this chapter, we will see how to create a project with Git source too.

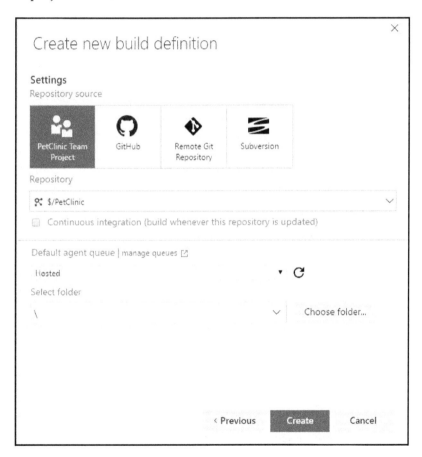

To set up CI, select the checkbox. So the build definition is going to be executed each time the repository is updated. What this essentially means is, any time a developer checks in the new feature implementation, or a bug fix, or any commit for that matter, it will result in the execution of the build definition.

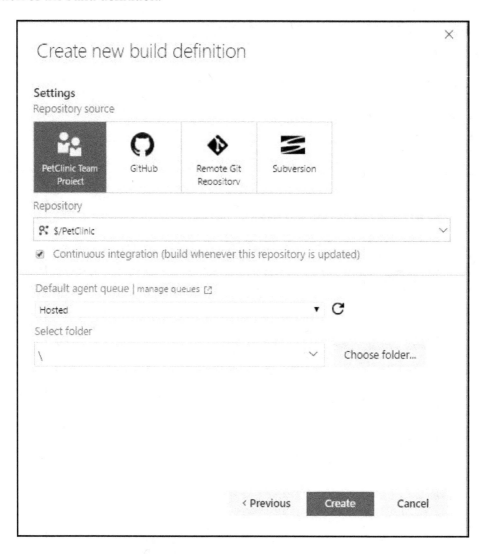

Keep the default agent queue as **Hosted** only. Agents are responsible for execution. We can set up our own agents, but in this book, we will only use **Hosted** agents for simplicity.

Click on **Create**:

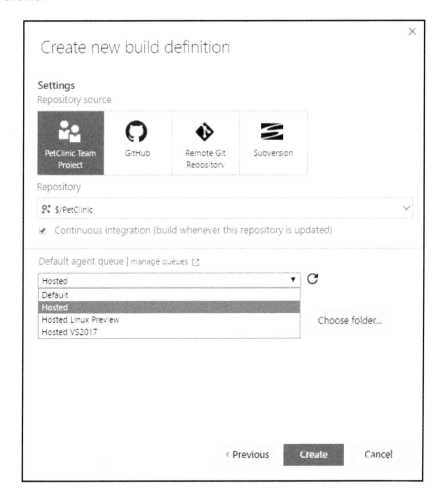

At this stage, our build definition for the sample Spring project is created, so we can automate the process of compilation of source code, unit test execution, and the creation of a package file. In the next section, we will cover how to configure the build definition so it can be executed successfully using the right set of files and folders.

Configuration of continuous build integration in VSTS

Once the build definition is created, we will configure the Maven task to give the path to `pom.xml` so build definition can use `pom.xml`, to compile the source code and create a package file.

Select **Maven pom.xml**. In the **Maven POM file**, give the path to `pom.xml` for the existing project:

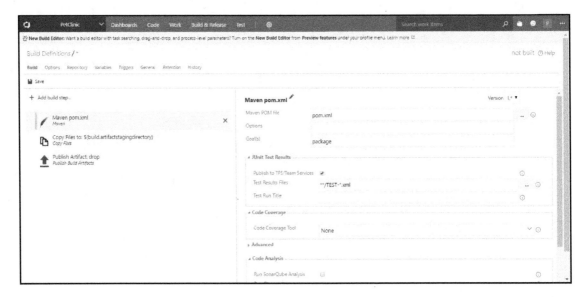

Click on the **...** icon to browse through the folders available in the existing project and select the path to `pom.xml`:

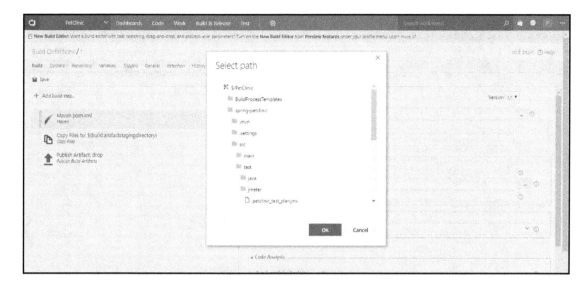

Scroll down; in our case, select `pom.xml` and click on **OK**:

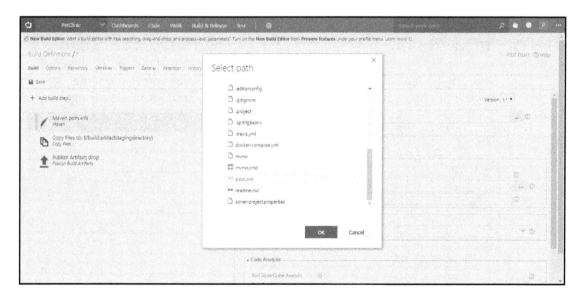

In the case of Maven, there are different goals such as `compile`, `test`, and `package`. We will give `package` here. If the default goal is available in `pom.xml`, then we don't need to explicitly mention it here.

Keep the **Test Results Files** setting as it is:

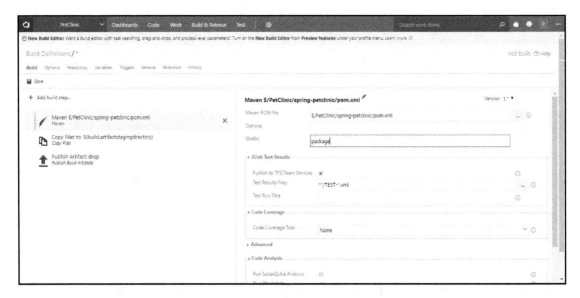

Select **Copy Files to: tasks** and keep **Source Folder** and **Target Folder** as it is. In the **Contents** box, enter `**/*.war`. It will copy the WAR file available in the source directory of the project from any path and copy it to the staging directory. We can use the same environment variables to access the WAR file in the release definitions while configuring continuous delivery:

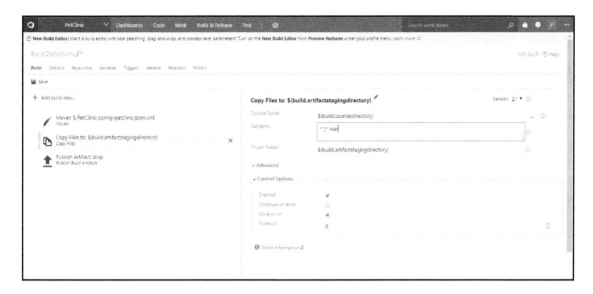

Select **Publish Artifact: task**. Keep the default setting as it is for now. It will publish the WAR file from the staging directory. Once it is published, we can utilize it in release definition:

In **Build Definitions**, multiple tabs are available, namely **Options**, **Repository**, **Variables**, **Triggers**, **General**, **Retention**, and **History**:

In the **Repository** tab, observe the settings related to the repository type and name. We already configured it for the `PetClinic` project in `Chapter 2`, *Getting Started with Visual Studio Team Services (VSTS)*:

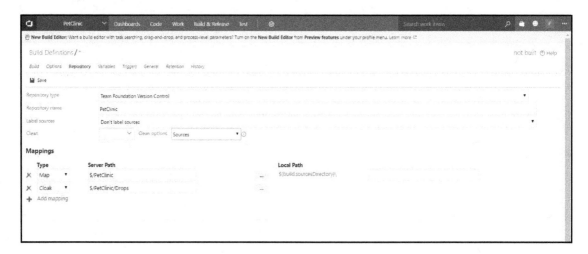

We can also give a label to the sources; for example, in the case of a successful build, provide a label to the build in a specific format:

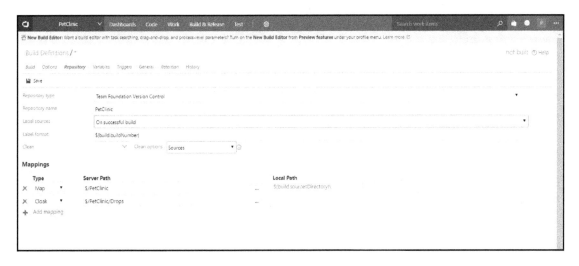

There are different options available here in **Repository type**, namely **Team Foundation Version Control**, **GitHub**, **External Git**, and **Subversion**.

Variables are similar to environment variables. Here, we can declare the key value pairs and can utilize them in the build definition.

To use these variables, we need to mention them in the **Build** section with $(VARIABLE_KEY). At the time of build definition execution, $(VARIABLE_KEY) will be replaced with the value mentioned in the **Variables** section. Often, such environment variables are useful if a specific value is used multiple times. It is easier to change it at a single place rather than manually changing it at all places.

For example, if we need to use FTP-related tasks, then it is better to provide the FTP URL and credentials in the **Variables** section and use them in the build definitions multiple times, rather than using them directly in the build definitions:

There are two ways to execute the build:

- Manually click on **Queue new build...**
- Schedule the build execution

In the **Triggers** tab, we can configure **Continuous integration (CI)**. In case we haven't configured CI during the new build definition creation, then we can configure it here.

In short, the **Triggers** tab provides different options to configure or schedule when the build should execute. So we can configure the builds to execute at the time of check-in of any feature or bug fix from the developers, or at the specific time configured in the **Triggers** tab.

The obvious is, why there are different ways to trigger a build at the time of check-in or at a specific time? The reason is, every time a developer checks in the code into the repository, it starts executing build definition, and that might not be the scenario we want to face. It is better to execute a build on a batch of changesets rather than executing it on each single changeset. Every check-in is considered as a changeset:

The preceding option was a trigger based on the check-in in the repository. To schedule CI at a specific time, select the **Scheduled** checkbox and configure a specific time based on the requirement.

In the scheduled triggers, we can set the time based on the 24-hour format, with minutes and time zone available in the list box. We can also select days when we want to execute the build definition. We can also add multiple times for the scheduled trigger for a given project:

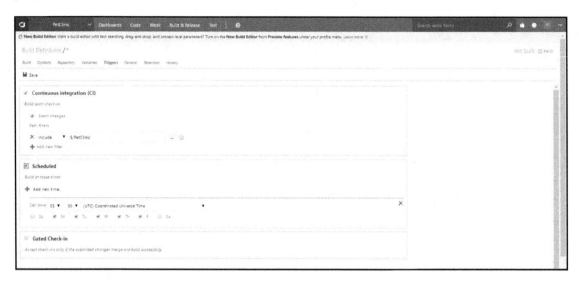

The **General** tab provides details on the default agent queue, authorization scope, build job timeout, and so on.

In case the build job takes more than 60 minutes, then it is better to increase the time limit here, otherwise the build definition execution will fail with time out.

There are some specific cases where the build takes a lot of time to complete all the tasks and in this case, we can increase the timeout:

The **Retention** tab provides options to configure what time you want to keep build record, source label, file share, symbols, and test results until. These rules are evaluated in this order:

Now, it is time to save our first build definition. Give a name to the build definition and provide a logical description. Click on **OK**:

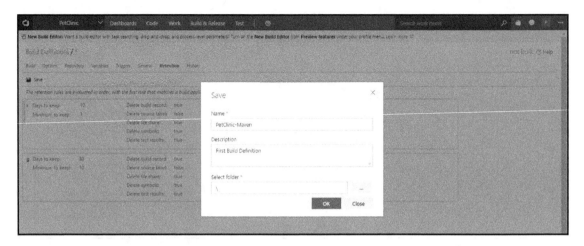

We have our first build definition that is ready to be executed. The given name appears after **Build Definitions** in the **Build** tab:

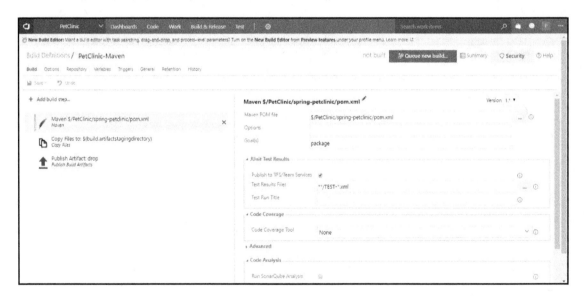

We can also provide permissions for the project by clicking on the **Security** button available on the **Build Definitions** page.

Click on **Close**:

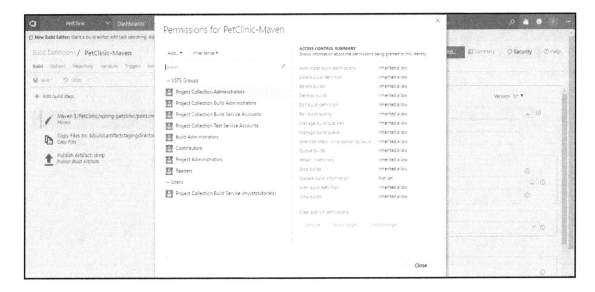

Executing build definition

Let's execute our first build definition for the sample Spring based project—`PetClinic`.

Click on **Queue new build....** Keep all the settings as they are and click on **OK**.

The queue suggests the agent selection that will execute the build definition. The **Source Version** is the changeset that needs to be used for execution. If no **Source Version** is given, then it will automatically take the latest changeset:

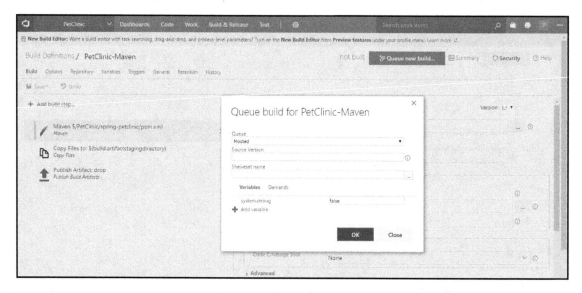

Build definition will be in a queue for a hosted agent. Once an agent is available, it will start execution based on the tasks defined in the build definition:

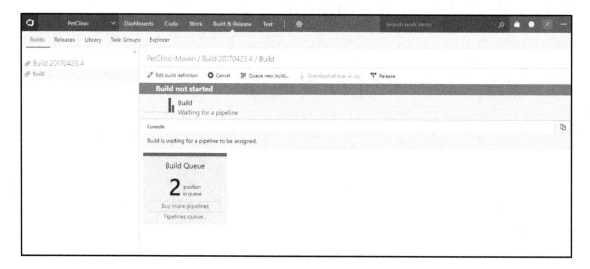

Once the agent is initialized, the build execution will start. Observe the logs and all tasks available in the left bar.

It will be executed in the following order:

1. **Initialize Agent**
2. **Get Sources**
3. **Maven $/PetClinic/NewPetClinic/pom.xml**
4. **Copy Files to: $(build.artifactstagingdirectory)**
5. **Publish Artifact: drop**
6. **Post Job Cleanup**

If any of the task execution fails, the build will fail. In our case, all tasks are executed successfully, hence the build succeeded:

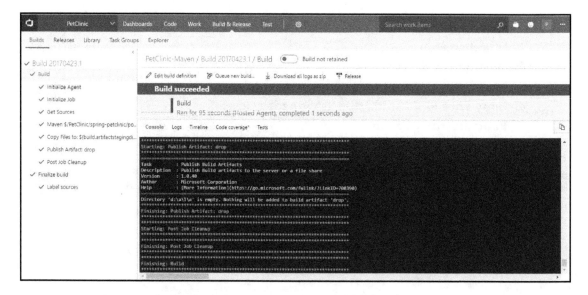

Click on the **Build & Release** section and we will find our build definition with its status, triggering point, pass rate, and history. Click on the build definition.

Sometimes, it is necessary to get all log files for troubleshooting on a local system. We can download all logs by clicking on the link and download all logs as a ZIP.

Verify the **Summary** portion. It provides details on repository, default queue, modification details, branches, recent history, and analytics:

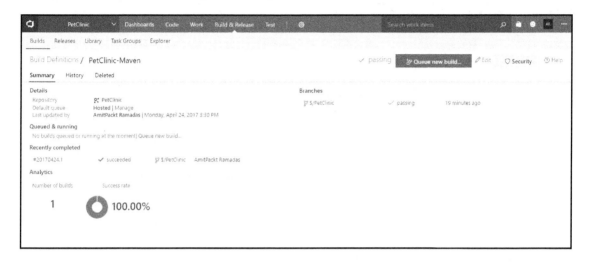

Click on the **Explorer** tab and we will get more details related to **Timeline**, **Artifacts**, **Tests**, and so on:

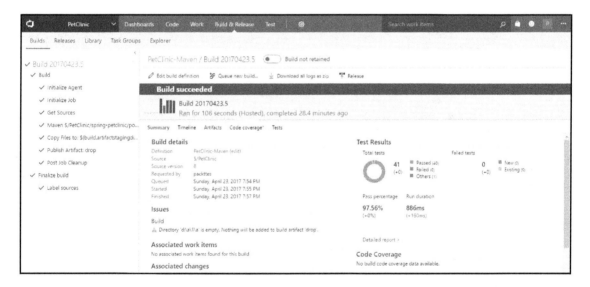

Click on **Timeline** to verify the duration each task took to be completed:

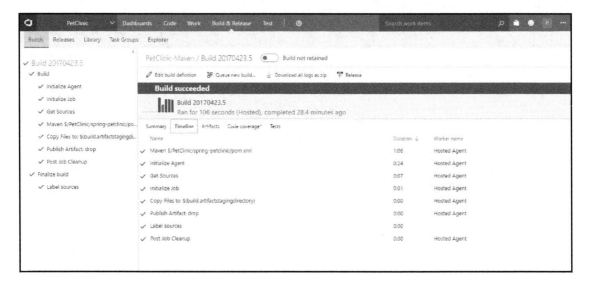

We configured the artifacts details in build definition tasks and based on it, we will find it in the **Artifacts** tab:

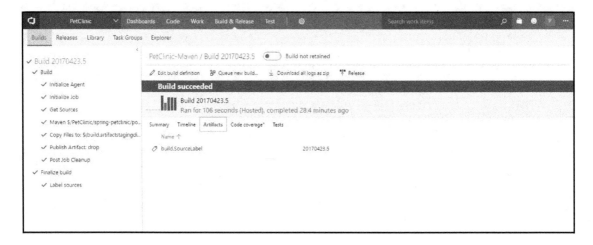

In this section, we have covered a build execution. Unit testing is also an important part of it that we will look into in the next section.

Unit test execution for automated testing

In the `PetClinic` example, unit tests are written in JUnit. Unit test cases individually and independently verify specific methods of an application. In build definition Maven tasks, the test configuration was kept as default.

After executing the build successfully, we can go to **Explorer** tab and click on the **Tests** links in the build execution logs to get more details on the test execution.

Verify the total number of tests, the passed and failed percentage, and the duration of test execution:

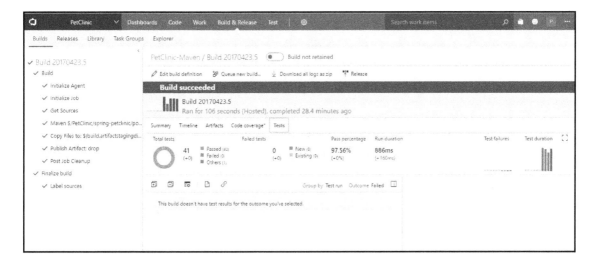

To get more details, click on the **Test** link on the top bar. Click on the **Test runs**.

Verify the **Completed** status of the test run in the **Recent test runs**. Double click on the entry:

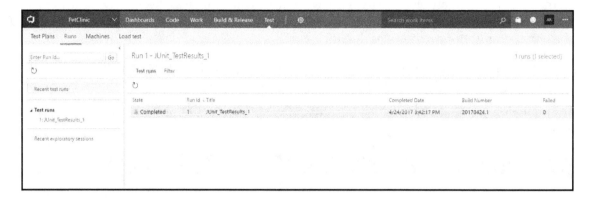

We will get the summary, run type, build version number, and outcome in the form of a chart showing passed and failed test results. In the following chart, it shows that all 41 unit tests have been executed successfully:

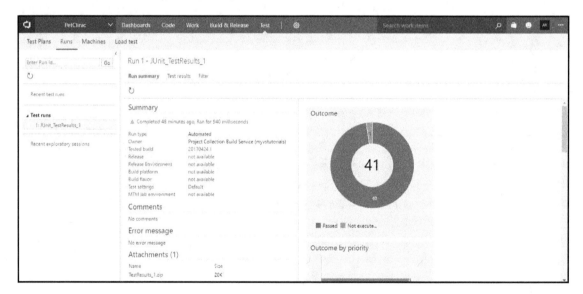

Click on the **Test results** tab to get results based on unit tests available for the project and the duration of execution of each of them:

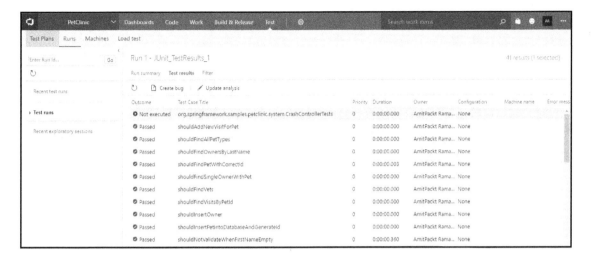

Hence, we have completed major tasks for CI. In the next section, we will discuss continuous feedback.

Continuous feedback on build execution

Build execution is important, but the significant part of the whole process is to get continuous feedback of the build execution status. For example, to send a notification in case of build execution failure or success to specific stakeholders.

On the VSTS Project, click on the settings icon, and it will bring up the **PetClinic Team** page:

Click on the **Notifications** tab:

Click on **+New**. Verify the template for the **Build** notification. Click on **Next**:

Configure the fields as per your need and click on **Finish**:

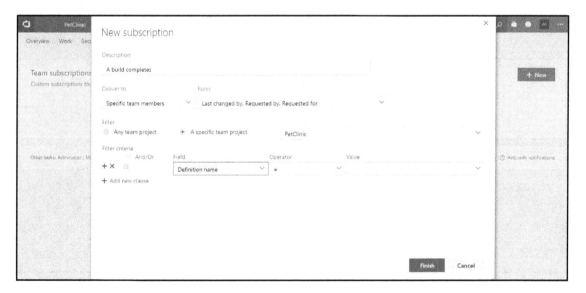

There are multiple notification templates available for the build status notification:

Similarly, we can create an notification when the build fails:

Verify all the created alerts in **Team subscriptions**:

For a self-exercise, observe whether all the alerts are triggered properly in terms of a specific event occurrence such as build success or build failure.

In the next section, we will cover how the Git project can be managed in VSTS.

Managing the Git project in VSTS

In this section, we will cover how to manage the Git project in VSTS; however, the build definition and its execution is for self-exercise.

On the main page of VSTS account, go to the **Projects** section. Click on **New Project**.

In **Create new project**, give **Project name**, select **Scrum** or **Agile** as the **Work item process**. Select **Git** as **Version control**. Click on **Create**:

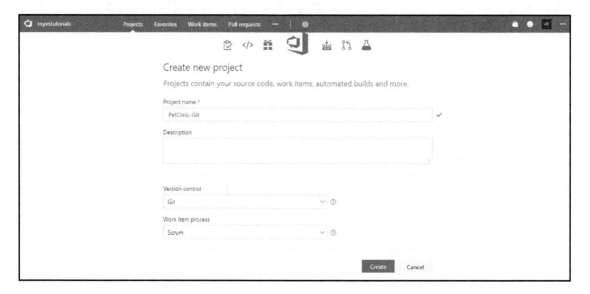

Wait till the project creation process completes in VSTS. Here is the screen for the newly created project:

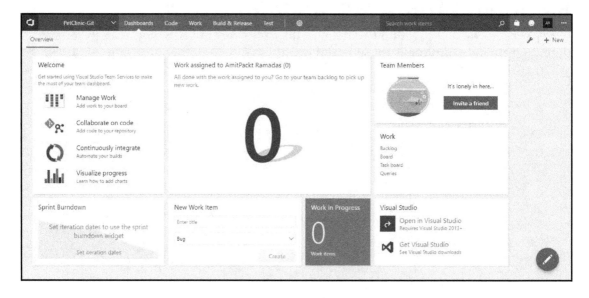

Click on the **Code** tab on the top bar and verify the details available in the **Files** section. Git related details are available:

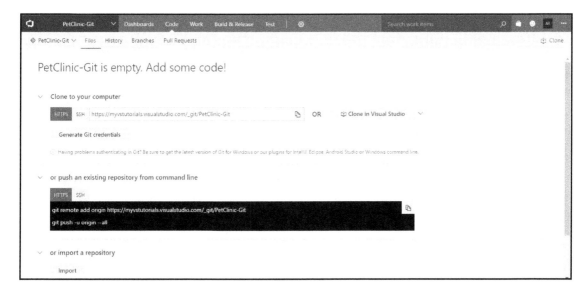

Verify the **History** tab as well. The repository is still empty as we haven't performed check-in:

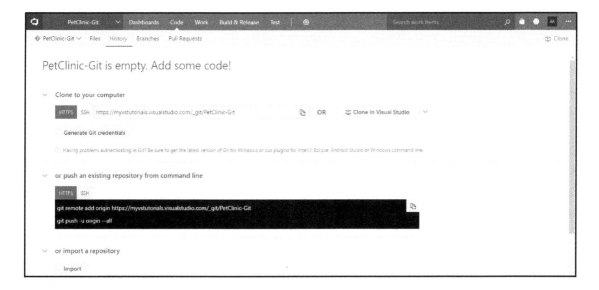

We will try to check-in the `PetClinic` code from the local system to Git available in VSTS. Before that, click on **Generate Git credentials** so we can use it from our local system to check-in the code into the Git repository available here.

Enter **User name (primary)** and **Password**. Click on **Save Git Credentials**:

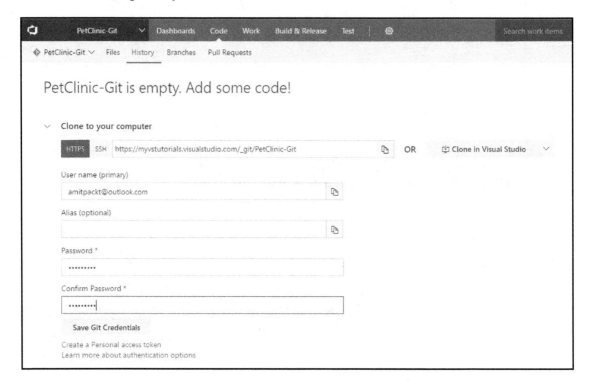

Go to the directory where the source code for the `PetClinic` project is available. Verify the files available in the directory. Initialize the Git repository with the `git init` command:

```
C:\Windows\System32\cmd.exe
Microsoft Windows [Version 10.0.14393]
(c) 2016 Microsoft Corporation. All rights reserved.

F:\##MicrosoftAzureBook\Pre-Finals\spring-petclinic-master>dir
 Volume in drive F is New Volume
 Volume Serial Number is 6A72-42C1

 Directory of F:\##MicrosoftAzureBook\Pre-Finals\spring-petclinic-master

18-09-2016  02:08    <DIR>          .
18-09-2016  02:08    <DIR>          ..
18-09-2016  02:08                45 .bowerrc
18-09-2016  02:08               192 .editorconfig
18-09-2016  02:08                61 .gitignore
18-09-2016  02:08    <DIR>          .mvn
18-09-2016  02:08               726 .springBeans
18-09-2016  02:08                31 .travis.yml
18-09-2016  02:08               134 bower.json
18-09-2016  02:08             7,112 mvnw
18-09-2016  02:08             5,186 mvnw.cmd
18-09-2016  02:08            17,112 pom.xml
18-09-2016  02:08             8,515 readme.md
18-09-2016  02:08                 0 Readme.txt
18-09-2016  02:08               332 sonar-project.properties
18-09-2016  02:08    <DIR>          src
              12 File(s)         39,446 bytes
               4 Dir(s)  249,993,940,992 bytes free

F:\##MicrosoftAzureBook\Pre-Finals\spring-petclinic-master>git init
Initialized empty Git repository in F:/##MicrosoftAzureBook/Pre-Finals/spring-petclinic-master/.git/

F:\##MicrosoftAzureBook\Pre-Finals\spring-petclinic-master>_
```

Verify `git status`. It will show untracked files:

```
F:\##MicrosoftAzureBook\Pre-Finals\spring-petclinic-master>git init
Initialized empty Git repository in F:/##MicrosoftAzureBook/Pre-Finals/spring-petclinic-master/.git/

F:\##MicrosoftAzureBook\Pre-Finals\spring-petclinic-master>git status
On branch master

Initial commit

Untracked files:
  (use "git add <file>..." to include in what will be committed)

        .bowerrc
        .editorconfig
        .gitignore
        .mvn/
        .springBeans
        .travis.yml
        Readme.txt
        bower.json
        mvnw
        mvnw.cmd
        pom.xml
        readme.md
        sonar-project.properties
        src/

nothing added to commit but untracked files present (use "git add" to track)

F:\##MicrosoftAzureBook\Pre-Finals\spring-petclinic-master>
```

Add the remote repository by executing the `git remote add origin`
`https://myvstutorials.visualstudio.com/_git/PetClinic-Git`.

We have to log in to our VSTS account:

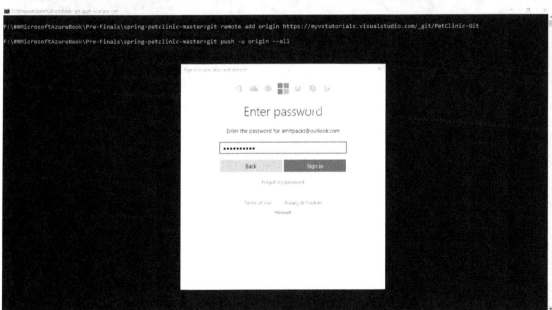

We have to configure the user if it is not configured already using the following commands:

- `git config --global user.email "amitpackt@outlook.com"`

- `git config --global user.name "amitpackt"`

Here is the output:

Add all files for the commit operation using the `git add -A` command:

Verify the status once again using the `git status` command:

Execute your first commit by using the `git commit -m "First Commit"` command:

After commit operation, we need to execute `git push` command:

Once the `git push` operation is successfully completed, go to VSTS and verify the files available for Git project – now we have all the files available in the VSTS account:

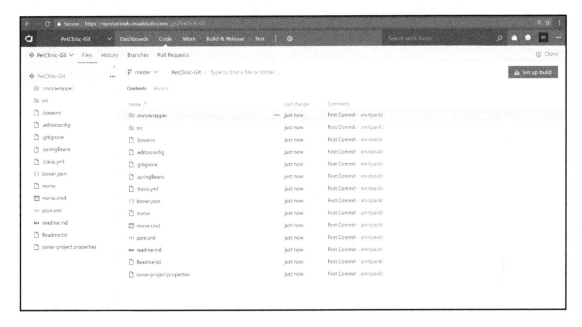

Go to the **Build & Release** section and click on **+New definition**:

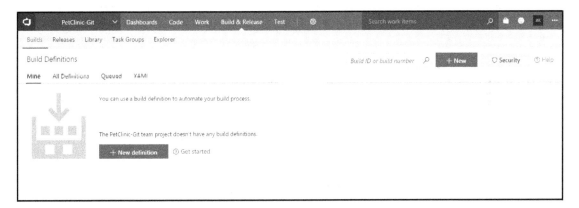

Select the **Maven** template for our Java-based project:

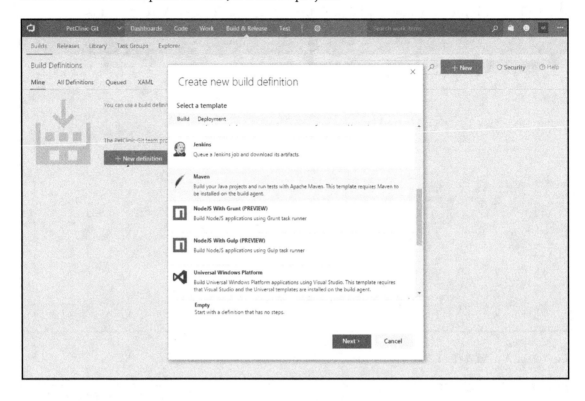

Select the Git repository:

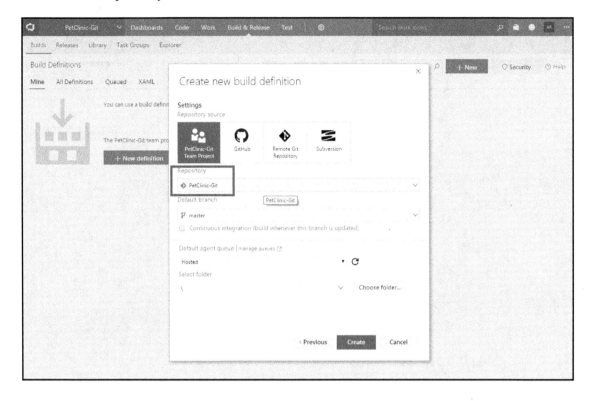

Check whether the tasks available in the **Maven** template are similar to the TFVC-based build definition:

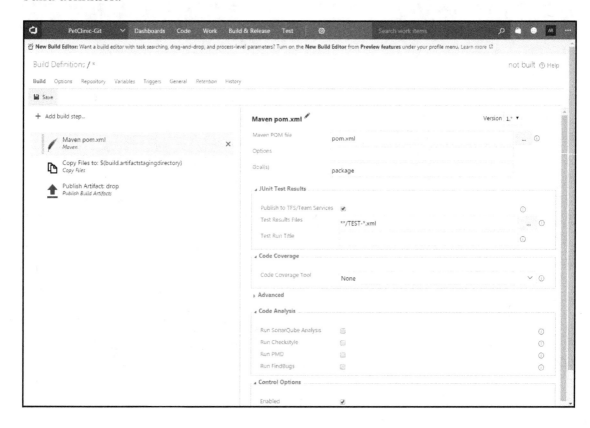

Click on the **Save** link and provide a name for the build definition:

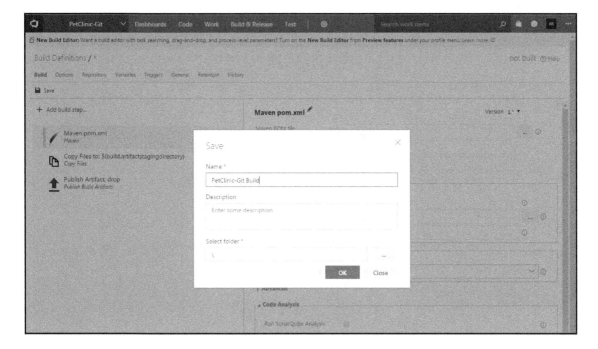

Check whether the build is saved and the name appears on the dashboard. Click on **Queue new build...**:

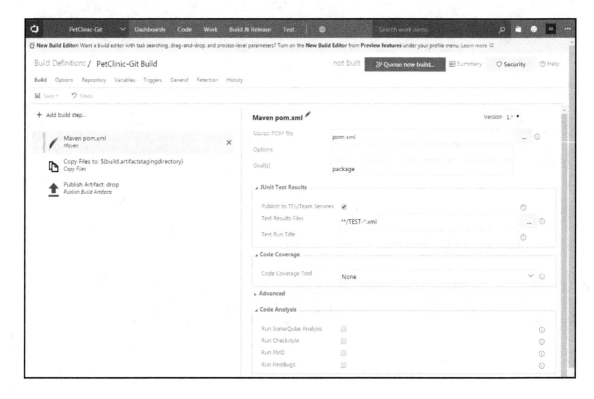

Keep settings as default and click on **OK**:

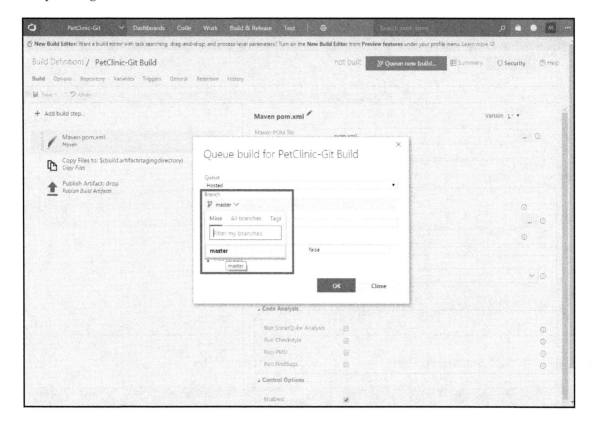

Click on the **Get Sources** section of the log and observe the Git-related operations:

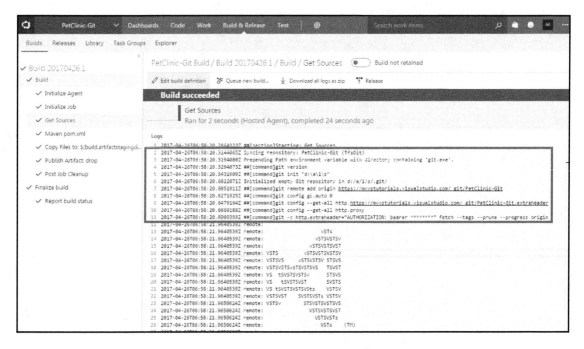

Verify the **Get Sources** section when it is successfully completed:

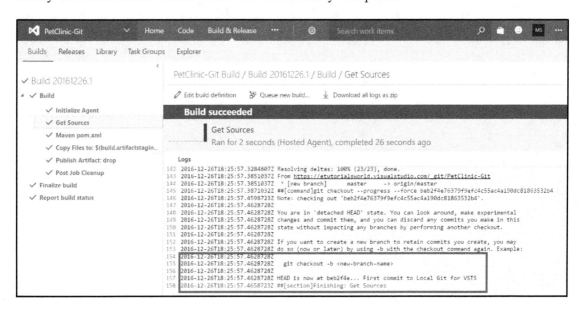

The rest of the processes are the same as we described in the preceding section, where TFVC is used as a repository.

In the next section, we will briefly cover task catalog and marketplace.

Task catalog and marketplace

In **Build & Release**, we can use many tasks after selecting a template. In the `PetClinic` build, we have used the **Maven** template for the build execution. It has a predefined set of tasks that needs to be executed. Based on the need, we can add more tasks from the task logs in the build definition.

All tabs contain all the tasks available to perform specialized tasks for application life cycle management:

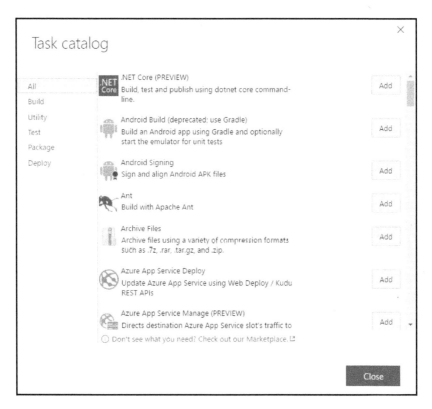

The **Build** tab in **Task catalog** contains tasks related to CI:

- **.NET Core (PREVIEW)**: This builds, tests, and publishes using .NET core command line
- **Android Build (deprecated; use Gradle)**: This builds an Android app using Gradle and optionally starts the emulator for unit tests
- **Android Signing**: This signs and aligns the Android APK files
- **Ant**: This builds with Apache Ant
- **CMake**: This builds with the CMake cross-platform build system
- **Gradle**: This builds using a Gradle wrapper script
- **Grunt**: This is the JavaScript Task Runner
- **Gulp**: This is the Node.js streaming task-based build system
- **Index Sources & Publish Symbols**: This indexes your source code and publishes symbols to a file share
- **Jenkins Queue Job**: This queues a job on a Jenkins server
- **Maven**: This builds with Apache Maven
- **MSBuild**: This builds with MSBuild
- **SonarQube for MSBuild - Begin Analysis**: (Deprecated) This fetches the Quality Profile from SonarQube to configure the analysis
- **SonarQube for MSBuild - End Analysis**: (Deprecated) This finishes the analysis and uploads the results to SonarQube
- **Visual Studio Build**: This builds with MSBuild and sets the Visual Studio version property
- **Xamarin.Android**: This builds an Android app with Xamarin
- **Xamarin.iOS**: This builds an iOS app with Xamarin on macOS
- **Xcode Build**: This builds an Xcode workspace on macOS
- **Xcode Package iOS**: This generates a `.ipa` file from Xcode build output

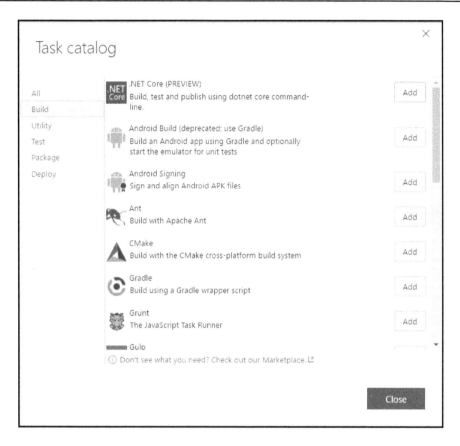

The **Utility** tab in **Task catalog** contains tasks related to specific operations that need to be performed for specialized tasks, as follows:

- Archive files using a variety of compression formats such as .7z, .rar, .tar.gz, and .zip
- Extract a variety of archive and compression files such as .7z, .rar, .tar.gz, and .zip
- Run a command line with arguments
- Run a windows .cmd or .bat script
- Run a PowerShell script
- Run a shell script using bash
- Copy build artifacts to a staging folder
- Copy files from a source folder to a target folder
- Use cURL to upload files with FTP, FTPS, SFTP, and HTTP

- Upload FTP
- Delete files or folders
- Download artifacts produced by a Jenkins job

The **Test** tab in **Task catalog** contains tasks related to testing related operations as follows:

- Run the load test in the cloud with VSTS
- Run the Apache JMeter load test in cloud
- Run a quick web performance test in the cloud with VSTS
- Publish test results to VSTS/TFS
- Run coded UI/Selenium/Functional tests on a set of machines (using Test Agent)
- Run tests with Visual Studio test runner
- Deploy and configure Test Agent to run tests on a set of machines
- Test mobile apps with Xamarin Test Cloud using Xamarin.UITest

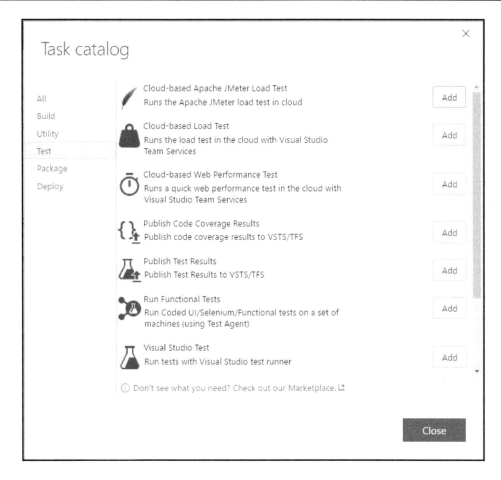

The **Package** tab in **Task catalog** contains tasks related to packaging resources:

- CocoaPods is the dependency manager for Swift and Objective-C Cocoa projects
- Run `pod install`
- Run the `npm` command
- Install or restore missing NuGet packages
- Create `.nupkg` outputs from `.csproj` or `.nuspec` files

- Upload `.nupkg` files to a NuGet server
- Restore Xamarin components for the specified solution

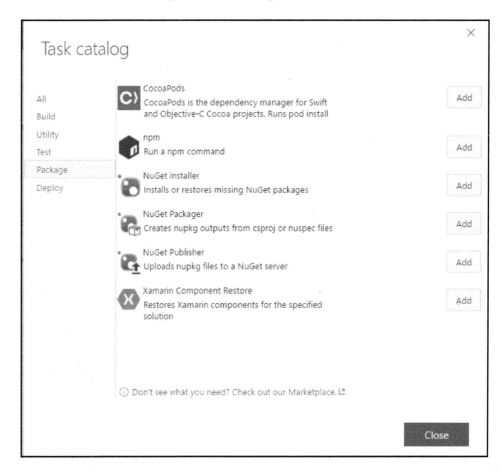

The **Deploy** tab in **Task catalog** contains tasks related to the deployment of the package to a specific environment:

- Update Azure App Service using Web Deploy / Kudu REST APIs
- Run a Shell or Batch script with Azure CLI commands against an Azure subscription
- Deploy an Azure Cloud Service
- Copy files to Azure blob or VM(s)
- Run a PowerShell script within an Azure environment
- Deploy, start, stop, and delete Azure Resource Groups

- Deploy Azure SQL DB using DACPAC, or run scripts using SQLCMD
- Copy files or build artifacts to a remote machine over SSH
- Execute PowerShell scripts on remote machine(s)
- Run shell commands or a script on a remote machine using SSH
- Copy files to remote machine(s)

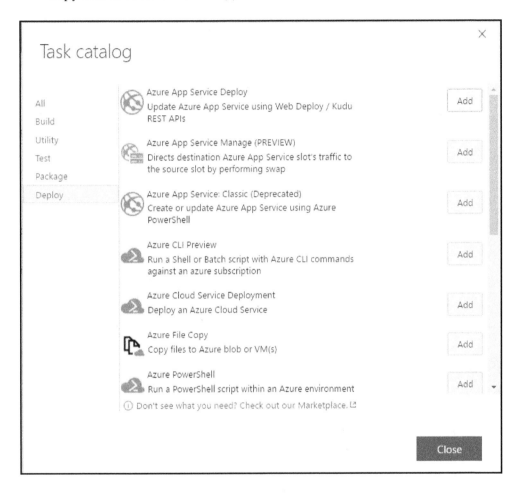

In case we need tasks that are not available in the **Task catalog**, we can go to **Marketplace** and utilize tasks available there.

 Visit **Marketplace** at `https://marketplace.visualstudio.com/search ?target=vsts&category=Build%20and%20release&sortBy=Downloads`.

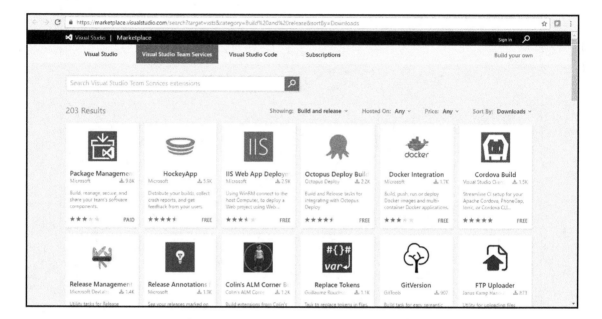

 To build your own task visit `https://www.visualstudio.com/en-us/doc s/integrate/extensions/overview`.

Summary

It is always better to fail at an early stage and recover sooner. In the case of application life cycle management, if we find issues at early stages, then we get more time to fix them, while severity and dependencies are less complex and can be easily sorted out.

> *Continuous effort – not strength or intelligence – is the key to unlocking our potential.*
> —*Winston Churchill*

In this chapter, we covered CI for a Java-based web application.

After configuring and executing CI for the `PetClinic` project, where code is shared via TFVC repository, the next step should be to create a deployment environment. The deployment environment can be a development, QA, staging, or production environment.

In the next chapter, we will create Microsoft Azure Web Apps (Azure App Service), configure Azure web app with programming language specific settings (in our case configuration related to Java application), create and configure – Dev, QA, UAT, Staging, and Prod, for isolated environment, cost benefit, and warmed up environment for application deployment.

We will also cover getting and changing deployment credentials for FTP for specific Azure Web Apps, basic monitoring of Azure Web Apps, configuring role-based access for secure access of Azure Web Apps, and scaling of Azure Web Apps resources. We will also look at Microsoft Azure Web Apps properties and Microsoft Azure Web Apps – App Service Plan in brief too.

> *Individual commitment to a group effort – that is what makes a team work, a company work, a society work, a civilization work.*
> —*Vince Lombardi*

Hence, the development and QA team's efforts covered us until now and the operation team's efforts in the coming chapters help to make changes in the existing culture.

We need to understand the fact that change doesn't come overnight, and expecting a mindset change in a day or a week is not feasible.

4
Continuous Development with Microsoft Azure Web Apps

Most people overestimate what they can do in one year and underestimate what they can do in ten years.

–Bill Gates

The Microsoft Azure App Service is a PaaS offering from Microsoft and it has an easy learning curve. In this chapter, we will discuss App Service (Microsoft Azure Web Apps) in detail. Web Apps are used to deploy applications in the process of CD and continuous development. It covers how we can create different web applications for environments that can be used to deploy web applications with cost benefits and isolation too. It also covers a brief description on providing secure access to all resources using role-based access that is significant from the security and governance perspective.

In this chapter, we'll cover the following topics:

- Creating Azure Web Apps
- Configuring Web Apps with programming language specific settings
- Deployment slots – development, QA, UAT, staging, and production
- Deployment credentials management for FTP
- Monitoring Azure Web Apps
- Configuring role-based access for secure access of Azure Web Apps
- Scaling Azure Web Apps
- Basic tasks to manage Azure Web Apps

Creating Azure Web Apps

Azure Web Apps is an App Service by Microsoft that can be used to deploy Java, ASP.NET, Node.js, PHP, and Python-based business web applications. The PaaS model comes with less management in the context of managing underlying resources. Hence, we need not worry about the infrastructure and we can focus on the innovations and improvements in the application logic.

App Service can be easily used in DevOps practices. VSTS can be used for continuous integration and CD or deployment using different tasks and different ways. VSTS has tasks for the application deployment in Azure App Service.

Azure Web Apps can scale and be made available in different geographies using manual and scheduled scaling operations and traffic manager simultaneously. The underlying resources can be based on Linux (in preview) or Windows and it provides this option while creating a web application. There are multiple pricing tiers available with different features and capacities to host web applications:

- **Free**: Try this for implementing **Proof of Concept** (**POC**)
- **Shared**: This is for basic web application or static websites
- **Basic**: This is suitable for the development/test environment
- **Standard**: This is suitable for web and mobile applications in the production environment
- **Premium**: This is suitable for enterprise scale and integration; it is the most expensive

> For more details, go to App Service pricing: `https://azure.microsoft.com/en-us/pricing/details/app-service/`.
> View full details for ASP: `https://azure.microsoft.com/en-us/pricing/details/app-service/plans/`.

Let's create our very first Azure web application:

1. Go to `portal.azure.com` and click on **App Services**. If the **App Services** menu item is not available in the left-hand sidebar, then click on **More services** at the bottom of the sidebar. Find **App Services** in the **Filter** and click on the star icon. It will be available in the left-hand sidebar now. We can also use search.
2. Click on the **+Add** link:

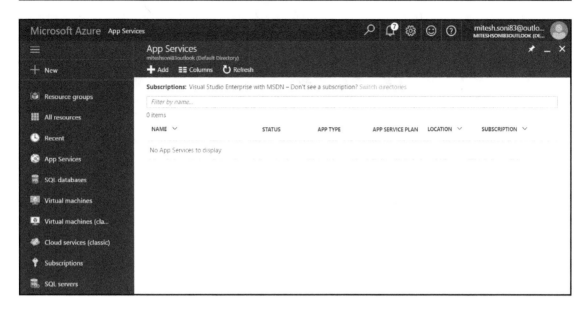

3. A pane with different options to create a web application will be opened. In our case, we will use an internal database, which is available with a sample application, so we don't need database still for understanding and demonstration, we will select the **Web App + SQL** template to create our Azure web application. Click on **Create**:

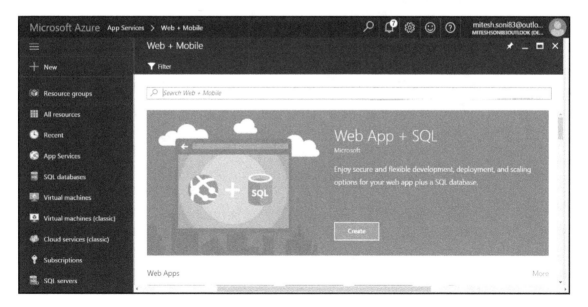

4. Give a name to the web application, select existing **Resource Group**, and keep the default setting in **App Service plan/Location**:

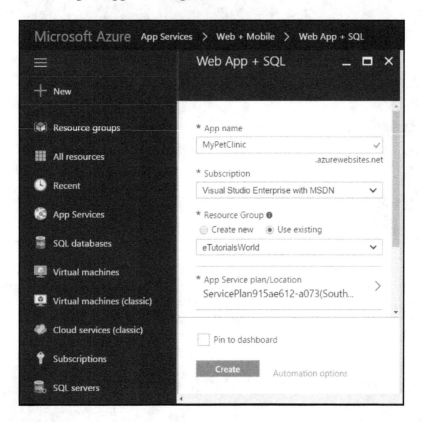

5. As we selected **Web App + SQL**, we need to select or create an Azure SQL Database.

   Click on **Create a new database**. Provide a name for the SQL database, **Pricing tier**, and **Target server** on which the SQL database will be available:

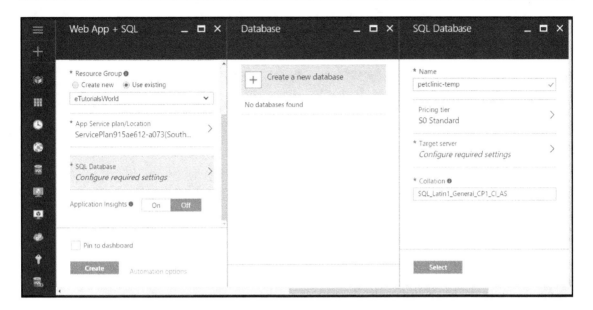

6. As no **Target server** is available, click on **Create a new server**. Provide a **Server name**, **Server admin login**, **Password**, and **Location**. Click on **Select**:

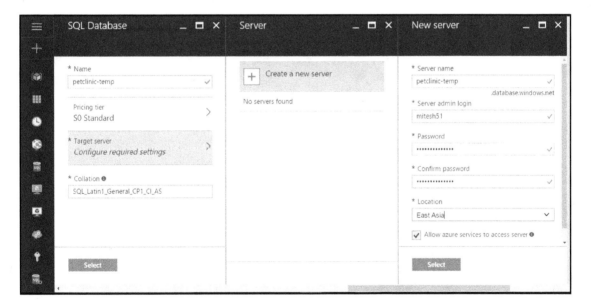

7. Verify that the newly configured server details are available in the **Target server** field. Click on **Select**:

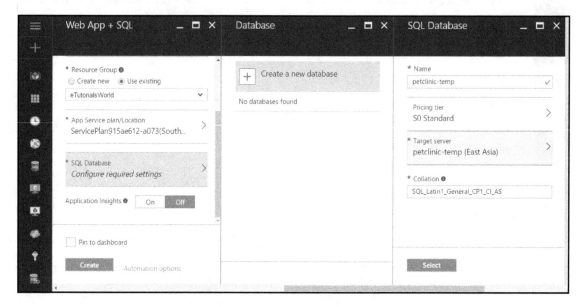

8. As all details are filled in, click on **Create**:

9. In the notification section, click on the existing activity to verify the status of your web application creation:

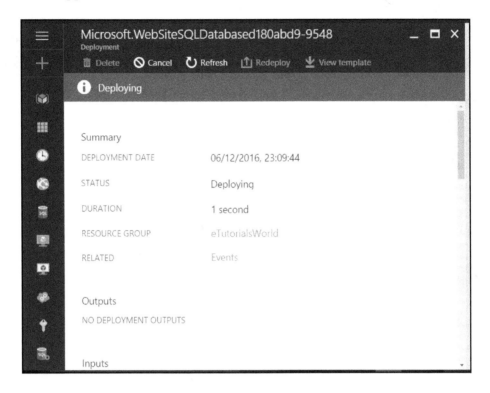

10. Wait for few minutes and get your first Azure web application ready in the **App Services** section:

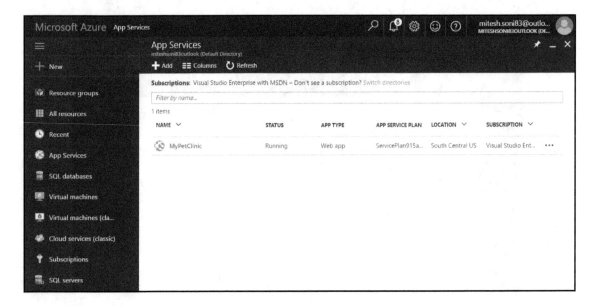

11. Select the `MyPetClinic` Azure web application in the **App Services** section. After creating a web application in Azure App Service, we will use it for application deployment.

In the **Overview** section, we can get details on **Resource group**, **Status**, **Location**, **Subscription name**, **Subscription ID**, **URL** of web application, and **App Service plan/pricing tier** associated with the Azure web application, username to access Azure web application resources using FTP, **FTP hostname**, and **FTPS hostname**. Click on the **URL** to visit the **Home** page of the Azure web application:

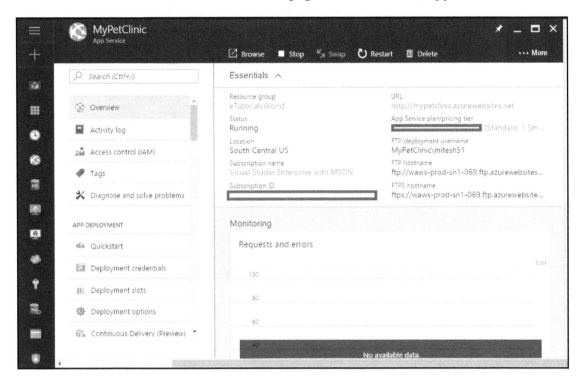

12. This is Azure web application with the default setting:

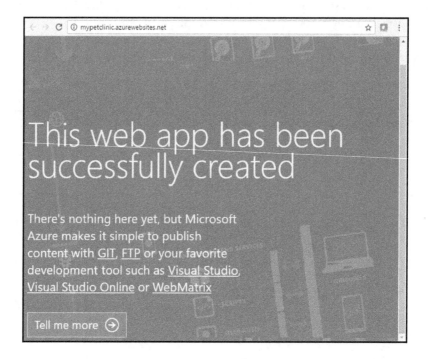

 To know more about Azure App Service, visit `https://docs.microsoft.com/en-in/azure/app-service/`.

Hence, we created Azure web application successfully with default settings. We have a sample Java-based web application so we need to tune Azure web application to provide the execution environment for the Java-based web application. In the next section, we will configure Azure web application with programming language specific settings.

Configuring Web Apps with programming language specific settings

Now, once we have created web application, we can configure it based on our needs. For example, we need to configure the web application based on a 32-bit or 64-bit platform, programming language, and so on.

1. Go to Azure web application in the Microsoft Azure portal.

2. Search for **Application settings** and click on it. It will open a **General settings** pane. Here we can configure the application runtime environment. There are different options available for configuration such as **.NET Framework version**, **PHP version**, **Java version**, **Python version**, and **Platform**:

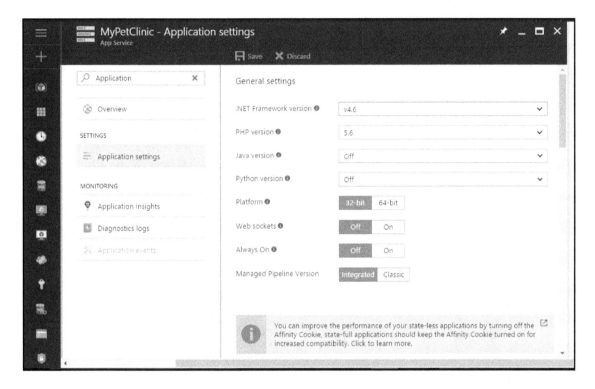

3. We are going to deploy a Java-based application, hence we will configure Java settings in this web application.
   Select **Java 8** in the **Java version** field:

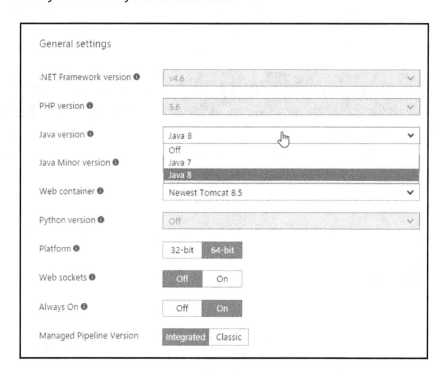

4. Select **Newest** in the **Java Minor version** field:

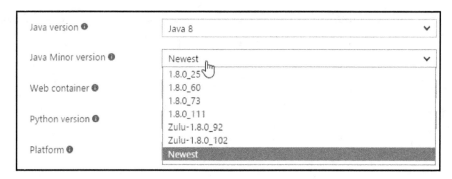

5. In **Web container**, select **Newest Tomcat 8.5**:

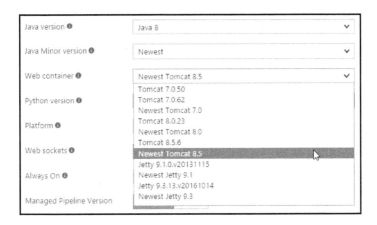

6. Select a **32-bit** or **64-bit** environment as **Platform**. Free and Shared pricing tiers can host a 32-bit environment only. The web application pricing tier has to be Basic or Standard for a 64-bit environment.

7. Enable the **Always On** switch for Azure Web Apps as they are unloaded if they are idle for some time, to conserve resources. If we enable this **Always On** switch, then web application will be loaded irrespective of the idle time.

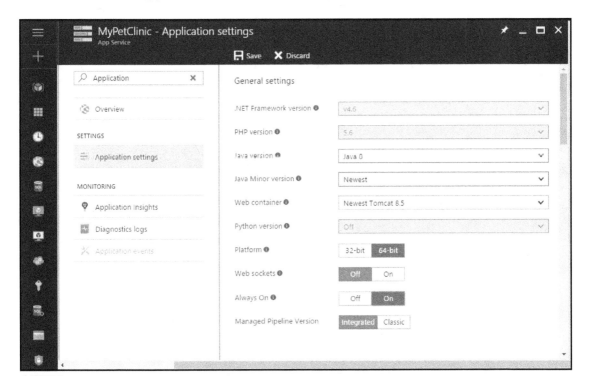

8. For a stateless application, we can keep the **ARR Affinity** switch **off** for better performance.

   Application Request Routing (ARR) is an IIS extension to manage traffic between users and active instances by keeping track of users. This affinity cookie keeps track of subsequent requests to manage requests and the requests are served by the same instance. Request client and server instance will communicate as long as a session is active. However, in the case of stateless applications, we need not keep track of subsequent requests as the requests can be served by any instance and there are no dependencies on data available on a specific instance.

9. Click on **Save**:

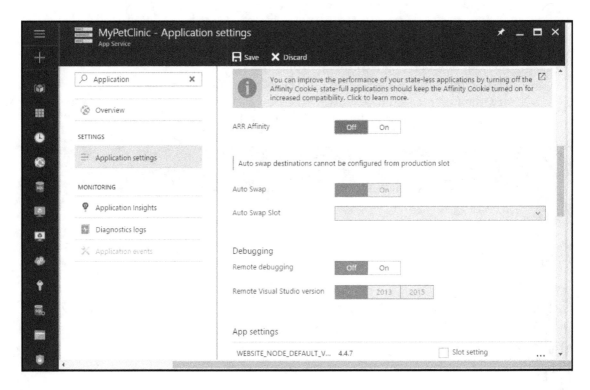

10. Visit the Azure web application URL and now we can see a Java-based environment available; hence, we can deploy a Java web application:

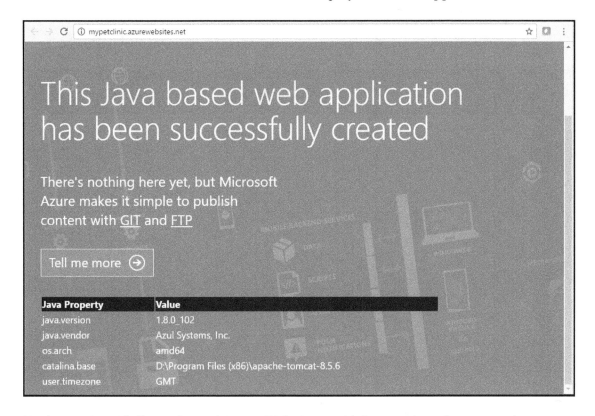

We have successfully configured Azure Web Apps with Java settings. In next section, we will discuss how deployment slots can be created.

Deployment slots – development, QA, UAT, staging, and production

App Service or Azure Web Apps is a main or production slot. In the Standard and Premium tiers, we can create deployment slots other than the main slot to deploy an application. We can use deployment slots for different environments before deploying an application into the main slot.

Slots are not different from a live web application. They have their own set of content, configurations, and hostnames. We can swap slots to roll back failures too.

1. In the Azure portal, go to the `MyPetClinic` Azure web application.
2. In the **APP DEPLOYMENT** category, click on the **Deployment slots** option:

3. Click on **+Add Slot**.

4. Provide a **Name** for the new slot and select **Configuration Source**:

   - **Don't clone configuration from an existing slot**
   - **mypetclinic**

Select **mypetclinic**, and all the configuration which is available in that Azure web application (main or production slot) will be done in a new slot. Click on **OK**:

5. In the normal scenario, we have different environments for application deployment. Examples include, QA, **User Acceptance Testing** (**UAT**), and staging. We can manage them using slots in Azure App Services. Create qa, uat, stage, or any other slot, based on requirements. Click on the dev slot and it will open up a side pane:

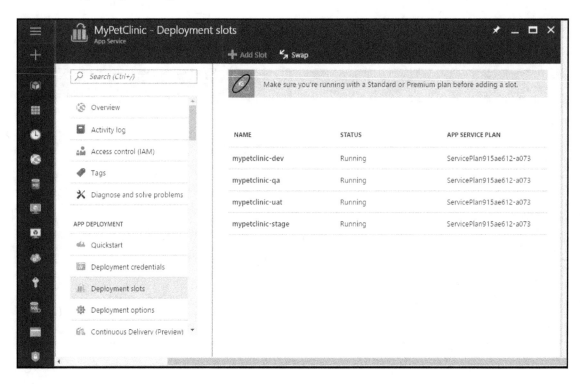

As we can see, it is same as a normal web application. All settings and configurations and everything are the same as are available in a normal Azure web application.

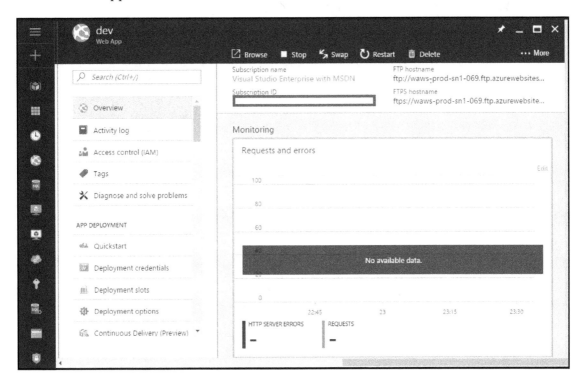

6. Click on **App Service plan** of the web application. It will show how many apps and slots are running on the same ASP.

We can change the ASP for a specific slot:

  Remember that a slot is a separate live web application running on the ASP.

We can have different settings for slots other than the main slots. We can select different repositories and deployments on the slots and manage them in isolation.

We can swap slots with each other. It helps to get warmed up and verify slots for production rather than providing fresh deployment on production. We can verify slots with production and the transition is seamless. Apparently, it changes only the pointer while requesting the slot.

There are a few settings in a slot that can be swapped such as **General settings**—such as **Java version**, **Platform**, **Web sockets**, **Always On**, **App settings**, **Connection strings**, and monitoring and diagnostic settings. We can configure **App settings** and **Connection strings** to stick to a slot, so, even when we swap the slot, those settings won't be swapped; for example: database settings, publishing endpoints, and SSL certificates.

Deployment credentials management for FTP

We can connect to Azure web application with FTP also. We can configure FTP tasks in the VSTS for the deployment of a package file.

Perform the following steps to get FTP-related details:

1. In the **Overview** section of the Azure web application we have created, copy **FTP hostname** or **FTPS hostname**.
2. Click on **More**.
3. Select **Get publish profile**. It will download a file that has details about FTP username and password, which is constant and can be used for FTP connection.

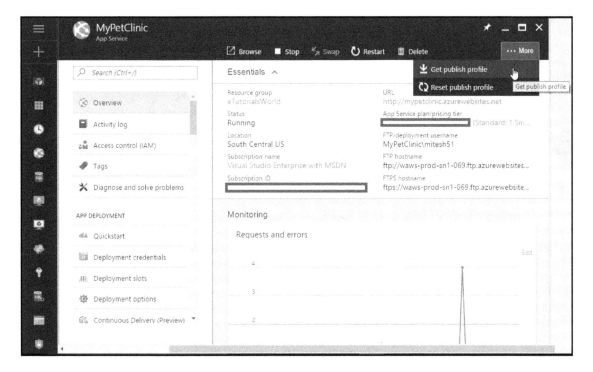

4. To set user specific FTP credentials, click on **Deployment credentials**, set username, and password:

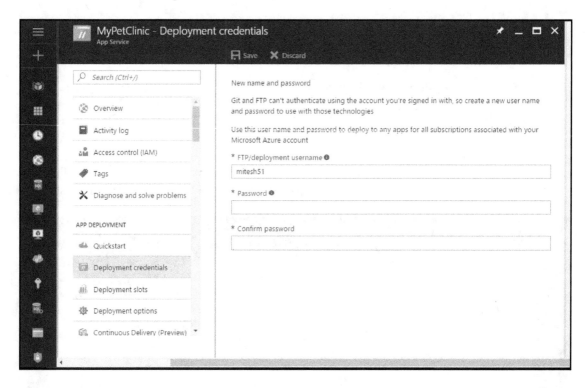

This username and password is for all subscriptions associated with the Microsoft Azure account, while the username and password in the publish profile file are per-site.

In the next section, we will cover the basic monitoring capabilities available in the Azure portal.

Azure Web Apps monitoring

Azure Web Apps provides the easy-to-analyze **Monitoring** section on the App Service dashboard itself. It gives basic details on the number of requests and errors. We can also customize based on available options by clicking on **Edit**:

1. In the **Overview** section of our web application, observe the **Monitoring** chart. It shows **Requests and errors**:

2. Select **Time Range**, **Chart type**, and the details we need to monitor in the chart.

3. Click on **OK**, and observe the change in the bar chart:

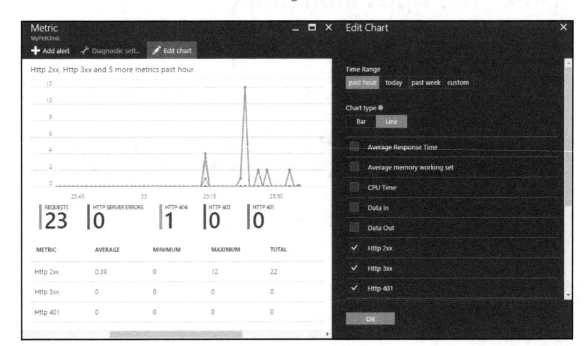

We configured Azure web application with basic settings. In the next section, we will configure the role-based access for secure access of Azure Web Apps.

Configuring role-based access for secure access of Azure Web Apps

Microsoft Azure **Role-Based Access Control** (**RBAC**) provides role-based authorization to access specific Azure resources or resource group. With Azure RBAC, we can provide access to resources based on need. For example, server-side developers get access to resources that are used to host the web application; the testing team will have access to only testing-related resources available in the Azure portal; the database team will have access to the SQL database.

There are three basic roles:

- **Owner**: This has full access to all resources
- **Contributor**: This is to create and manage all resources, but it has no privilege to grant access to others
- **Reader**: This is to view available resources

A few important things to note:

Microsoft Azure subscription has one **Azure Active Directory** (**Azure AD**) that has many users, groups, and applications associated with it. We can grant access to users and groups for available Azure resources at three different levels:

- Subscription
- Resource groups (It may contain multiple resources such as virtual machines, SQL databases, and Azure Web Apps)
- Individual resources such as Azure Web Apps

Let's configure our Azure web application with Azure AD so it can be accessible to the users who are allowed to access it and also configure role-based access to users:

1. Go to Azure **App Services** and click on the MyPetClinic web application.
2. Click on the **Access control (IAM)**.
3. It will give the list of users who have the **Owner** role. We need to add users so click on the **+Add** link to add the users.

4. Select a role as **Contributor**:

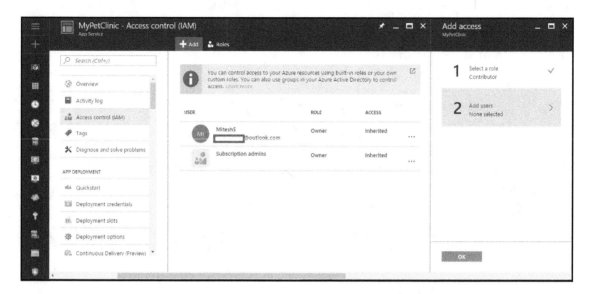

5. It will open a pane with users; search for the user we want to give access to. Select it and click on **Select**:

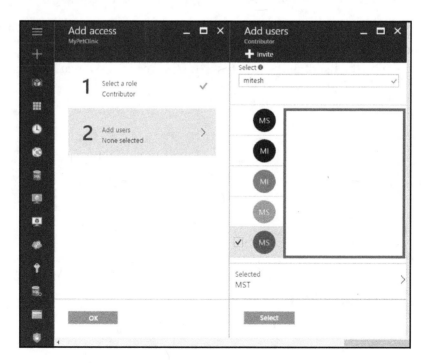

6. Verify the newly added user in the list of **Access control** (**IAM**). The user can manage Azure web application as they are given **Contributor** rights:

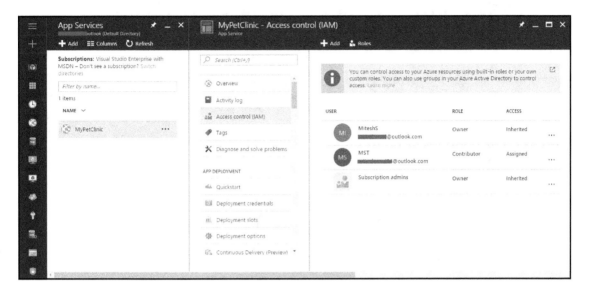

Let's see how to configure Azure web application, so access to the application can be restricted to specific users only available in the Azure AD:

1. In the **SETTINGS** section, click on **Authentication / Authorization**. **App Service Authentication** is **Off** by default. Enable **App Service Authentication** by switching it **On**:

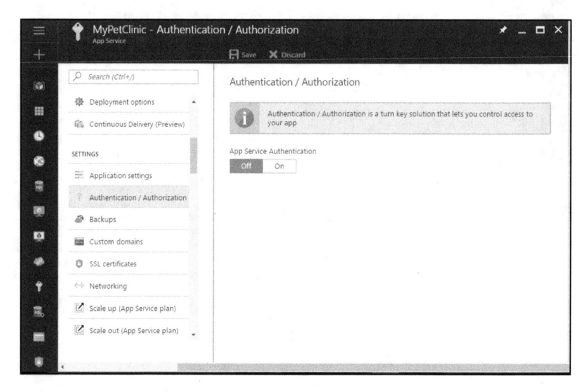

2. In **Authentication Providers**, select **Azure Active Directory**. In the next pane, select **Express** in **Management mode**.
3. Select **Create New AD App** as we haven't created any app in Azure AD to map it with Azure web application.
4. Provide the name of the application for Azure AD and click on **OK**:

5. Observe the value in the **Action to take when request is not authenticated** label. **Allow Anonymous requests (no action)** is the selected value:

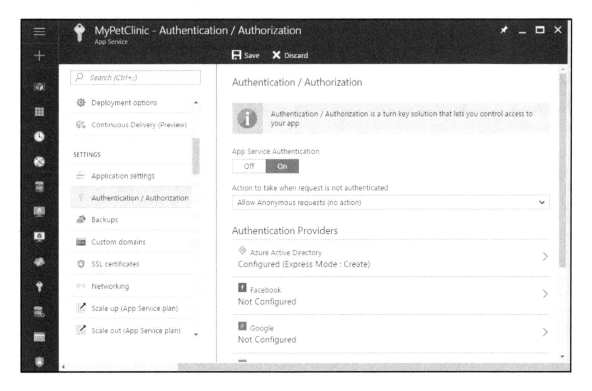

6. Change the value to **Log in with Azure Active Directory** and save the configuration:

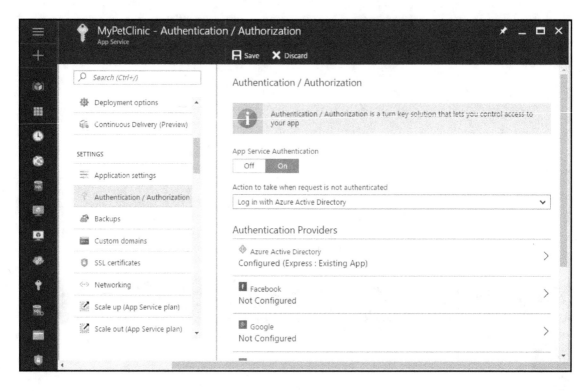

7. Visit the Azure web application URL and we will be redirected towards the login page and not the web application home page.

Give a valid e-mail and password configured in Azure AD and access the Azure web application:

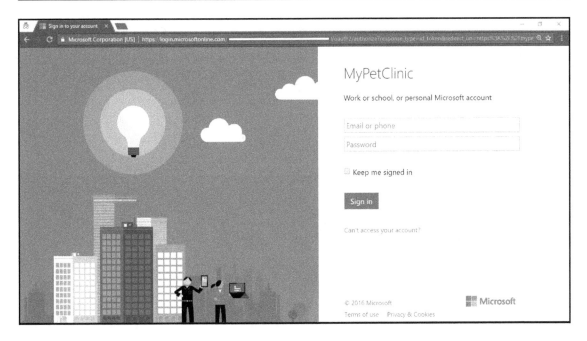

In this section, we covered how to provide the required access to the Azure web application resources to specific users and also how to restrict access to the Azure web application itself for users using Azure AD. In the next section, we will cover how to scale Azure Web Apps resources so the requests load can be managed efficiently.

Scaling Azure Web Apps

The scaling up and down or scaling in and out operations are required to effectively utilize underlying resources based on the requirements. For example, for an online shopping website, we can predict that it will have a huge number of requests during festival days. It may have a moderate number of requests on normal weekdays. In such a scenario, it is better to keep more resources available to manage user requests and decrease the number of resources on normal days. If we can automate this scale in and scale out operation, then it is the best utilization of resources and customers also won't face any issues.

Both the operations are performed on the ASP.

Scaling up and down

In this option, we can increase the number of cores, RAM, storage, the number of instances, slots, backup, and other services.

To scale up, go to Azure web application and select **Scale up** (**App Service plan**).

The selected pricing tier will have a blue border around it. Change the higher pricing tier based on your requirements. Click on **Select**:

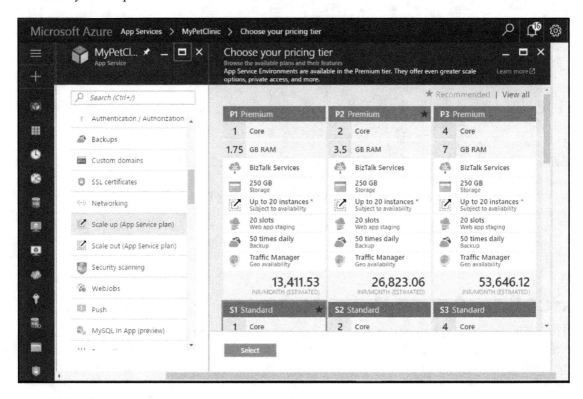

To scale down, go to Azure web application and select **Scale up** (**App Service plan**).

The selected pricing tier will have a blue border around it. Change the lower pricing tier based on your requirements. Click on **Select**.

This is how we can achieve scale up and scale down operations in Azure Web Apps.

Scaling in and out

Scaling in and out is a more efficient option. We can increase the number of instances serving Azure web application and decrease instances manually or based on CPU percentage and other parameters. In the Basic and Standard pricing tier, we can increase instances up to 20 while the **App Service Environment** (**ASE**) limit is 50. We will discuss ASE in the next chapter.

To scale out, go to Azure web application and select **Scale Out** (**App Service plan**).

In **Scale by**, we can select **an instance count that I enter manually**. Provide the number of instances via the slider:

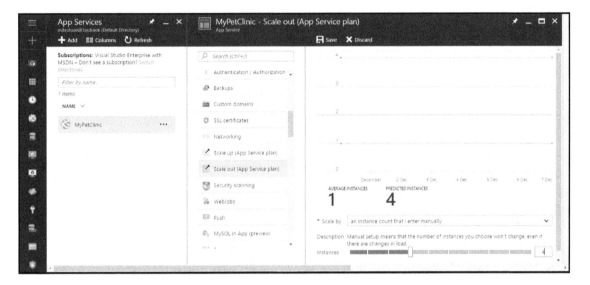

In **Scale by**, we can select **CPU Percentage**.

Provide the number of instances via the slider. We can select the minimum and maximum number of instances.

Select **Target range** of the CPU that should be used for the scale in and scale out operations:

When we don't require more instances because of less load on the application, then we can decrease the number of instances and that is the scale in operation. We can do it manually and also automatically as we do in scale out operations.

We saw how we can perform scale up and scale out operations in this section. In the next section, we will see some important properties for Azure Web Apps.

Basic tasks to manage Azure Web Apps

As we have covered the main topics, namely creating Azure Web Apps, configuring web application with programming language specific settings, deployment slots – development, QA, UAT, staging, and production, deployment credentials management for FTP, Azure Web Apps monitoring, configuring role-based access for secure access of Azure Web Apps, and scaling Azure Web Apps, let's now see how we can perform some other tasks to manage and maintain Azure Web Apps.

Microsoft Azure Web Apps properties

There are specific scenarios where we may need to connect to some web services available behind the firewall and installed on-premise.

To consider security, we need to whitelist IP addresses from the sources where the request is originating:

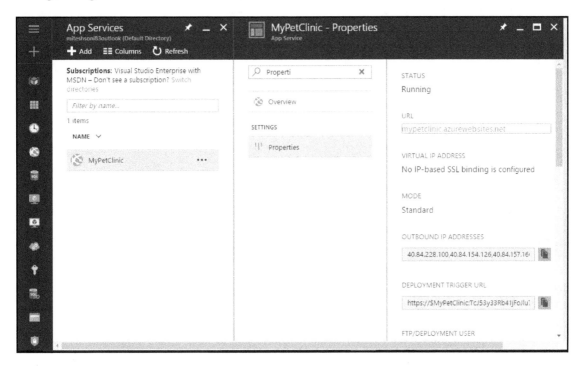

We can use **OUTBOUND IP ADDRESSES** to whitelist behind the firewall, so applications hosted on Azure Web Apps can access the resources available on-premise.

Microsoft Azure Web Apps – App Service plan

Azure **App Service plan** (**ASP**) is the main source of the runtime environment. Azure Web Apps can share an ASP and all scaling up and scaling out operations are performed on the ASP:

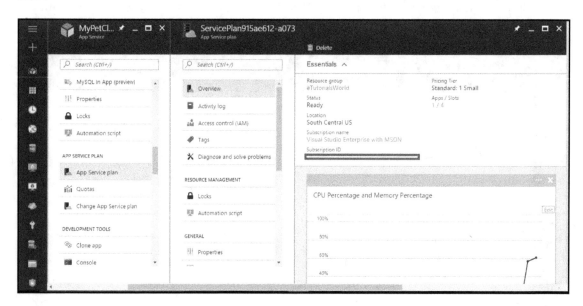

In the next section, we will cover the Microsoft Azure App Service backup and restore feature.

Azure Web Apps backups

While we are discussing the platform to deploy a Java-based web application, we need to cover all the features available to keep the Azure web application available to the users all the time. In the case of disaster, it is far easier to restore an app if the backup is taken. The Microsoft Azure App Service backup and restore feature allows us to take a backup and restore the web application to the state when the backup was taken. It can also manage web application configuration, web application content, and the SQL database connected to Azure web application. We need a Microsoft Azure storage account and container to utilize the Microsoft Azure App Service backup and restore feature.

The Microsoft Azure App Service backup and restore feature is available in the Standard pricing tier or higher.

In **SETTINGS**, click on **Backups**. No backup is configured yet. Click on **Configure**:

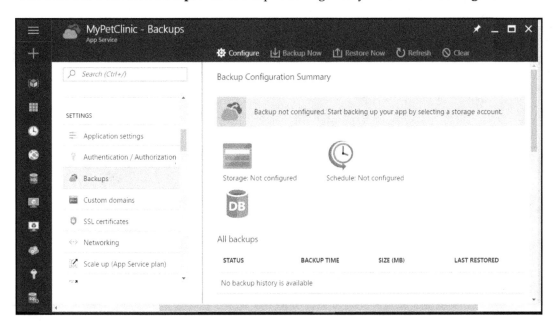

We need a storage account and container for backup, hence we will configure **Storage Settings** first and then **Schedule Settings** and **Database Settings**:

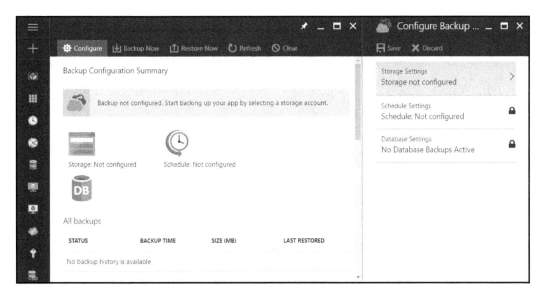

Click on +**Storage account**:

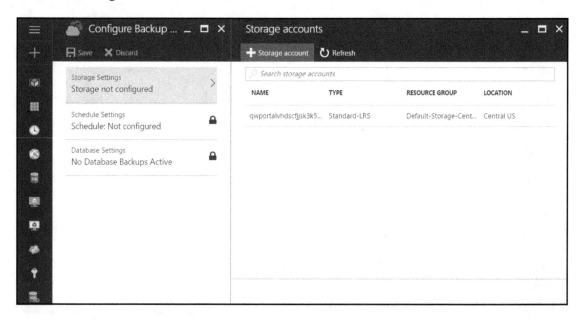

Provide a **Name** for the storage account, click on **Standard** performance, and configure **Locally Redundant Storage** (**LRS**) as replication and **South Central US** as **Location**. Click on **OK**:

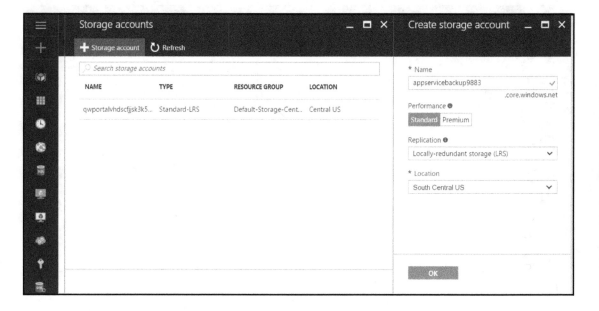

Once the storage account is created, click on **+Container**:

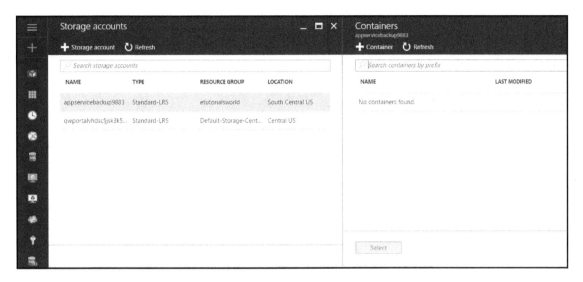

Provide a **Name** for the container and configure private access for the new container. Click on **Create**:

Select the `petclinic` container:

Once **Storage Settings** are configured. Click on **Schedule Settings**:

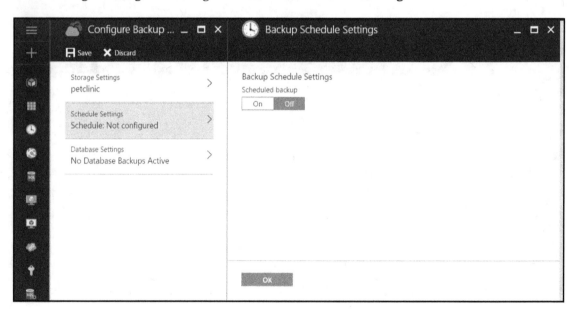

Enable the backup schedule by clicking on **On**. Configure the **Frequency**, **Unit of Frequency**, date, time, and **Retention** of the backup schedule. Click on **OK**:

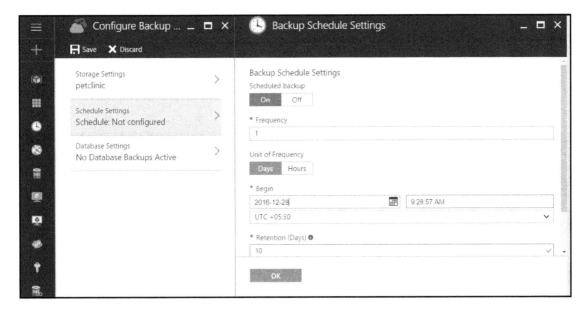

Click on **Database Settings**. We have the web application with SQL database, so select **defaultConnection**. Click on **OK**:

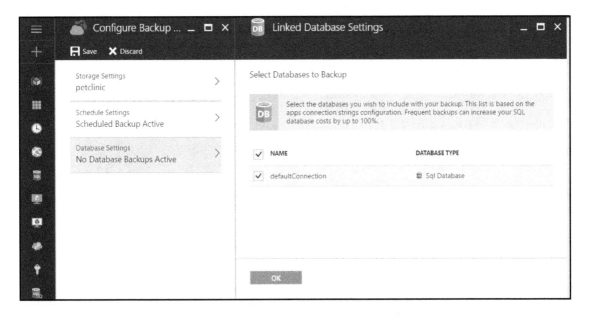

The Azure SQL database business continuity model includes the point-in-time restore point. It means that backups are retained for x number of days based on the pricing tier, as follows:

- **Basic**: Any restore point within 7 days
- **Standard**: Any restore point within 14 days
- **Premium**: Any restore point within 35 days

Save the **Backup** schedule settings:

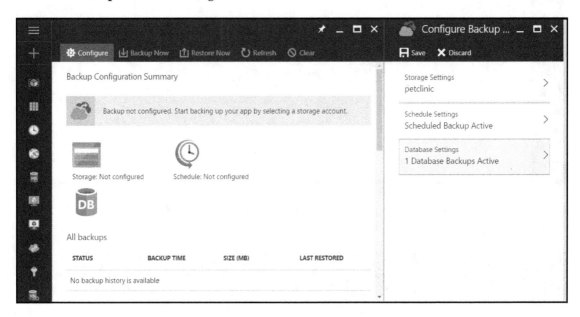

Verify the **Backup Configuration Summary**. **Storage** and **Schedule** are configured.

For testing, let's take a back up now:

1. Click on the **Backup Now** option:

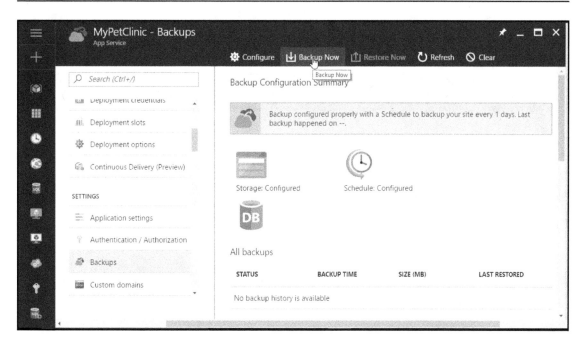

2. Verify the status of the existing backup. It is showing **InProgress**:

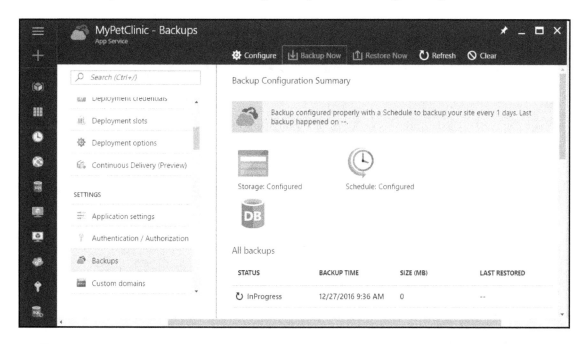

3. Click on the **InProgress** backup to get more details on its status. Observe **TRIGGER TYPE**:

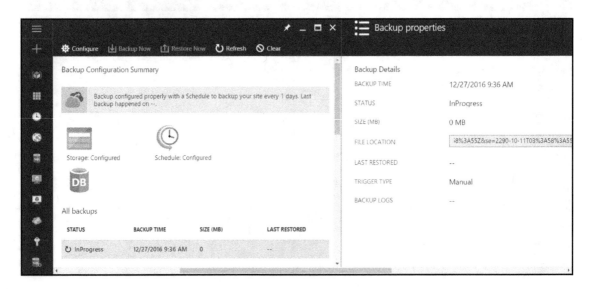

4. A successful backup process will take some time. Verify the status in the Azure portal:

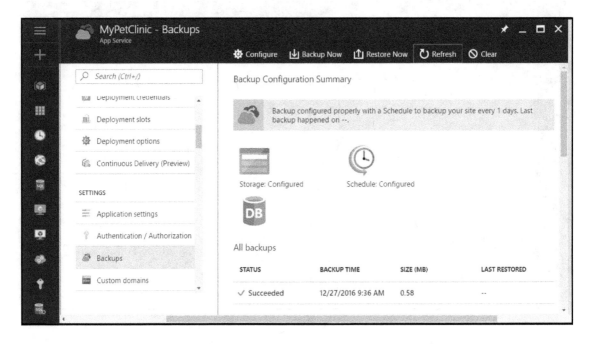

5. Click on the backup line and verify the overall status with backup size:

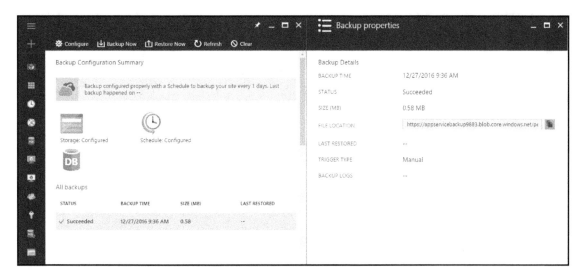

Once we have a backup ready for Azure web application, we can use it to restore the web application.

Azure Web Apps restore

To restore Microsoft Azure web application, the ASP should be in the Standard or Premium pricing tier.

On the **Backups** pane, click on **Restore Now**:

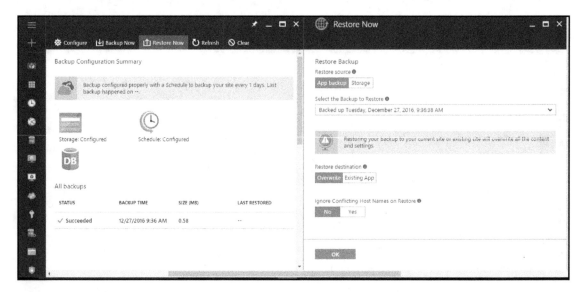

Click on **Storage** and select the backup we have created. Click on **OK**:

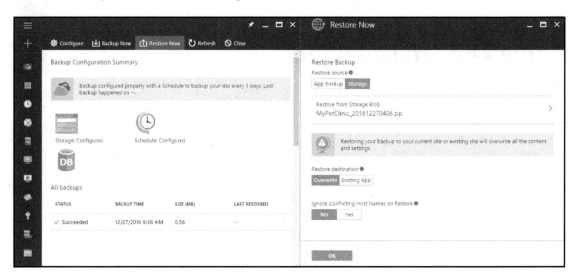

This is how we can make a backup and restore the backup.

Azure Web Apps custom domains

Azure Web Apps has a unique subdomain. It is `azurewebsites.net`. For development, QA, and stage, we can manage with a unique subdomain, but for the production application, it is essential to have a custom domain.

We can map a custom domain to the Azure web application using Azure portal. By default, the name of Azure web app will be `<webapp_name>.azurewebsites.net`. To map a custom domain, go to Azure web application in the Azure portal, go to **SETTINGS** and click on **Custom domains.**

We can purchase domains and add a hostname too:

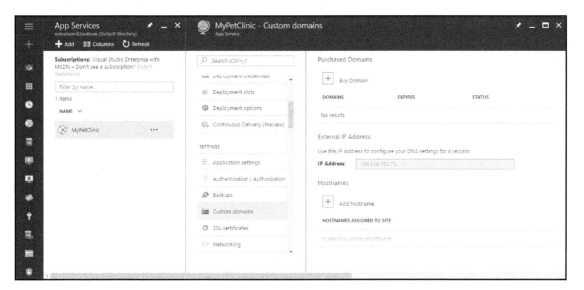

 To get more details on a custom domain, visit the following resources available in Microsoft Azure Documentation. Map a custom domain name to an Azure application `https://docs.microsoft.com/en-us/azure/app-service-web/web-sites-custom-domain-name.`
Configuring a custom domain name for a web app in Azure App Service using Traffic Manager `https://docs.microsoft.com/en-us/azure/app-service-web/web-sites-traffic-manager-custom-domain-name.`

Azure Web Apps SSL certificates

As we know, Azure Web Apps or Azure App Service comes with a unique subdomain, `azurewebsites.net` and it gives a wildcard certificate too. However, we can purchase and manage an SSL certificate from the Microsoft Azure portal itself for custom domains. Go to Azure web application in the Azure portal, go to **SETTINGS**, and click on **SSL certificates**:

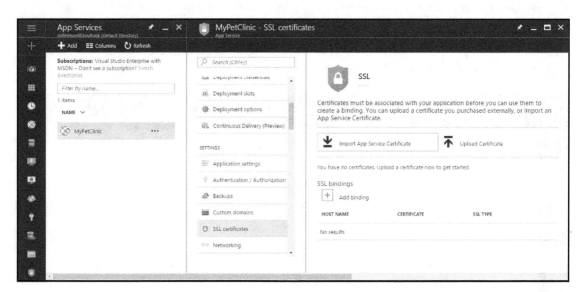

 For more details on buying and configuring an SSL certificate for your Azure App Service refer to `https://docs.microsoft.com/en-us/azure/app-service-web/web-sites-purchase-ssl-web-site`.

Azure Web Apps networking

Azure **Virtual Networks** (**VNets**) allow us to keep Azure resources in a non-internet routable network. The main benefit of VNets is that we can control and restrict the overall access to Azure resources to and from. We can connect to on-premise resources too with VPN.

VNET Integration allows us to configure a web application so that it can access a web service or database available in Azure VNets.
There are three options available in **Networking**:

- **VNET Integration**: This is to access Azure resources available in or through Azure VNets
- **Hybrid Connections**: This is to access applications in private networks
- **App Service Environment**: This is to host Azure web application in an Azure VNet

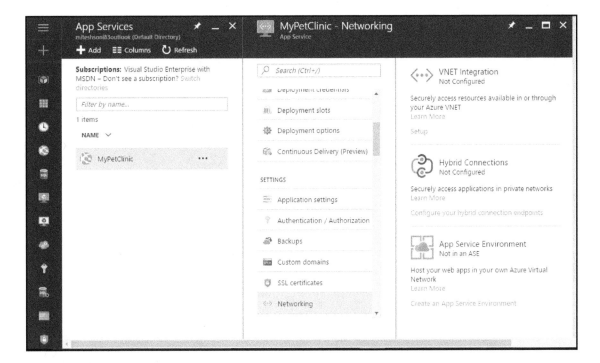

 Azure Web Apps and networking is out of the scope of this book as the focus is on end-to-end automation of **Application Lifecycle Management** (**ALM**). To get more details on how to integrate Azure web application with an Azure VNet, visit `https://docs.microsoft.com/en-us/azure/app-service-web/web-sites-integrate-with-vnet`.

Azure Web Apps security scanning

Web vulnerability scanning services powered by Tinfoil Security can be utilized in Azure App Services to make web applications more secure. Tinfoil Security is built into the Azure App Service management and available in the Azure portal itself.

1. Go to the Azure management portal.
2. Select the `MyPetClinic` web application.
3. Go to **SETTINGS** and click on **Security scanning**:

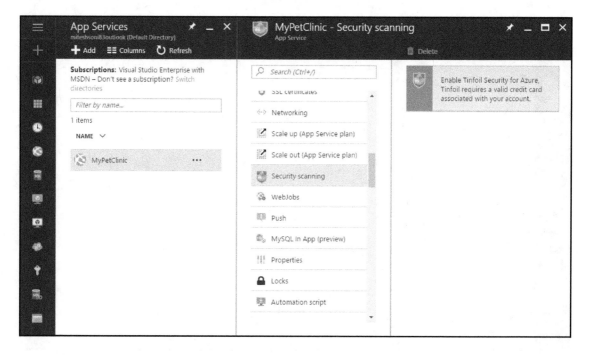

We need to have a credit card associated with the account to get the benefit of this service.

> To get more details on web vulnerability scanning for Azure App Service powered by Tinfoil Security, visit `https://azure.microsoft.com/en-us` `/blog/web-vulnerability-scanning-for-azure-app-service-powered` `-by-tinfoil-security/`.

Azure Web Apps locks

Let's consider a scenario where there are multiple people who are given the same kind of access to Azure web application or other resources. What if someone who is authorized to access the Microsoft Azure resources accidentally deletes the resources available in the Azure portal?

To avoid such a scenario, we can set the lock level to CanNotDelete or ReadOnly.

- **CanNotDelete:** This lock level allows users to read and modify resources, but authorized users can't delete the resource
- **ReadOnly**: This lock level allows only read permissions and authorized users can't delete the resource

Let's try to apply the lock level on the Azure web application we have created:

1. Go to `MyPetClinic` Azure web application. Go to **SETTINGS** and find **Locks**.
2. Click on **Locks**.
3. Click on **+Add**.
4. Provide **Lock name** and **Lock type**.
5. Click on **OK**:

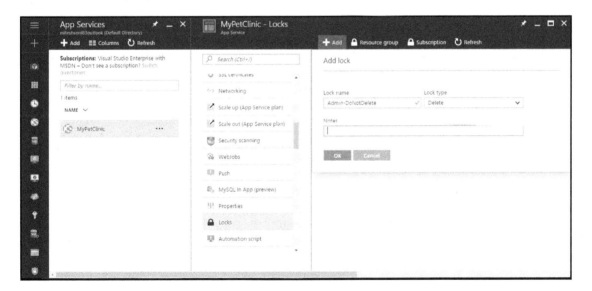

6. Go to the **Overview** section of Azure web application and try to delete the web application.

We will get a notification of **Failed to delete web app**:

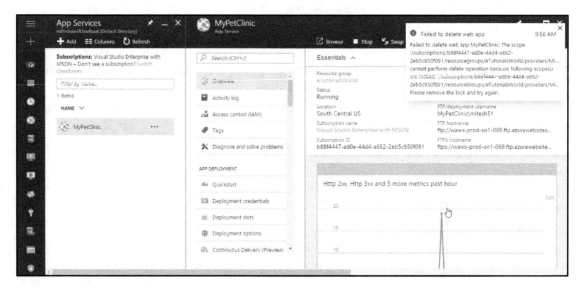

If we read the complete message, then we will see the reasons: **... cannot perform delete operation because following scope(s) are locked....**

Azure Web Apps console

We can manage our web application environment in **Console**.

Console is available in the **DEVELOPMENT TOOLS** category of Azure web application. We can execute commands in this section:

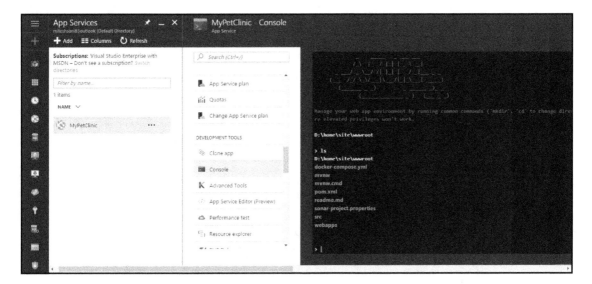

We executed the `ls` command. This command gives us the list of files and directories available in the existing folder. We can see all the files and folders available in the `wwwroot` directory of our `MyPetClinic` Azure web application.

We have covered most of the basic tasks required to manage Azure Web Apps.

Summary

Let's revise what we have covered until now.

In this chapter, we saw how to create Azure web applications and configure web applications with programming language specific settings, deployment slots for managing different environments in a cost-effective manner, use deployment credentials for FTP, basic Azure Web Apps monitoring, configure role-based access for secure access of Azure Web Apps, scaling up and down Azure web application resources, scaling in and out Azure web application resources, Microsoft Azure Web Apps properties, Microsoft Azure Web Apps – ASP, Azure Web Apps backups and restore from the backup, and overview of Azure Web Apps custom domains, SSL certificates, networking, security scanning, locks, and console:

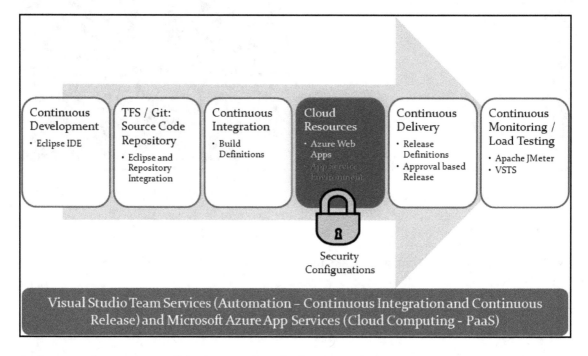

In the next chapter, we will look into ASE which is considered more secure than a normal Azure web application. An ASE is more secure and has a higher number of instances while scaling operations at the time of peak load. We will cover how to create an ASE and how to deploy Azure web applications into it.

5
Azure App Service Environments

Most people overestimate what they can do in one year and underestimate what they can do in ten years.

—Bill Gates

This chapter is a bit theoretical, but it covers a premium service of Microsoft Azure platform that can be used for specific use cases that Azure Web Apps may not be able to handle effectively. Other than that, it is important to know why we are covering Azure Web Apps and **App Service Environment** (**ASE**). The reason behind that is it is equally important to have an environment ready for package deployment. When we consider it in the context of Java, we need to deploy the WAR file in a different environment. Here, we are dealing with PaaS so we need not worry about installing a runtime environment, else we will also need to find ways to automate it.

This chapter not only covers how to create ASEs but also provides a detailed comparison of Azure Web Apps and ASEs to enhance security. Security is one of the most important parts of application life cycle management, and hence this service increases the value in the context of DevOps. The following topics are covered in this chapter:

- Overview of ASEs
- Creating and configuring ASEs
- Enforcing HTTP redirection to HTTPS on Azure Web Apps
- Filtering traffic by IP and dynamic IP restrictions
- Comparing ASE and non-ASE (Azure Web Apps) environments

Overview of ASEs

An ASE provides a dedicated and isolated environment to run Azure App Service. ASE is a premium service offered in Microsoft Azure. It provides more instances to scale if Azure Web Apps is hosted in an ASE. In Azure Web Apps, we have a **Networking** section where we can integrate Azure Web Apps with Azure VNet. In ASE, we can host Azure Web Apps in the VNet itself. In other words, ASE can be created in the subnet of a VNet as they are deployed in a VNet created by the account owner.

The benefit of hosting Azure App Service or Azure Web Apps in the ASE is that we can configure security for Azure Web Apps the way we do it for Azure VNet. In simple terms, we can use **Network Security Groups** (**NSGs**) to make it more secure. We can create NSGs with inbound and outbound rules to control traffic to Azure Web Apps. Thus, we can create a hybrid cloud scenario where Azure Web Apps can communicate with on-premise resources over a secure connection.

It also provides more instances in scaling. Up to 50 instances can be used in ASE while scaling out. Hence, it is useful if we have requirements of high scaling. All these 50 instances are dedicated to the same subscription in which ASE is created.

ASE is made up of two main components:

- **Front end compute resource pools**: Front end pools can be used for load balancing and SSL termination in ASE.
- **Three worker compute resource pools**: When we create ASE, three worker pools are created. We can host multiple instances in each worker pool based on the availability of resources and create ASP. Once ASP is created for ASE resources, we can use it in a similar way we use normal ASP. Worker pools provide us the facility to choose different sizes of compute resources based on the needs of applications. Applications with a similar kind of needs can be hosted on a specific worker pool where we can create multiple ASPs.

It is better to deploy an application in Azure Web Apps and in ASE and conduct performance testing with the same kinds of parameter before choosing any of these two environments for hosting an application. The main reason for this is the performance of the environment. If performance is the main criteria, then it is better to verify the performance and then go for the final choice out of the two.

Before we move ahead with creating ASE, we need to remember few things:

- By default, ASE is created with two front end instances and two worker pool instances.
- We can't run workloads in the front end.
- We can configure a total of 55 instances in an ASE:
    - Two instances are used for the front end (*55-2=53*); we can't directly access front end pool instances or take remote access of them. We can only change the number of instances in the pool.
    - Each worker pool is given one additional instance that is not utilized in ASP, but it is used for fault tolerance. As we have three worker pools in ASE, three instances are needed (*53-3=50*). We can't directly access worker pool instances or take remote access of them. We can only change the number of instances in the pool.
- Front end and worker pool instances take 2-3 hours to provision.
- We can move Azure Web Apps from one worker pool to another worker pool.
- We can create multiple ASEs within a single Azure region and across multiple Azure regions.
- The number of instances in the front end and worker pools can be specified during ASE creation, or we can increase the size of instances manually and by auto scaling.
- ASE comes with one IP address that can be utilized for IP SSL.
- Only one ASE can exist in a subnet.
- The subnet used to host the ASE must not contain any other compute resources.
- We can keep ASE and VNet in different resource groups.
- The VNet must have at least eight addresses or more.
- When we delete an ASE, it deletes all the contents within it.
- In an ASE, you have four size options, P1, P2, P3, and P4.

 Once we add instances to the ASE, the price is calculated based on it. Even if we don't use these instances in ASPs, we need to pay as we have assigned these instances in the pools.

We know that we can host Azure Web Apps in standard ASP and an ASP created in ASE. However, we can't move Azure Web Apps from a standard ASP to ASE directly. We can use backup and the clone feature to achieve the deployment of an application in standard ASP to ASE.

Creating and configuring ASEs

Let's create an ASE with following:

- Front end pool with two P2 compute resources
- Worker pool 1 with two P1 compute resources
- Worker pool 2 with zero P2 compute resources
- Worker pool 3 with zero P3 compute resources
- Single IP address to be used for IP SSL
- VNet with 512 addresses using an RFC 1918 private address space; subnet with 256 addresses

To create an ASE follow, these steps:

1. In the left sidebar, find **App Service Environments**.

If it is not available, then click on **More services** and filter **App Service Environments**. Click on the star icon to bring that link on the left sidebar.

2. Click on **+Add**. Enter **Name** for the ASEs, select **Subscription**, and select **Resource Group** (we already created the eTutorialsWorld resource group) by clicking on **Use existing**:

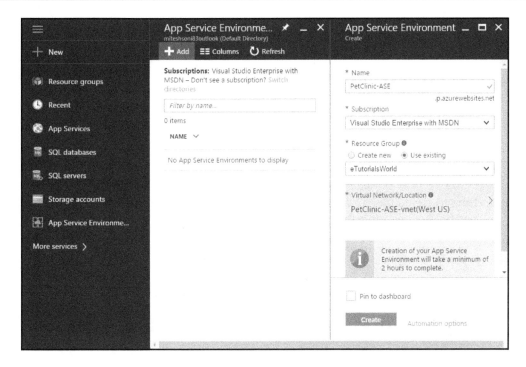

3. Click on **Virtual Network** and on **Create New**. Enter name for the **Virtual Network** and select a **Location**. Click on **OK**:

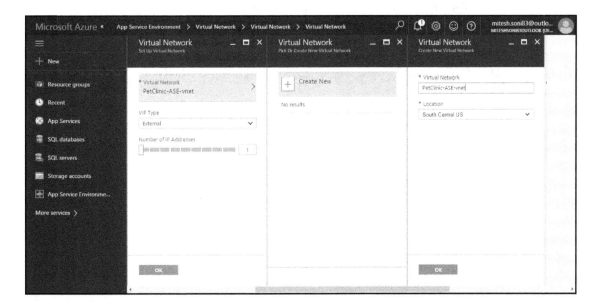

Once we have configured VNet with the proper location, we can go back to the pane where other details of ASEs are available.

Observe one notification available on the pane. It says that **Creation of your App Service Environment will take a minimum of 2 hours to complete**. In other words, a minimum 120 minutes of the creation of an environment. The reason it takes so much time is that it is dedicated to a subscription and the resources are isolated.

4. Click on **Create**.

   Have a cup of coffee or go for lunch/dinner, as this will take time. However, the time to create has decreased comparatively, but 120 minutes is given in the notification, so it's better to wait and watch.

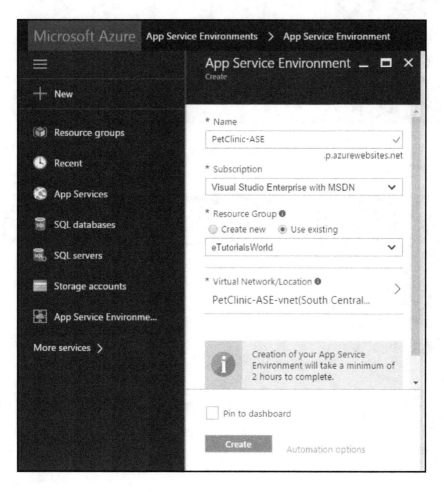

In the notifications, click on the latest work in progress notification to see the existing progress of the ASE that we created recently.

Verify the status and duration. Observe the blue bar and information message **Deploying**. Look at the **Inputs** section in this notification window. It has **WORKER1SIZE** and **WORKER1COUNT** as well.

5. To get details as the time goes by, click on **Refresh** to get details of the progressing state of the ASE deployment:

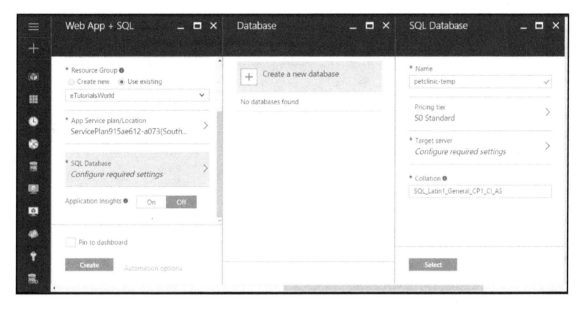

Once ASE is ready, we can verify it in the list of ASEs available in the **App Service Environments** section in Azure portal.

Select the ASE created recently and click on the **Overview** section.

A side pane that contains basic information related to ASEs and also **Monitoring** (**Front End Metrics**) will be opened.

If we monitor it closely, ASE has a subdomain name that is
`<Name_of_ASE>.p.azurewebsites.net`. We can see VNet we created and the location that was selected for this.

 It is important to note that ASEs doesn't host Azure App Service or Azure Web Apps. It is the ASP that is used to host Azure App Service or Azure Web Apps.

In our case, ASEs doesn't have any ASPs. As there is no ASP, we don't have any Azure Web Apps or slots deployed in the ASP, so there are no Azure Web Apps that belong to this ASE:

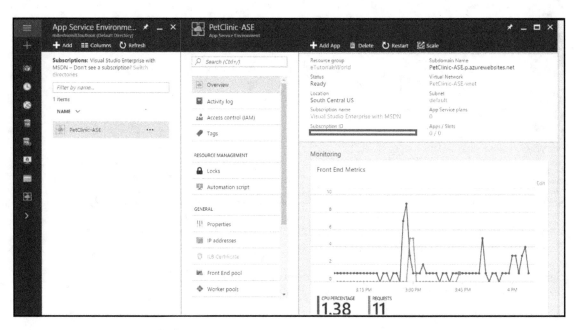

Let's see what activity has been performed since we clicked on the **Create** button of ASEs. We can see **Write HostingEnvironments** operations in the log in the last hour:

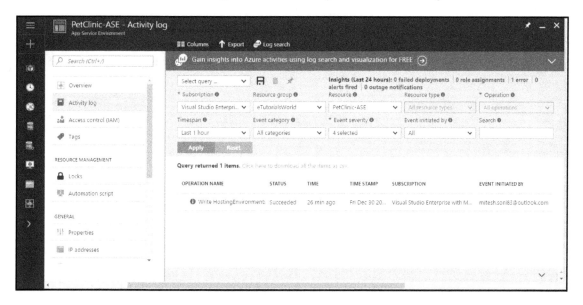

ASE is created in a subnet of a VNet. It is not about connecting Azure Web Apps with any network. It is about the created Azure Web Apps in the VNet.

In Azure Web Apps, we discussed how outbound IP addresses can be used to access on-premise resources with the use of whitelisting those four outbound IP addresses. The problem is that those four IP addresses are generic and not dedicated to a specific customer or subscription or an Azure web application.

In the case of ASE, we can use the IP address given in **Properties** for whitelisting to access on-premise resources, and we can manage access to on-premise web services with confidence:

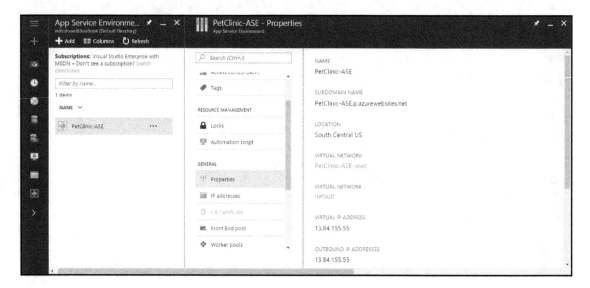

Each default configuration of an ASE comes with a single IP address. This allocated but unassigned IP address is available in the **GENERAL** section of ASEs.

We can increase up to 10 IP addresses in **App Service Environments** in Azure portal and utilize them:

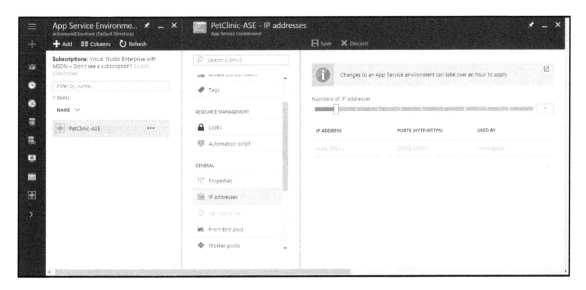

After discussing front end and worker pools in the **Overview** section, if we are still searching where we will get them in the Azure portal and in ASEs, then we are at their doorstep.

ASEs – front end pool

In **App Service Environments**, go to the **GENERAL** section. Here, we will get **Front End pool**.

Click on **Front End pool**, and we will get a side pane with all the details about **PetClinic-ASE - Front End pool**.

Remember that the front end pool is also a collection of compute instances.

Observe the **Resource group**, **Status**, **Location**, and **App Service Environment** of the front end pool.

If we remember the default **Pricing Tier**, we can have the minimum instances we have for front end pool, which is **P2** and 2 instances. We can choose a higher level of pricing tier for the front end pool, but not the lower pricing tier.

The **Monitoring** section shows CPU percentage, memory percentage, and the number of requests the front end pool has dealt with:

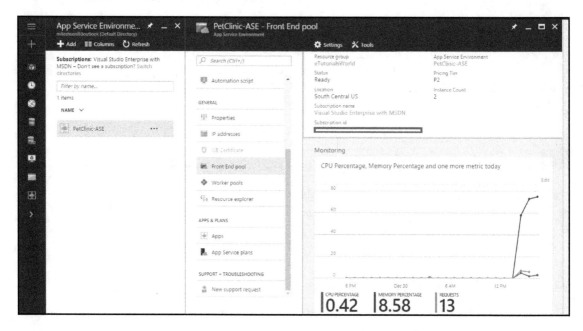

Front End pool also has settings and a set of operations associated with it.

Click on **Settings**, and it will open a side pane with available settings that we can view or change. We can perform the scale up/down or scale in/out operations:

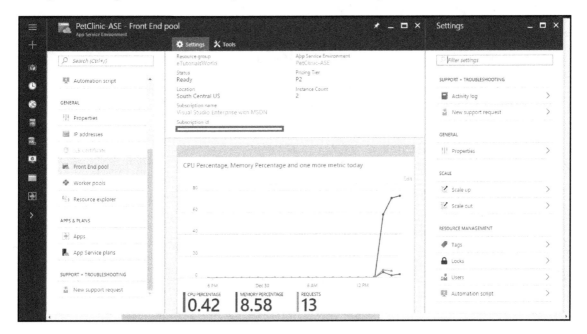

Let's verify **Front End pool**.

Go to **App Service Environments**, click on the ASE that we created, click on **Front End pool** in the **GENERAL** section of the ASE settings, and click on **Scale up** in the **SCALE** section in **Settings** of a front end pool.

Here, we can choose the scale size.

This section shows different instances that ASEs can have for a front end pool. The P1 instance is grayed out, because we can't select it in the case of **Front End pool**. The minimum size supported in the front end pool for ASEs is P2:

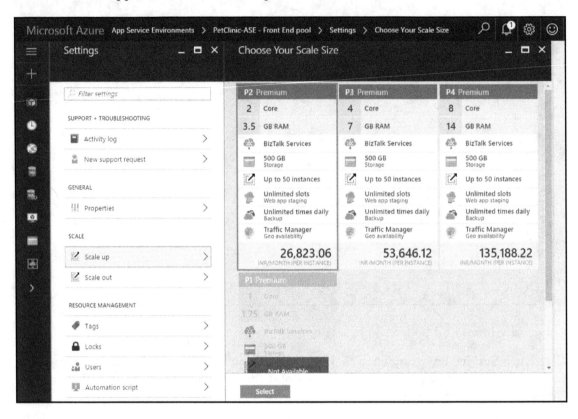

We can also modify scale out settings the way we do in ASP for Azure Web Apps or Azure App Service.

We can scale it manually, or by CPU percentage, or by other metrics:

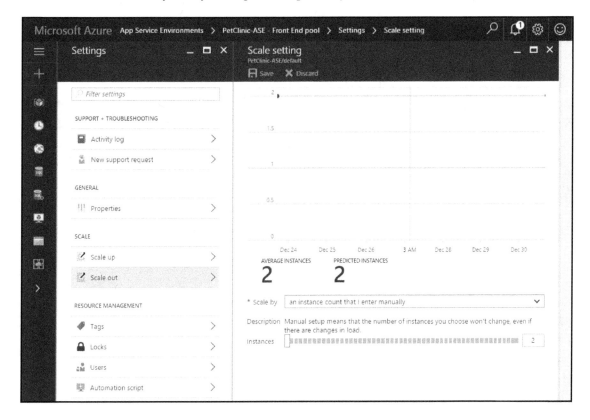

Now comes the turn of worker pools.

ASEs – worker pools

As we already know, there are three worker pools in an ASE. The pool of resources physically hosts the ASPs. To get details of the worker pool specific to ASEs, click on the ASE created recently and go to the **GENERAL** section; click on **Worker pools** and we can see **Worker pool 1**, **Worker pool 2**, and **Worker pool 3**:

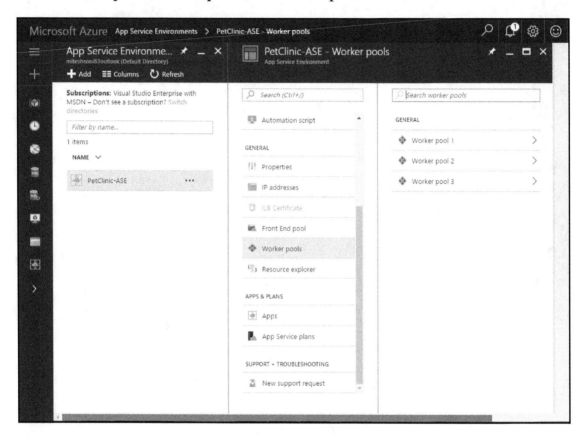

With the default ASE settings, we can have instances created on only **Worker pool 1** and not other worker pools.

To get the **Worker pool 1** details, click on it, and it will open a side pane with its details. In a front end pool, we have a restriction that we can't select scale size P1. However, in the case of worker pools, we don't have that restriction. We can utilize all scale sizes such as, P1, P2, P3, and P4. By default, **Worker pool 1** has **P1** instances and the **Instance count** is 2. As there is no ASP created out of this worker pool, we can't host any Azure Web Apps, hence application count is showing 0.

When we click on **Settings**, we get the same kind of options that we got in the front end pool:

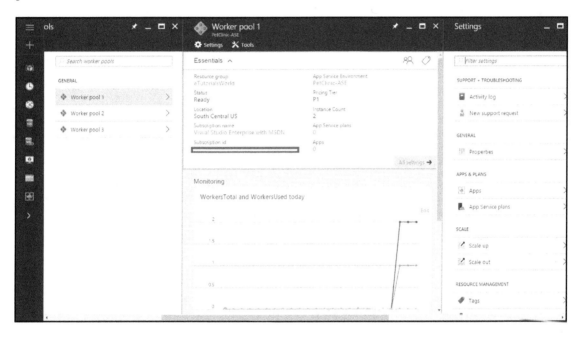

Click on **Scale up** in the **Worker pool 1** settings to verify existing scale size and other options. We can see that there is no grayed out section of scale size in **Worker pool 1** as we have in **Front End pool**.

The existing scale size is P1, and we can select any other scale size if we need it:

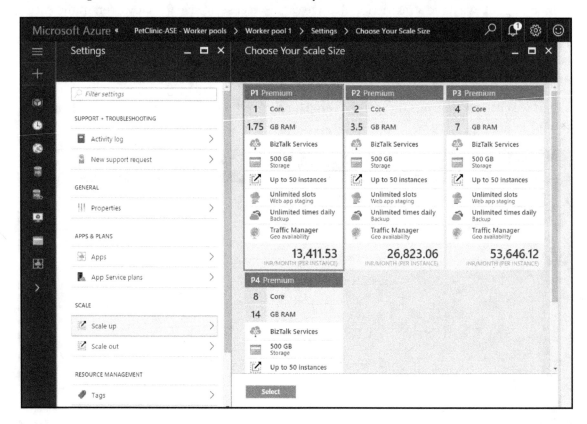

We can also modify the **Scale out** settings the way we do in ASP for Azure Web Apps or Azure App Service.

We can scale it manually, or by CPU percentage, or by other metrics:

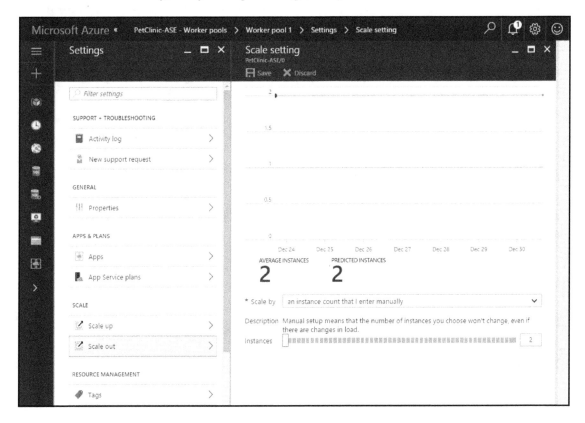

Let's verify what **Worker pool 2** has!

As expected, it has zero instances because in the default ASE only **Worker pool 1** has an instance allocated, and that is 2. However, the **Pricing Tier** is associated with **Worker pool 2**. It is important to remember that it is a default setting and if we need, we can change the scale size from P2 to P3, P2 to P4, or P2 to P1:

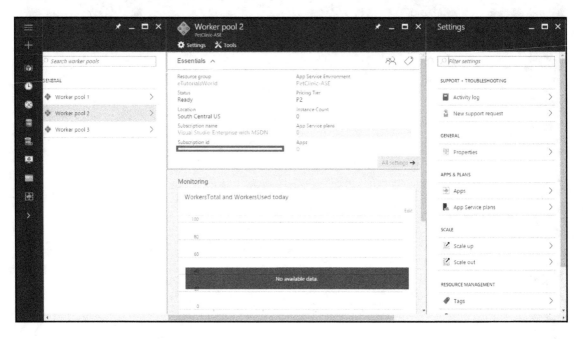

Let's verify what **Worker pool 3** has!

As expected, it has zero instances because in the default ASE only **Worker pool 1** has an instance allocated, and that is 2. However, the **Pricing Tier** is associated with **Worker pool 3**. It is important to remember that it is a default setting and if we need, we can change the scale size from P3 to P2, P3 to P4, or P3 to P1:

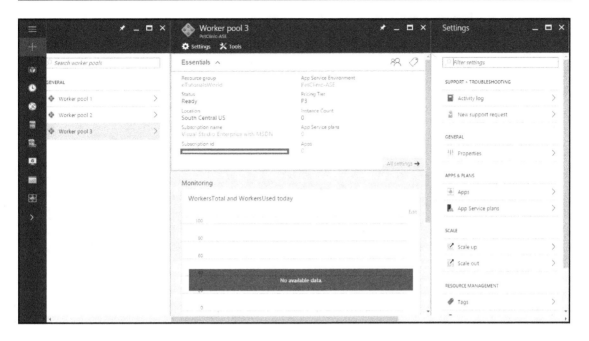

We can't associate multiple scale sizes to **Front End pool** or **Worker pools**.

ASEs – app service plan

As we have verified all default configurations of ASEs, let's verify the same things in the main window of ASEs in Azure portal.

It has zero **APP & SLOTS COUNT** and zero **PLAN COUNT** as we are yet to create ASP and then host Azure Web Apps in ASEs:

As we iterated multiple times that we need to create ASP first in ASEs.

Click on **App Service plans** in the left sidebar; if it is not available, click on **More services** and filter **App Service plans** and open it.

Click on **+Add**. Observe carefully here. The pane opened by clicking on **+Add** has all the same details and options that we used while creating a normal ASP.

The question is, how to create ASP in ASEs?

It is **Location** and **Pricing tier**:

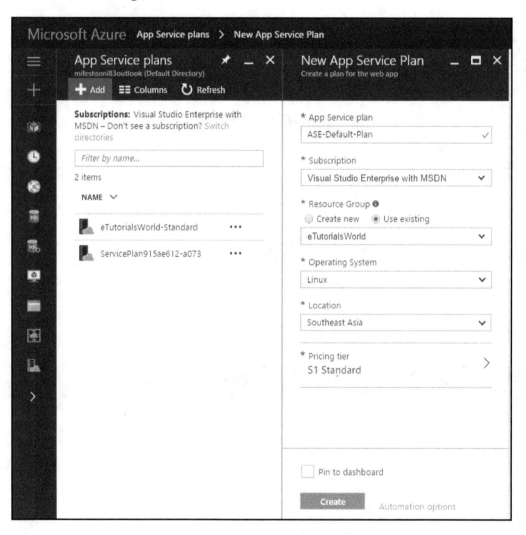

We can select **Worker pool** that has available instances to host ASP can be utilized in the **Pricing tier**:

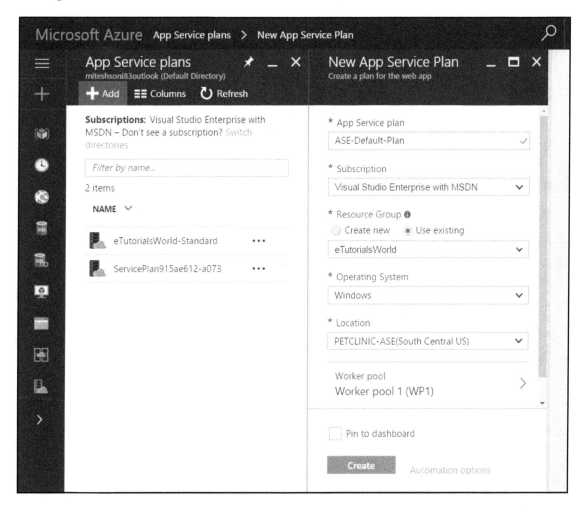

How do we bring the **Worker pool 1 (WP1)**?

Select the **PETCLINIC-ASE(South Central US)** ASE in the **Location** field. The moment we select ASE in **Location**, it will change the pricing to **Worker pool**.

Now the obvious question is, where does pricing come into picture in this case?

Remember that, we have scale sizes in **Front End pool** and **Worker pool**. This is used for pricing:

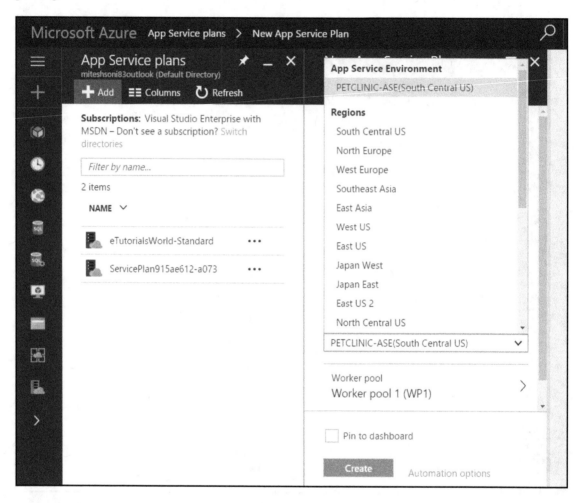

Then click on **Worker pool**. It gives us the list of worker pools available. Surprise!

Why does it have only **Worker pool 1 (WP1)**? In our ASE, we have three worker pools. The reason is, even though we have three worker pools in ASEs, not all the worker pools are allocated instances. Only **Worker pool 1** has an instance, and that also has two instances, as we saw in an earlier section.

Again, there is a surprise here. **Worker pool 1 (WP1)** shows only one instance available, even though we have two instances in Worker pool 1. The reason is, ASE uses one instance for fault tolerance, and so we can't use it for hosting ASP. We will discuss this in a later section regarding the number of instances available in the worker pools, and, how many of these are actually usable considering fault tolerance.

Select **Worker pool 1 (WP1)** and click on **Create**:

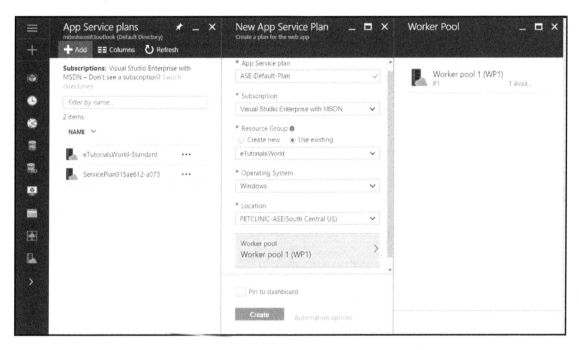

This will create a new ASP that is hosted in ASEs. We can see the newly created ASP named `ASE-Default-Plan` in the list of ASPs available:

Click on the newly created ASP, and we can see **Pricing Tier** is **P1**. That is expected, as we have selected **Worker pool 1**, which has scale size **P1** selected:

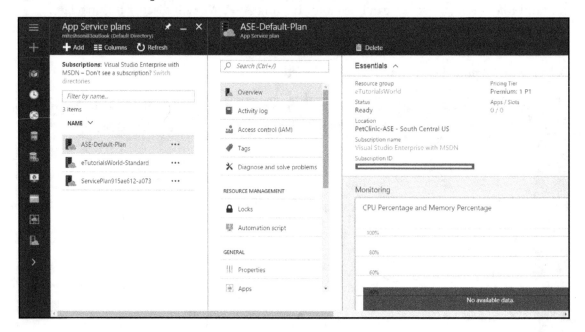

Now, let's go to **App Service Environments** in Azure portal to check whether any modifications are there.

If we observe carefully, **PLAN COUNT** has increased from 0 to 1, as we have one ASP in our ASE:

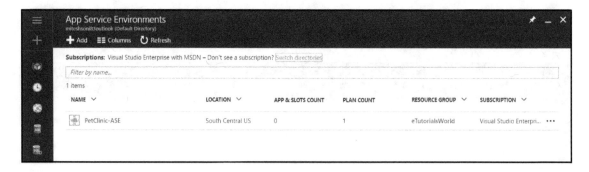

Click on the ASE and verify the **Overview** section with the details of **App Service plans** too. It also shows 1:

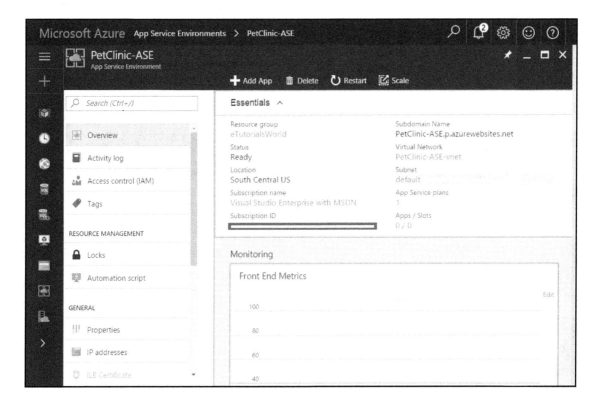

Now it is game time.

What do we need to create an App Service or Azure web application?

Yes, we need ASP. So, in other words, we can use ASP created in ASEs and create Azure Web Apps, and it is that simple to create an Azure web application in the ASE.

In other words, our web application will be in VNet. How?

ASP is created in ASEs; ASE is created in the VNet that has a subnet:

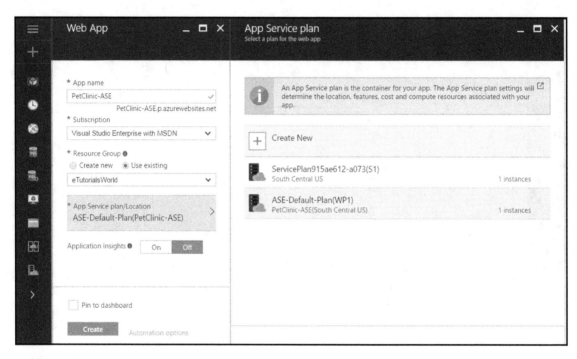

Select ASP created in ASEs and click on **Create**:

Wait for a while!

In Azure **App Services**, we will have the Azure web application that is created in ASEs. Verify the location. We selected this location while creating ASEs:

Let's go to **App Service Environments** in Azure portal and verify the changes in the list of ASEs. Now it shows 1 in **APP & SLOTS COUNT**:

In the next section, we will see how to configure the Azure Web App so we can host our Sample JEE application in it. It is not different than the way we do it in the normal Azure App Service.

ASEs – configuring Azure Web Apps

As we have created Azure Web Apps in the ASE, our next task is to configure the Azure Web Apps.

Click on `PetClinic-ASE` in the **App Service** section and go to **Application settings**.

Configure the **Java version**, **Java Minor version**, **Web container**, **Platform**, and **Always On** properties.

Save the settings. Click on the **Overview** section and visit the public URL assigned to Azure Web Apps hosted in ASEs:

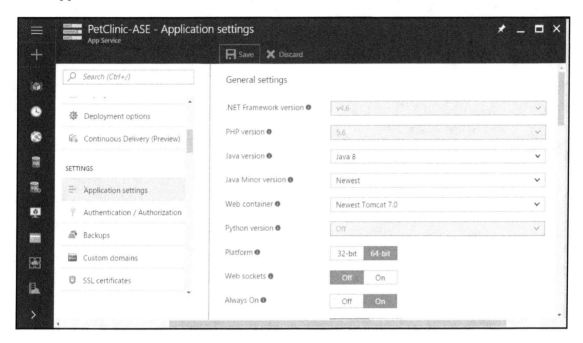

Observe the URL and compare it with the normal Azure Web Apps URL.

Here, we have `<Azure_Web_App_Name>.<App_Service_Environment_Name>.p.`

`azurewebsites.net.`

Everything else is similar to what we have in normal Azure Web Apps.

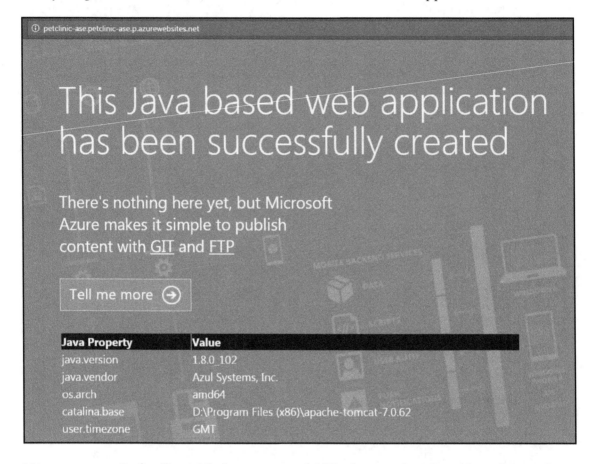

Now, we are quite familiar with the concepts of ASEs, front end pools, and worker pools. We also know that Azure Web Apps is in a VNet now as the ASEs are created in a VNet.

ASEs – virtual network

Let's try to see the different aspects of VNet involved in the ASE.

Go to the ASE that we created, click on **Virtual Network**, and then click on **Address space**. Here we will get the default address space used in VNet:

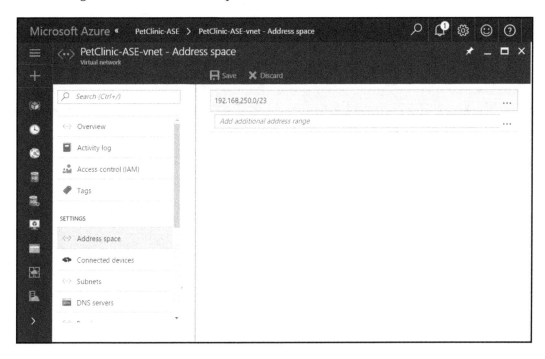

In the ASE, click on **Virtual Network**, go to **SETTINGS**, and click on **Subnets** to get details on the subnet used in this ASE:

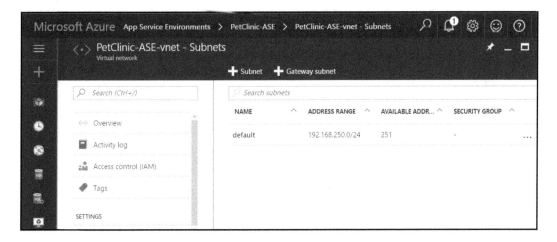

Here, we will get details on **Address range (CIDR block)**, **Available addresses**, **Network security group**, and other details:

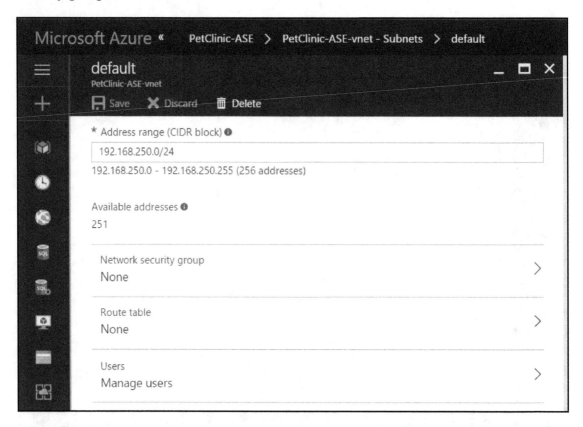

The reason that we are discussing VNet and subnet more in detail is to configure better security. One of the main reasons to have ASEs is better security.

Why and how?

We know we have hosted Azure Web Apps in the ASE that is in VNet. Hence, we can apply all security-related configurations in the Azure web application that is available for VNet. We can achieve this by configuring NSG.

We can see that no NSG is assigned in our ASE. So our next task is to create NSG and assign it to subnet so we can control inbound and outbound traffic to Azure web application / ASEs:

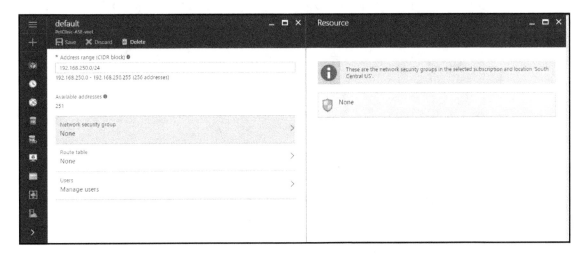

Click on **More services** in the left sidebar of Azure portal, filter **Network security groups** and open it. As of now, there is no security group available. Let's create one NSG.

Click on **+Add**:

Give **Name, Subscription, Resource group,** and **Location**. Click on **Create**:

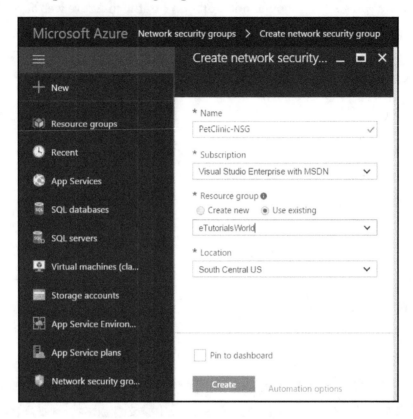

Wait until we get the notification of the creation of NSG. We can see the newly created NSG in the list of **Network security groups**:

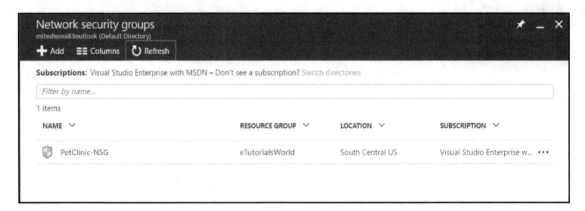

Let's explore NSG. Click on the NSG that we have created.

We can see that no security rules (inbound or outbound) are configured, and this NSG is not associated with any subnets either:

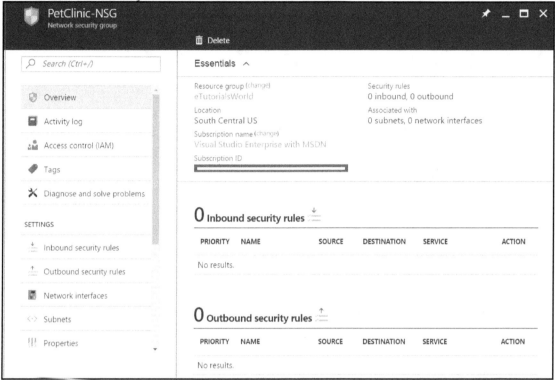

ASEs – network security groups

Let's configure **Inbound security rules** and O**utbound security rules**.

In the **SETTINGS** section, click on **Inbound security rules** and click on **+Add**.

Here, we can give the name of the rule and the priority of the rule in the case of execution. To get detailed information on priority, click on the small icon after the label:

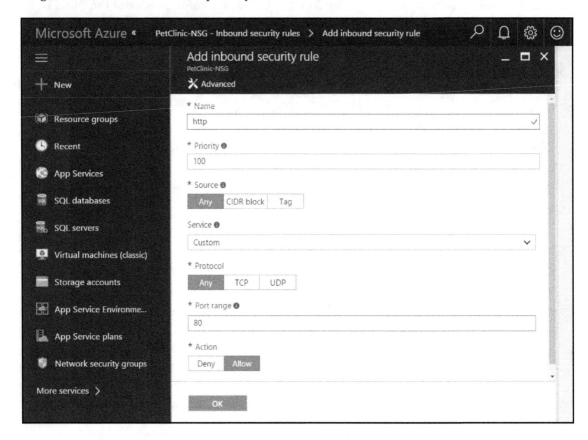

We can select from which source traffic should be allowed or restricted, for which protocol, the port range or port number along with the action. The following rule is just an example where any source is allowed to access any port. Observe the **Priority** given to this:

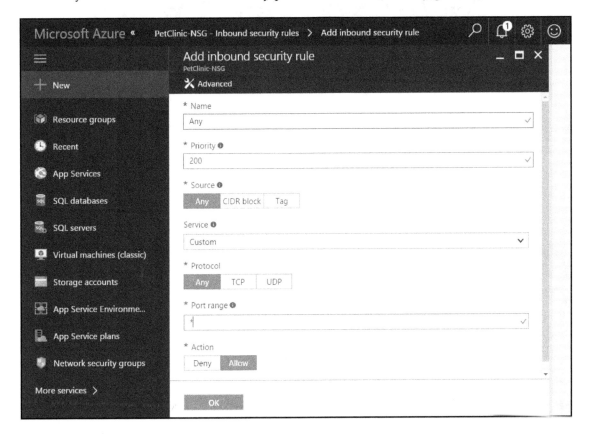

Let's configure another rule for the **HTTPS** protocol and give it **Priority** as well:

Let's verify the list of inbound security rules and their priorities:

There are **Default rules** also that are already configured. To make default rules visible, click on the **Default rules** link in the **Inbound security rules** pane.

All these rules are applied in the sequence of priority assigned to them:

Similarly, we can control outbound traffic too. **Outbound security rules** also have a default set of rules that is visible when we click on **Default rules**:

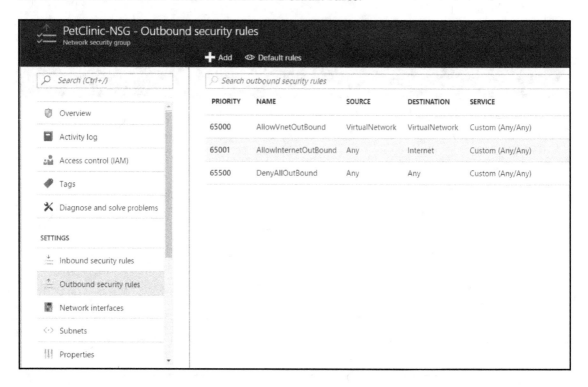

Let's verify the NSG again, and we can see three inbound security rules are added and visible on the main pane of NSG:

 To get more details on NSGs, go to `https://docs.microsoft.com/en-us` `/azure/virtual-network/virtual-networks-nsg`and also refer to *Azure Network Security Groups (NSG) – Best Practices and Lessons Learned* at `https` `://blogs.msdn.microsoft.com/igorpag/2016/05/14/azure-network-s` `ecurity-groups-nsg-best-practices-and-lessons-learned/`.

Now, we will assign NSG to the subnet available in ASEs.

Configuring NSG in ASE subnet

Once we have created a NSG, we can assign it to the subnet we have in ASEs.

Go to ASE, then click on **Virtual Network,** and then click on **Subnets**, and go to the default subnet. Click on **Network security group**.

Now we can see the NSG we created in the list, and we can assign it to this subnet:

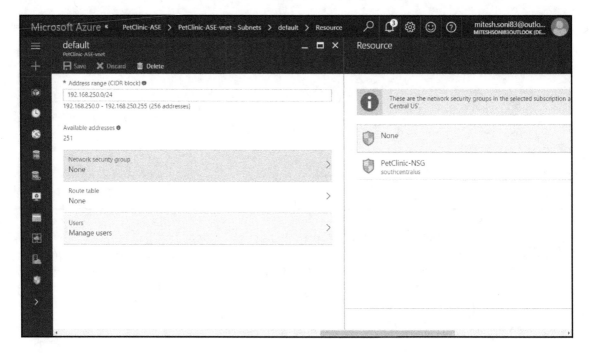

After selecting the **Network security group**, click on **Save**:

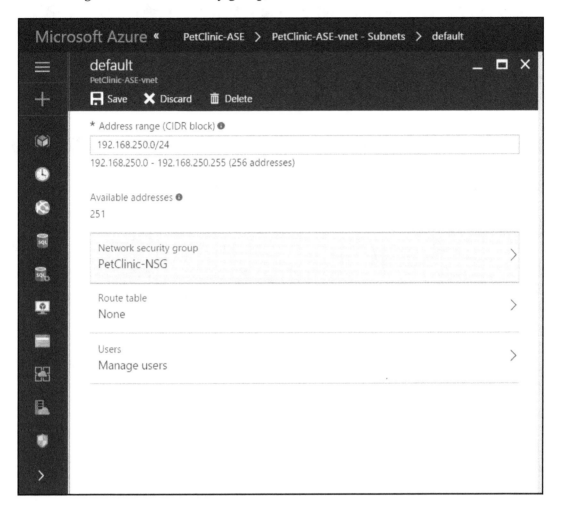

Once we are ready with Azure Web Apps hosted in ASE, the rest of the things are similar to Azure Web Apps. Even the **Continuous Delivery** (**CD**) process is also the same.

We only need to select the Azure web application that we created in ASE while configuring the task **Deploy Azure App Service**.

We will cover this part in detail in the next chapter, where we will look into deploying a WAR file into Azure Web Apps and ASE using VSTS.

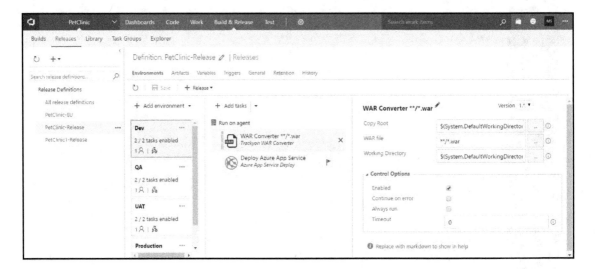

To delete an ASE, go to Azure portal and click on **Delete**. It will ask for confirmation and once we delete it, all the resources in that ASE will be deleted.

So, we covered all the basic details regarding ASEs. As we are discussing securing App Service or Web Apps, we will also discuss how to configure Azure Web Apps to increase security. However, it is necessary to keep a lock on ASE as it may contain many applications, and deleting an ASE will delete all of them.

Enforcing HTTP redirection to HTTPS on Azure Web Apps

By default, Azure App Service does not enforce HTTPS. We can enforce HTTPS redirection by configuring the rules in the `web.config` file.

In our normal Azure Web Apps URL, add `scm` after the name of the Azure web application. It opens a Kudu editor:

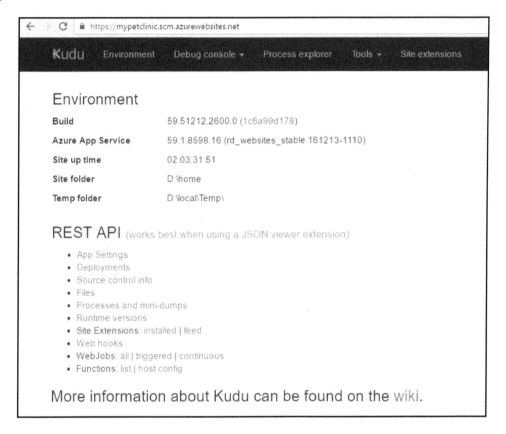

Go to **Debug console** and navigate to the `wwwroot` directory in the Kudu editor.

Create `web.config` by executing the `touch web.config` command in the console:

Click on the Edit icon of the file and we can add the following content to redirect HTTP to HTTPS:

```xml
<?xml version="1.0" encoding="UTF-8"?>
<configuration>
  <system.webServer>
    <rewrite>
      <rules>
      <!-- BEGIN rule TAG FOR HTTPS REDIRECT -->
        <rule name="Force HTTPS" enabled="true">
          <match url="(.*)" ignoreCase="false" />
          <conditions>
            <add input="{HTTPS}" pattern="off" />
          </conditions>
            <action type="Redirect" url="https://{HTTP_HOST}/{R:1}"
              appendQueryString="true" redirectType="Permanent" />
        </rule>
      <!-- END rule TAG FOR HTTPS REDIRECT -->
      </rules>
    </rewrite>
```

```
      </system.webServer>
    </configuration>
```

Save it:

Visit the application URL and you will be redirected to the HTTPS-based URL:

In the next section, we will cover how to filter traffic by IP and also regarding dynamic IP restrictions to secure Azure Web Apps by adding rules in the `web.config` file.

Filtering traffic by IP and dynamic IP restrictions

We may want to restrict access to Azure Web Apps. We can achieve this using the `<ipSecurity>` element. We can define which IP addresses can access Azure, and the action to take in case of a violation of that rule:

```xml
<configuration>
  <system.webServer>
    <security>
      <ipSecurity allowUnlisted="true" denyAction="NotFound">
        <add allowed="true" ipAddress="xxx.xxx.xxx.xxx"
          subnetMask="255.xxx.xxx.xxx"/>
      </ipSecurity>
    </security>
  </system.webServer>
</configuration>
```

```
Kudu    Environment    Debug console    Process explorer    Tools    Site extensions                    M S

Save    Cancel         web.config

1    <?xml version="1.0" encoding="utf-8"?>
2 ▾  <configuration>
3 ▾    <system.webServer>
4 ▾      <rewrite>
5 ▾        <rules>
6 ▾          <rule name="Force HTTPS" enabled="true">
7              <match url="(.*)" ignoreCase="false" />
8 ▾            <conditions>
9                <add input="{HTTPS}" pattern="off" />
10            </conditions>
11            <action type="Redirect" url="https://{HTTP_HOST}/{R:1}" appendQueryString="true" redirectType="Permanent" />
12          </rule>
13        </rules>
14 ▾      <security>
15 ▾        <ipSecurity allowUnlisted="false" denyAction="NotFound">
16            <add allowed="true" ipAddress="1.39.10.51" subnetMask="255.255.255.0" />
17          </ipSecurity>
18        </security>
19      </rewrite>
20    </system.webServer>
21  </configuration>
22
```

Dynamic IP restrictions allow us to block access to Azure Web Apps based on different scenarios as follows:

- To deny access by maximum concurrent requests
- To deny access by maximum requests within the specified time period

To configure dynamic IP restriction, make the following changes to the `web.config` file:

```xml
<configuration>
  <system.webServer>
    <security>
      <dynamicIpSecurity>
        <denyByConcurrentRequests enabled="true"
        maxConcurrentRequests="10"/>
        <denyByRequestRate enabled="true" maxRequests="10"
        requestIntervalInMilliseconds="2000"/>
      </dynamicIpSecurity>
    </security>
  </system.webServer>
</configuration>
```

Click on **Save**:

```xml
<?xml version="1.0" encoding="utf-8"?>
<configuration>
    <system.webServer>
        <rewrite>
            <rules>
                <rule name="Force HTTPS" enabled="true">
                    <match url="(.*)" ignoreCase="false" />
                    <conditions>
                        <add input="{HTTPS}" pattern="off" />
                    </conditions>
                    <action type="Redirect" url="https://{HTTP_HOST}/{R:1}" appendQueryString="true" redirectType="Permanent" />
                </rule>
            </rules>
            <security>
                <ipSecurity allowUnlisted="false" denyAction="NotFound">
                    <add allowed="true" ipAddress="1.39.10.51" subnetMask="255.255.255.0" />
                </ipSecurity>
                <dynamicIpSecurity>
                    <denyByConcurrentRequests enabled="true" maxConcurrentRequests="100" />
                </dynamicIpSecurity>
            </security>
        </rewrite>
    </system.webServer>
</configuration>
```

In the next section, we will compare ASE and non-ASE (Azure Web Apps).

Comparing ASE and non-ASE (Azure Web Apps)

The following are some but not all the differences between ASE and non-ASE:

	non-ASE	ASE
Virtual Network	Azure Web Apps are hosted in a multitenant environment. We can configure Azure Web Apps to integrate it with VNet.	ASEs are created in the VNet, so Azure Web Apps are hosted in Azure VNet.
Resource layers	There are instances that can be utilized directly in ASP.	In ASE, we have two layers: **Front end pool**: This is used for load balancing and SSL termination **Worker pools**: There are three worker pools in ASE. Instances available in the worker pools are used in the creation of ASP, and then we can host Azure Web Apps in the ASP.
Support for NSGs	Azure App Service / Azure Web Apps is a PaaS and not hosted in VNet. Hence, we can't configure inbound and outbound rules.	As ASE is in VNet, we can configure the subnet with NSG. Hence, we can configure inbound security rules and outbound security rules.
Instance size(s)	Only three types of instance can be used in Azure Web Apps: P1, P2, and P3. P4 instances can't be used in the non-ASE environment.	In front end pool, we can utilize P2, P3, and P4 instances, while in worker pools, we can utilize P1, P2, P3, and P4 instances.
Number of instances	In the Standard plan, we can have 10 instances. In the Premium plan, we can have 20 instances.	In ASE, we can utilize 50 instances, while in one ASE a maximum of 55 instances can be created.
Time to create	Normal App Service are created instantly.	ASE takes 2-3 hours to be created, and hence we need to wait until ASE is created.

Summary

Security is not a tool, a technology, or a one-time job, but an ongoing process. In this chapter, we discussed how to create ASE that is more secure than non-ASE or a normal Azure App Service. App Service is a PaaS offering from Microsoft Azure. ASEs offer App Service in the VNet and hence we can configure NSG to make the environment more secure.

In other words, we can configure inbound and outbound security rules for traffic that flows inwards and outwards.

So far, we have covered continuous development using the Eclipse IDE and its integration with source code repository in VSTS. We also discussed how to perform continuous integration, how to create Azure Web Apps in a non-ASE environment, and how to manage Azure Web Apps as well.

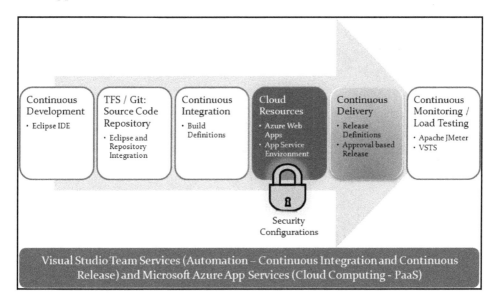

We need to understand that in ASE and non-ASE scenarios, only the hosting environment differs. Azure Web Apps related tasks and operations are same.

Our next goal is to deploy a package file in an environment that we have created that is Azure Web Apps in ASE or non-ASE.

In our case, it is a Java application, so we will need to deploy a WAR file in Azure Web Apps. In the next chapter, we will see how to achieve continuous delivery / continuous deployment using an approval-based workflow.

6

Continuous Delivery to Azure Web Apps and ASE Using VSTS

It's fine to celebrate success but it is more important to heed the lessons of failure.
—Bill Gates

This chapter will present how to deploy an application in Azure Web Apps and ASEs using VSTS. It also includes the security and governance aspects while deploying in different environments to ensure that only authorized persons can perform the deployment operation, and the process has to be verified.

This chapter will cover end-to-end automation visualization for deploying an application in the PaaS offering of Microsoft Azure.

- Overview of CD and continuous deployment
- Configuration of Microsoft Azure subscription
- Build and release automation
- Environment with release tasks
- Security and governance with approver setup
- End-to-end automation process execution
- Continuous feedback on release execution

Overview of CD and continuous deployment

CD and continuous deployment are normally used interchangeably. However, there is a minor difference.

CD is the application deployment into an environment that is not production, so it can be development, QA, stage, pre-production, and so on.

Continuous deployment is the application deployment into the production environment.

We need to understand the way an application is deployed in production and non-production environments manually and then try to automate that process. The automated approach of application deployment doesn't change. It is all about the location where the application is getting deployed.

CD makes the application package production ready. Continuous deployment goes through end-to-end automation for release management and manual intervention is not required.

A minor difference is the manual approval process in the environment that makes CD and continuous deployment different from each other. In the case of a production environment, it is better to have the manual approval process just before application deployment.

In the upcoming sections, we will see how to deploy the application package (the WAR file in our case, as it is a JEE application) in Microsoft Azure Web Apps.

Configuration of Microsoft Azure subscription

We will first go to our VSTS account. Here, we need the following things to be accomplished:

- Configure our Microsoft Azure subscription so we can connect to Azure Web Apps from VSTS
- Create a release definition that achieves the task of application deployment in Azure Web Apps

In the **Recent** section, click on `PetClinic`:

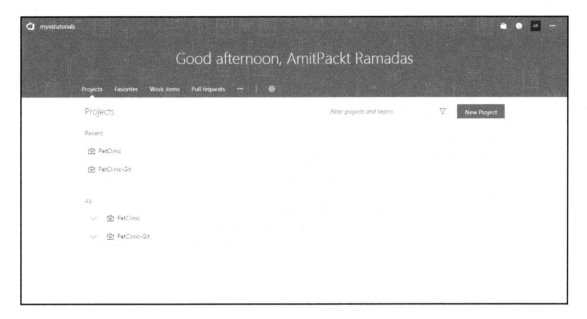

It will open the **Dashboards** page for the project created in VSTS:

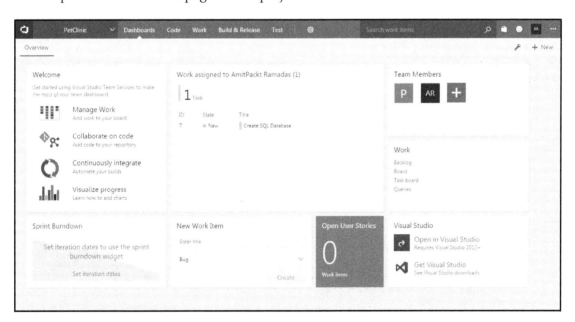

In the top bar, click on **Build & Release**, which will open a menu. Click on the **Releases** menu item:

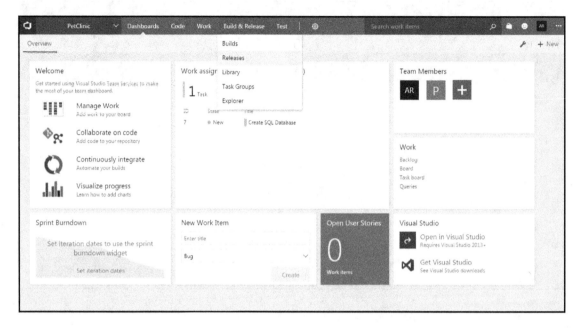

Click on the **Releases** link on the page.

As this is a new account, there is no release definition, so this section is empty. We can create a new release definition so that we can automate application deployment into Azure App Service or ASEs.

The way we have build definitions for continuous integration, we have release definitions for continuous release, CD, or continuous deployment. Release definitions contain different tasks that can be used for application deployment in the target environment.

So, let's create a new release definition. Each release definition can contain one or more environment, and each environment can contain one or more tasks to deploy an application.

Click on **+New definition**:

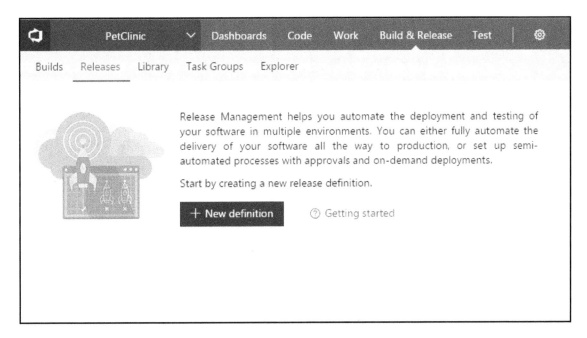

Once we click on **+New definition**, it will open a dialog box with deployment templates that can be used for deployment automation.

We are going to deploy the WAR file into Azure App Service / Azure Web Apps, so select **Azure App Service Deployment**. Click on **Next**:

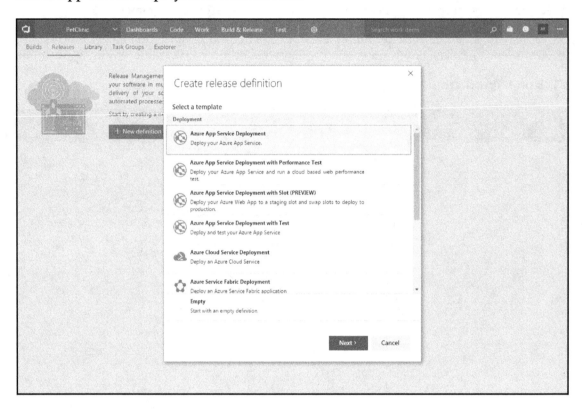

Let's remember few things from earlier chapters before explaining this deployment automation.

We created a build definition `PetClinic-Maven` that compiles the source code, executes unit test cases, and creates a WAR file. The WAR file is our artifact. This artifact is the result of the build definition execution.

Now, in release definition, we need to select where the artifact will come from, and that is from **Build**. Select the `PetClinic` project.

In **Source (Build definition)**, all build definitions related to the `PetClinic` project will be available. We will select `PetClinic-Maven`.

In a nutshell, we want to achieve continuous integration and CD here. This means that when a developer checks in new code or a bug fix in the repository, it will automatically trigger a build definition. The build definition will compile source files, execute unit tests, if any, perform static code analysis if Sonar is configured, and create a WAR/package file. This is an artifact. Once the build definition is completed successfully, it will trigger a release definition to deploy an artifact or a WAR file into Azure Web Apps that is hosted in ASE or non-ASE.

Click on the **Continuous deployment (create release and deploy whenever a build completes)** checkbox.

Click on **Create**:

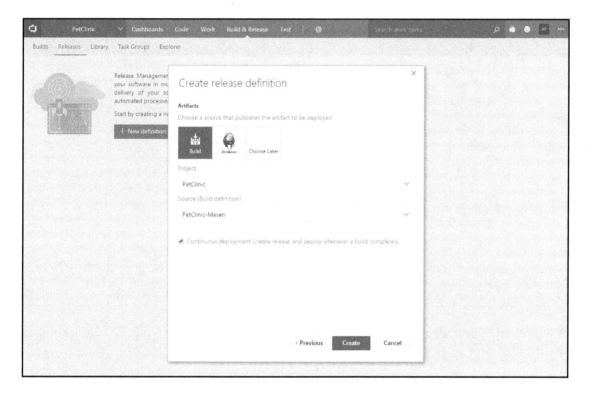

This will open a release definition in edit mode. We selected **Deploy Azure App Service**. The first thing that is required is to configure Azure subscription with VSTS.

Click on the task, and see there are fields named **AzureRM Subscription** and **App Service Name**. We need to configure our Azure subscription here, and the App Service names will appear in the list automatically.

Click on the **Manage** link next to the **Azure subscription** field:

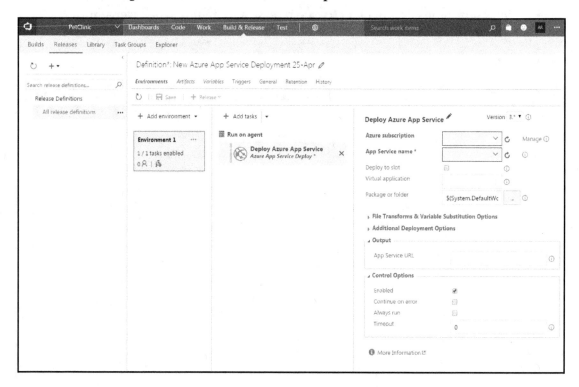

It will open a **Services** page in the VSTS portal. As of now, there is no service configured, so the list is empty:

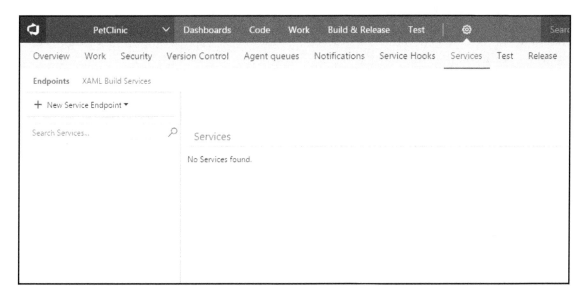

Click on **+New Service Endpoint**. A menu will open; select the **Azure Resource Manager** item from the menu to configure Azure subscription:

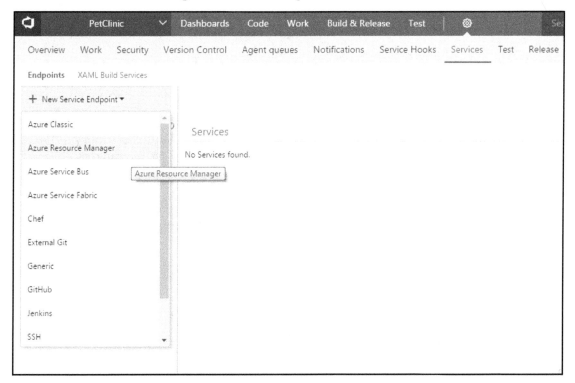

As we are already logged in, the VSTS and Azure account will get a subscription name in the list. Give the connection name that we will use in the release definition task to connect to the Azure account.

Click on **OK**:

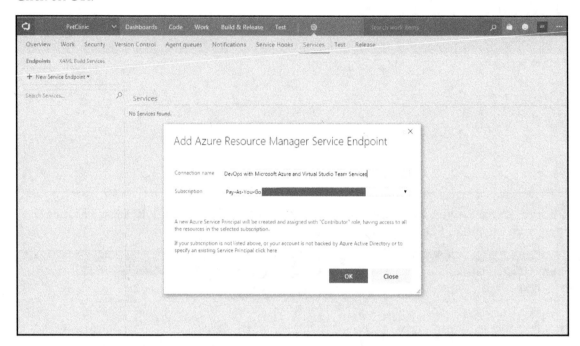

The purpose of adding the Azure subscription here is to get a list of resources available in that subscription to VSTS so we can configure them for deployment. In our example, we need a list of Azure Web Apps that are hosted in ASEs or non-ASE so we can deploy the PetClinic application to Azure Web Apps.

Once we close the box to add an Azure **Resource Manager** (**RM**) endpoint, we can see the list of endpoints in **Services** under **Endpoints**. Now we have our Azure RM subscription configured successfully:

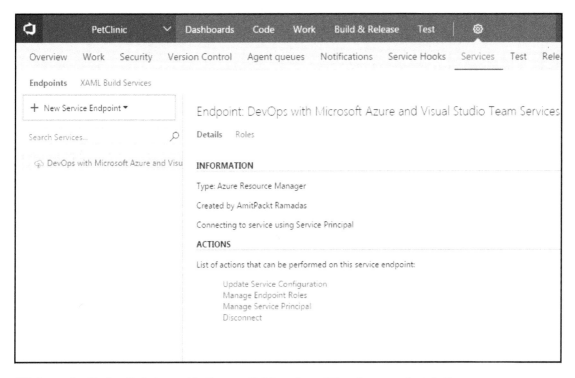

Click on the **Roles** link to verify the available roles of the Azure subscription:

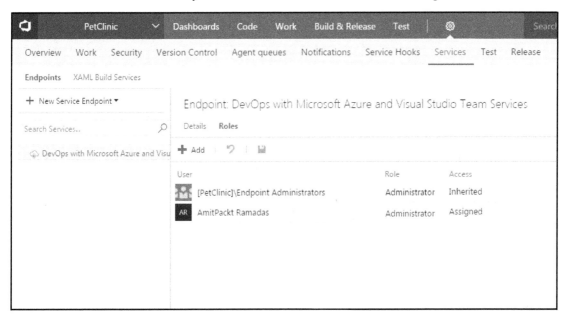

Now go to **Release Definitions** and click on the list box of **Azure subscription**, and now our newly added endpoint is available in the list.

Select the endpoint:

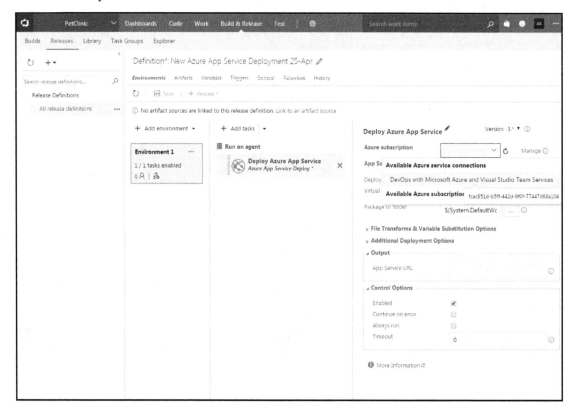

So far, we have configured Azure subscription endpoint in VSTS, so we can use it in a release definition to deploy the artifact in Azure App Service hosted in ASE and non-ASE.

In the next section, we will cover how to automate artifact deployment into Azure App Service when the build definition is executed successfully.

Build and release automation

Our main idea is to automate end-to-end activities that play a role in application life cycle management. To be precise, we want to have a scenario where the following activities are automatically executed with some workflow or approvals once developers commit some code for feature development or bug fixes:

- Continuous integration:
    - Compilation of source files
    - Execution of unit tests
    - Static code analysis

- CD:
    - Workflow-based application deployment into different environments, where one or more approvals are needed to deploy in a specific environment

- Continuous testing:
    - Load testing with VSTS or Apache JMeter

We have already configured **Azure subscription**. Once it is completed successfully, we can select **App Service Name**. Click on the down arrow, and Azure Web Apps available in the configured Azure subscription will be available in the list.

It is important to note that the list in **App Service Name** can have Azure Web Apps hosted in ASE or non-ASE. In simple terms, it doesn't matter whether Azure Web Apps are hosted in ASE or non-ASE. We only need to select **App Service Name** and that's it.

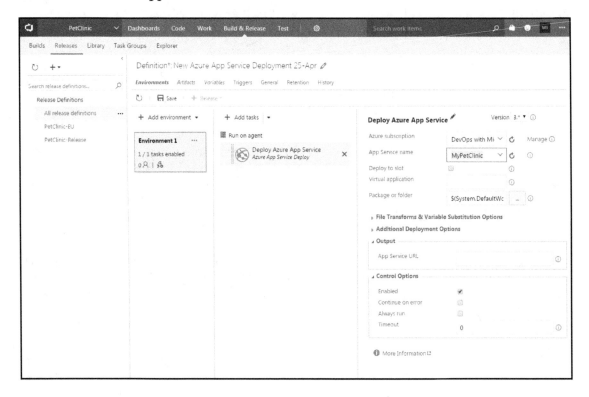

Go to **Package or Folder** and click on the three dots (**...**). Go to the `PetClinic-Maven`, and select the WAR file created after the successful execution of the build definition.

Our release definition will pick this WAR file and deploy it in Azure Web Apps.

Click on **OK**:

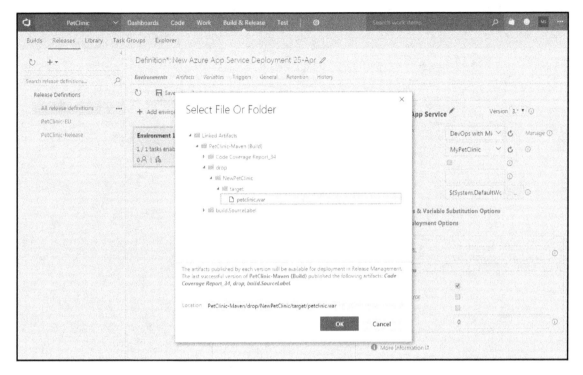

Now, we are all set to execute the release definition, but before that we need to save the release definition:

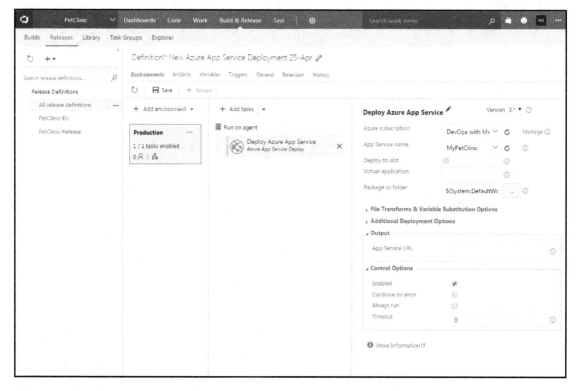

Click on the **Save** button and it will open a new dialog box. Provide a **Comment** and click on **OK** to save the release definition in VSTS:

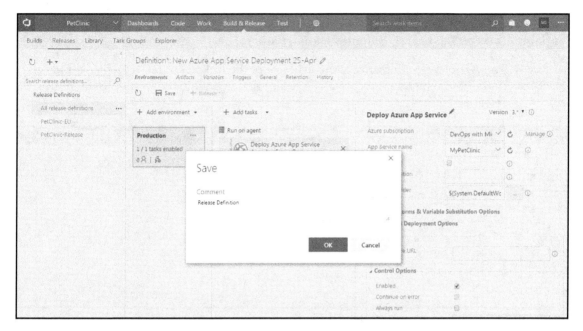

Verify that you have saved the release definition:

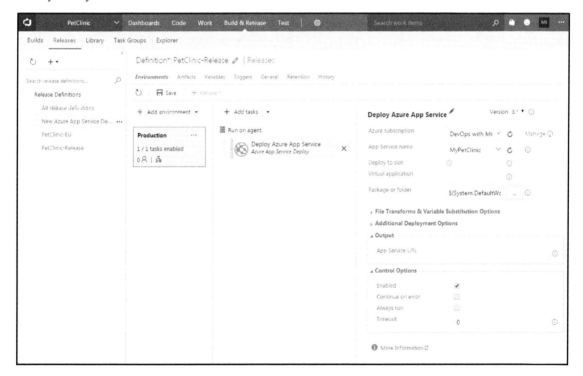

Before executing the release definition, let's look at other tabs/panes, such as **Artifacts**, **Variables**, **Triggers**, **General**, **Retention**, and **History**:

- The **Artifacts** section shows the artifacts of the linked sources (such as build definition, which will create a WAR file) that are available for deployment in releases:

- The **Variables** section can be used to create environment variables, and we can store parameters such as FTP hostname and other details:

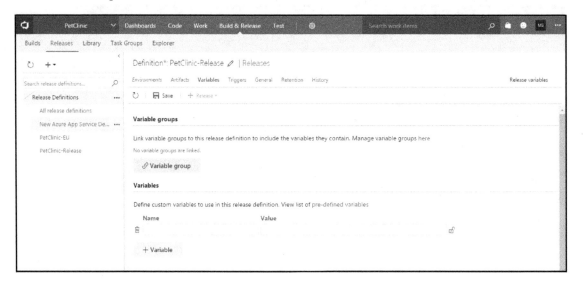

- The **Triggers** section allows us to set when a new release should be created. We can set it when a new artifact version is available, or in other words, when build definition execution is successfully completed:

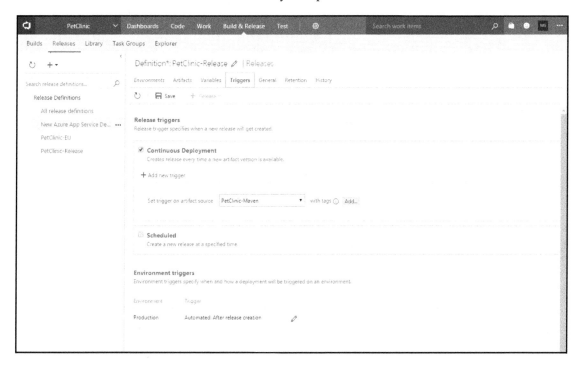

We can also schedule release definition execution based on the day and time specified with the time zone:

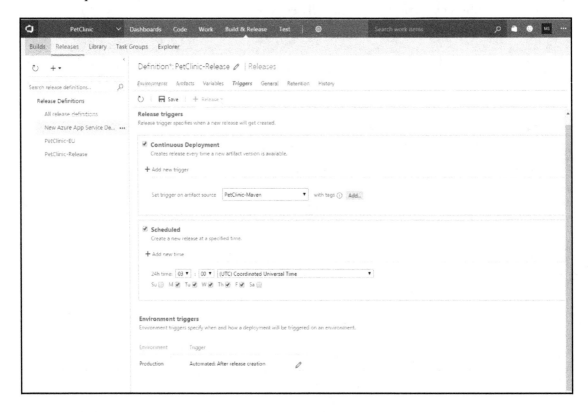

- The **General** section allows us to set **Release name format**. We will keep the default format for release name:

- The **Retention** section allows us to define the retention policy for releases deployed to different environments in the release definition:

- The **History** section will provide details on the changes made to the release definition, on which date, by whom, and comments, if any:

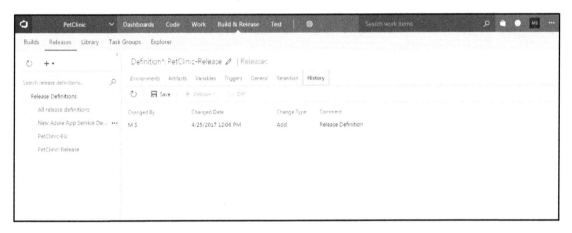

To check end-to-end automation, we will start the build definition execution. So, once it is successful, it will trigger a release definition. Save the release definition and click on **Queue new build...**:

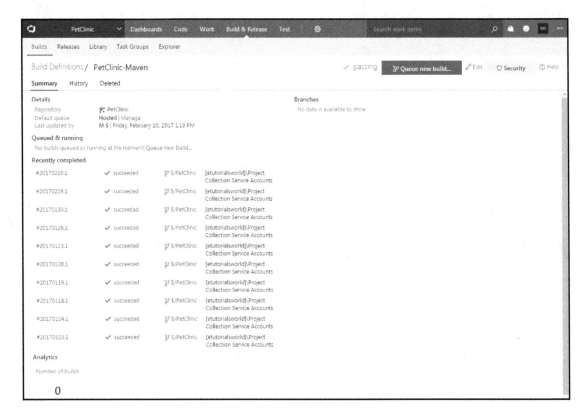

The **Queue build for PetClinic-Maven** build definition will trigger the release definition if it is completed successfully. Click on **OK**:

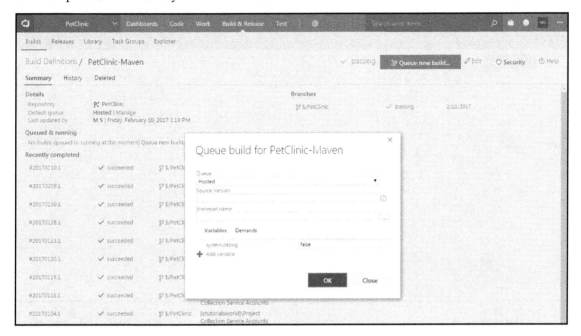

Once the build definition is successfully completed, the `PetClinic-Release` release definition will be triggered. Its job is to deploy the `.war` artifact into Azure App Service.

Deployment failed! Let's find out why this deployment has failed:

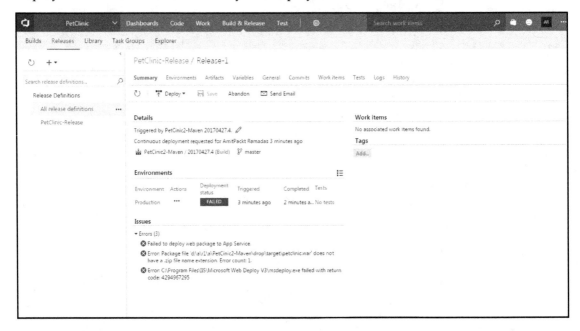

Verify **History** first. We can see that the release definition was triggered, but deployment has failed:

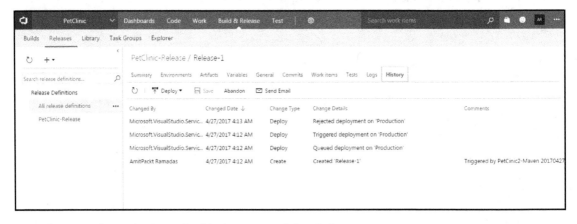

Let's find out from the logs the likely cause of this failure.

Go to the **Logs** section and verify the release definition execution steps. It clearly indicates that it is the final deployment operation that has failed:

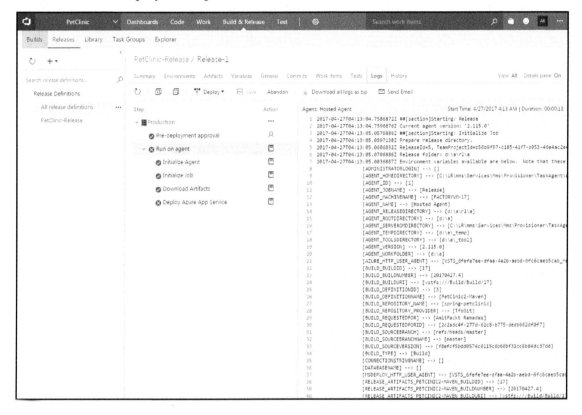

Click on the failed step, that is, **Deploy Azure App Service**:

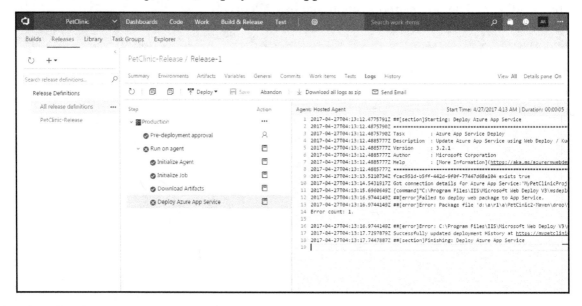

After closely examining the logs, we can see that it is mentioned that `.war` does not have a `.zip` file extension.

Remember, we selected `petclinic.war` and not `petclinic.zip`. It seems to deploy a WAR file with this task. We need to have a ZIP file and not a WAR file.

How do we solve this?

If we convert the WAR file into ZIP file, then it can be done, and it should happen automatically:

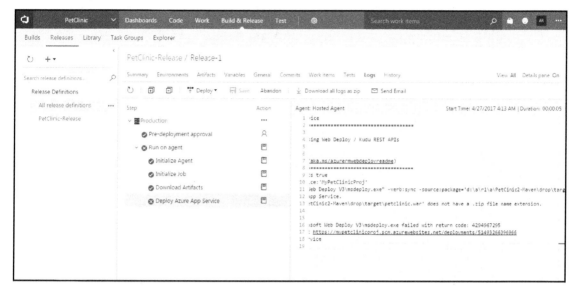

The question is, how?

Trackyon task to convert a .war file into a .zip file

The best way should be any task that can convert `.war` into a `.zip` file. So let's do it:

1. Click on **+Add tasks** and click on the **Marketplace** link:

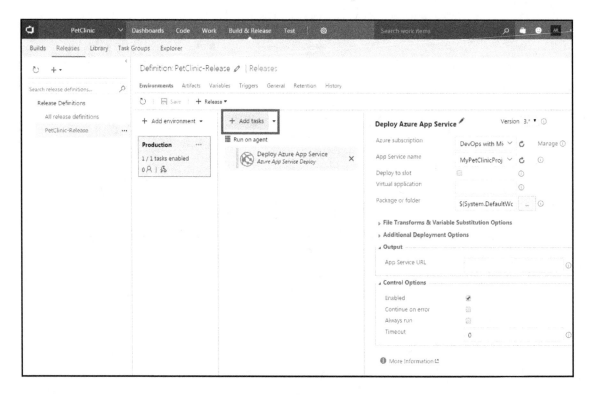

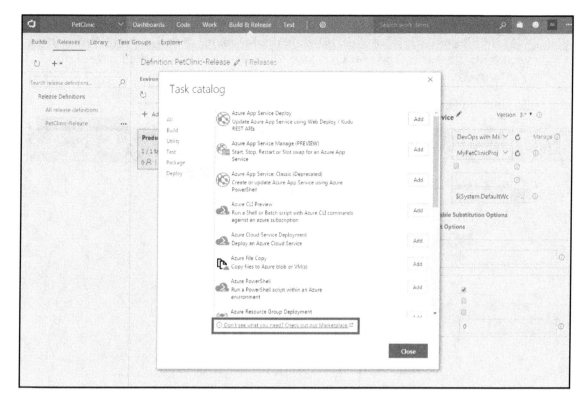

It will open a new window of **Marketplace** window.

2. Find Trackyon Advantage:

Observe carefully the **Usage** part, as it says the WAR converter task converts WAR files into ZIP files. Hence, before deployment, we will convert WAR files into ZIP files using the Trackyon task. Once that is done, our deployment on Azure Web Apps should work.

3. Click on **Install**:

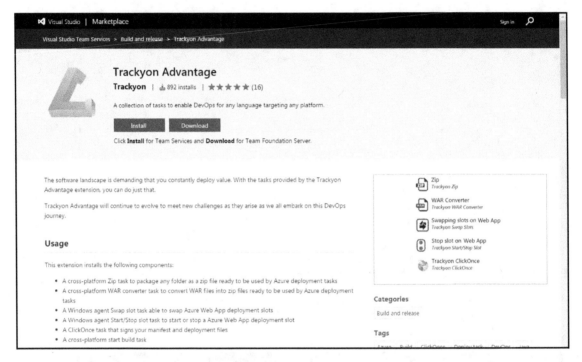

4. Select the VSTS account where we want to install Trackyon Advantage.

5. Click on **Continue**:

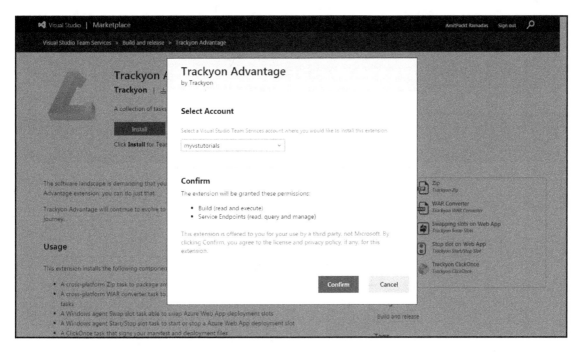

6. Click on **Proceed to the account**. Click on **Close**:

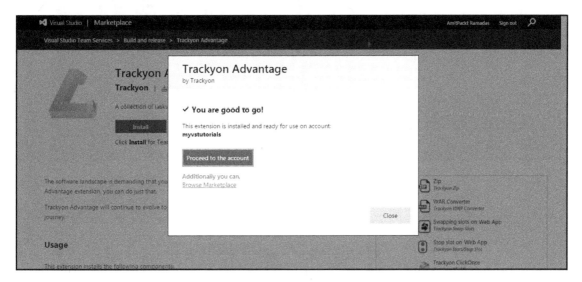

After installation, our next task is to add that task to the release definition. So, before deployment into Azure Web Apps, the WAR file is converted into a ZIP file:

1. Select the **Trackyon WAR Converter** task.
2. Click on **Close**:

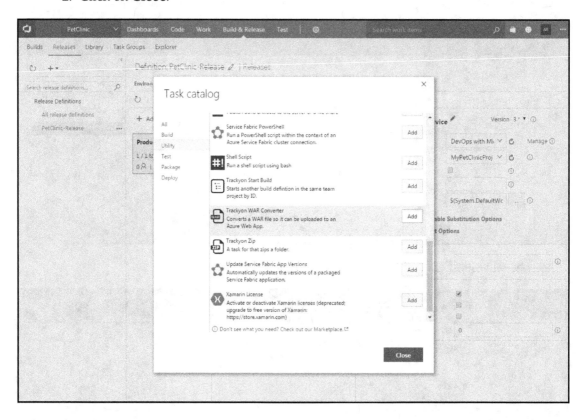

3. Select the folder where the WAR file is located:

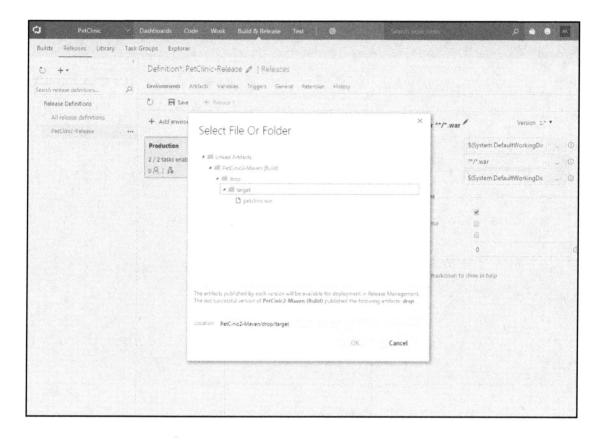

4. Select the folder where the ZIP file should be created:

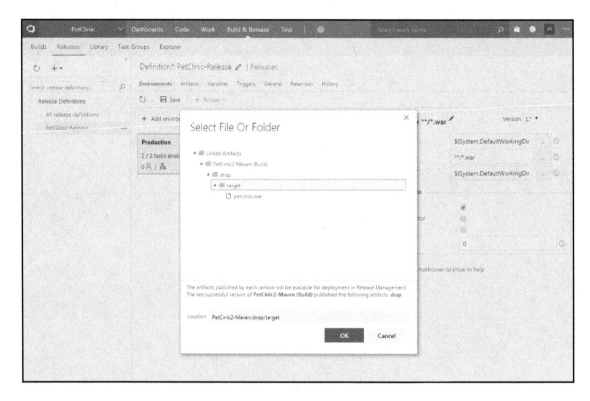

Now our release definition has two tasks to perform.

5. The first task converts the `.war` file into a `.zip` file, and the other task deploys the `.zip` file into Azure Web Apps:

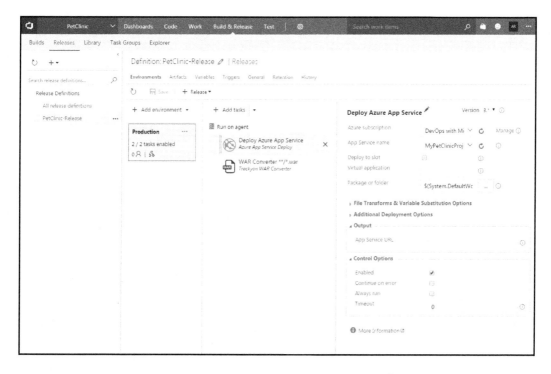

6. Go to the `PetClinic-Maven` build definition and click on **Queue new build...**:

7. The build will start when the hosted agent is available:

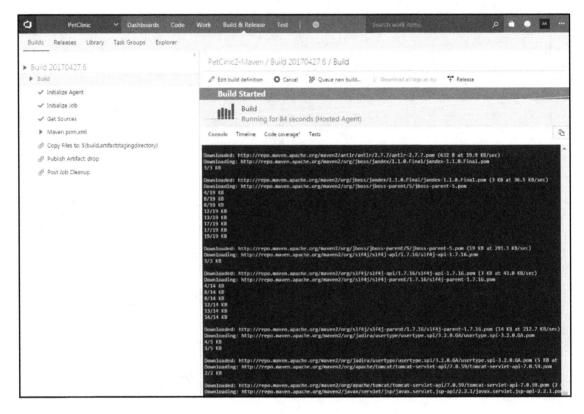

Wait until the build execution has completed successfully.

As we configured our release definition for CD, the successful build definition execution will trigger our release definition to achieve end-to-end automation.

Note the build number, **Build 20170427.6**:

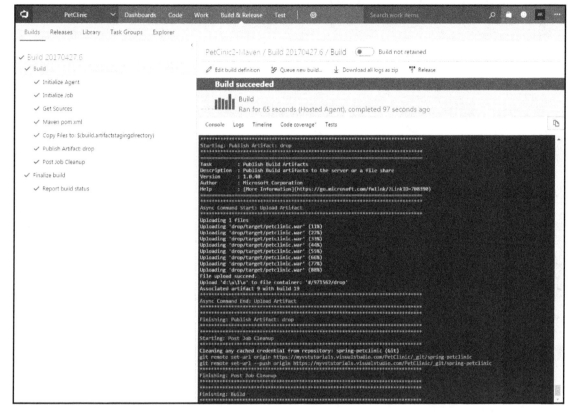

This build will trigger the release definition if completed successfully.

Continuous release – deploying the application in Azure Web Apps

Go to **Releases** and check the latest release definition. Look at the **Build** column to verify the build number.

Double-click on **Release-11** to get more details on the release definition execution in VSTS:

Now let's verify the details we have on the release definition execution in VSTS.

In **Details**, verify the build number that triggered the execution of the release definition. It also provides details on the user who requested continuous deployment.

The **Environments** section provides details about the environment the release definition has deployed to. It also shows the **Deployment status**—when the release definition was triggered, when it was completed, and whether any test execution was there. In our case, there are no test cases in the release definition:

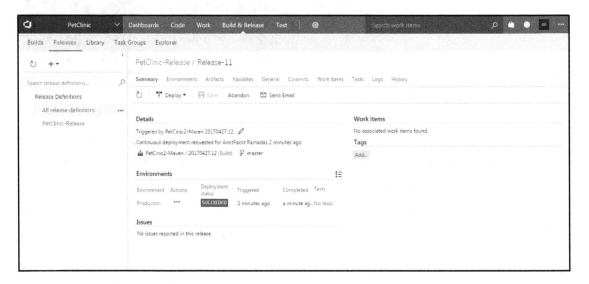

To get more details about the release definition execution, click on **Logs**. It will have series of steps that have been executed during release definition execution.

If the approval mechanism is set, then it will ask for approval first; once approval is given, it will **Run on agent**. It will initialize the agent first. Once the agent is available for the release definition execution, it will download the artifact or WAR file from the source folder.

As we already know that we can't deploy the WAR file directly, based on our configuration, it will convert the WAR file into a ZIP file. Once we have a ZIP file of our package, then our **Deploy Azure App Service** task will deploy the application package into Azure Web Apps:

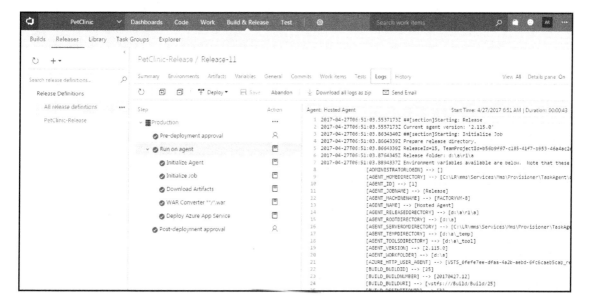

Click on the individual step to get a detailed log of the step execution. Let's see what the **WAR Converter **/*.war** step does:

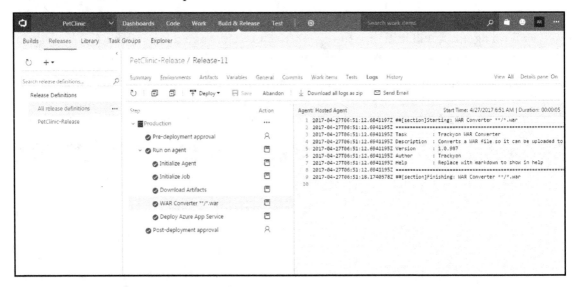

Similarly, the **Deploy Azure App Service** step execution will give details on how the deployment process is executed:

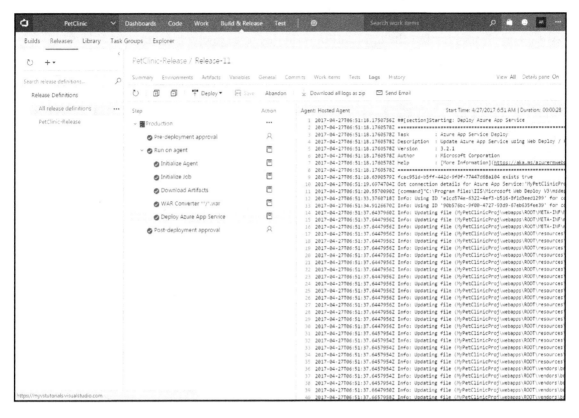

As there is no post-deployment approval configured, it is auto-approved, and hence the build execution is successful:

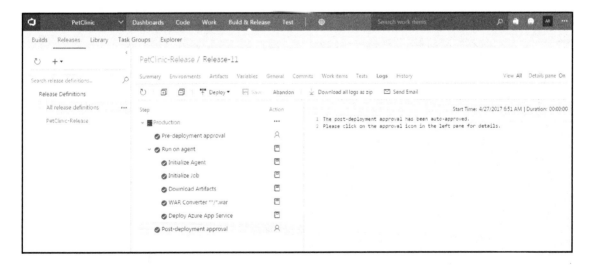

We already know the Azure web application URL, or we can get it from the Azure portal. Visit it and check whether the application is deployed correctly or not:

So, until now, we have configured end-to-end automation for application life cycle management using continuous integration and continuous deployment.

In the next section, we will cover how to create multiple environments and deploy an application into them using VSTS.

Environment with release tasks

We have configured automated deployment in the production environment. What if I need to deploy into multiple environments?

Let's remember how we are managing different environments in Azure Web Apps.

Any guesses?

Yes, you are right!

Deployment slots. We use deployment slots for different environments. So we should create multiple environments in the release definition and perform the deployment.

So, the next question should be, how do we create an environment that we can use for package deployment in a specific deployment slot in Azure Web Apps?

In the release definition, click on **+Add environment** and select **Create new environment**. We can select **Clone selected environment** if we want to have the same tasks as the existing environment in the new environment:

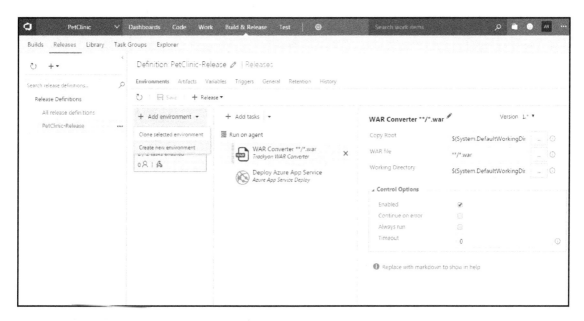

In the new environment, let's keep pre-deployment approval automatic.

Select **Trigger** to deploy automatically whenever a deployment to the previous environment is successful. We can rearrange or rename it once all the environments are configured.

Select the **Hosted** agent for release definition execution.

Click on **Create**. Change the name of the environment by double-clicking on the name of the environment. Based on the environment, the rest of the deployment details can be configured:

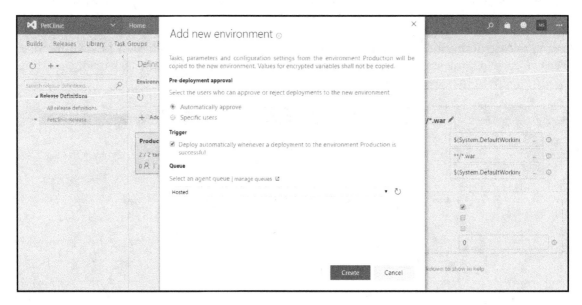

Change the existing environment name to **Dev** and click on (**...**). It will open a menu and select the **Clone selected environment** option.

In case of a new environment, what if we want to keep approvals before the deployment process takes place?

In the **Pre-deployment approval**, select **Specific users**. All the users available in the VSTS account are eligible for approval rights. We can give any name from that list.

Select **Trigger** to deploy automatically whenever a deployment to the previous environment is successful. We can rearrange or rename it once all environments are configured.

Click on **Create**. Change the name of the environment to **QA** by double-clicking on the name of the environment. Based on the environment, the rest of the deployment details can be configured:

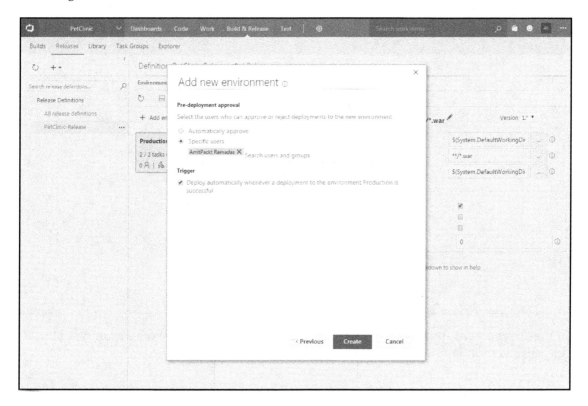

Configure the **UAT** environment in a similar fashion.

To assign approvals manually to any environment, select the environment, click on (**...**), and select **Assign approvers...**:

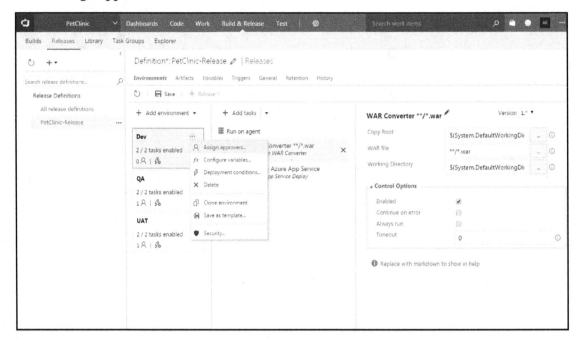

In **Pre-deployment approver**, we can specify users who can approve the execution of the release definition for the deployment.

Click on **OK**:

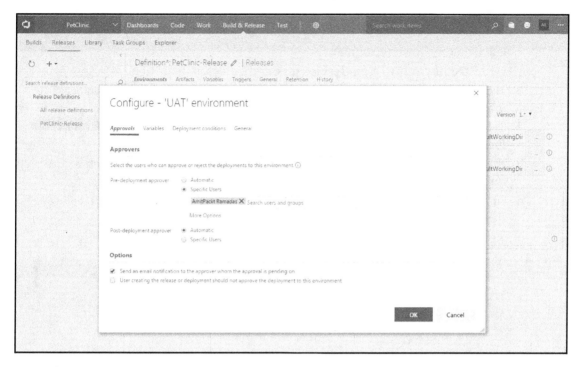

We only need to configure where to deploy the WAR file in different environments that we have created recently:

Let's start with **Dev** environment:

1. Click on the **Dev** environment.
2. Go to **Deploy Azure App Service** task in the release definition.
3. **Azure subscription** and **App Service name** are already configured, as we did that exercise earlier.
4. To deploy the WAR file into a specific slot, **dev** in this case, let's click on the **Deploy to Slot** checkbox.
5. It will ask for the **Resource Group**. Select the resource group in which Azure web application is available.
6. In the **Slot** list, all the slots created for Azure Web Apps will be listed. Select the **dev** slot.
7. Keep the rest of the details as they are and save the release definition:

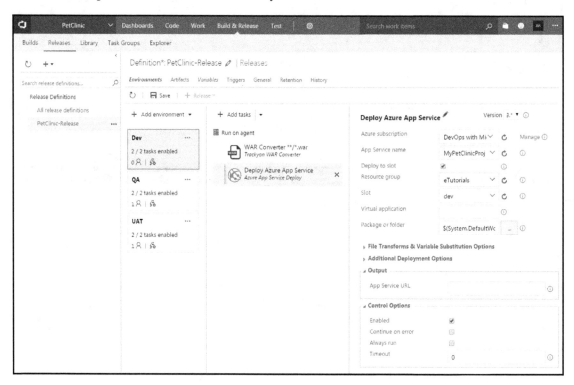

Now, let's configure the **QA** environment:

1. Click on the **QA** environment.
2. Go to **Deploy Azure App Service** task available in the release definition.
3. **Azure subscription** and **App Service name** are already configured, as we did that exercise earlier.
4. To deploy the WAR file into a specific slot, **qa** in this case, let's click on the **Deploy to Slot** checkbox.
5. It will ask for the **Resource Group**. Select the resource group in which Azure web application is available.
6. In the **Slot** list, all the slots created for Azure Web Apps will be listed. Select the **qa** slot.
7. Keep the rest of the details as they are and save the release definition:

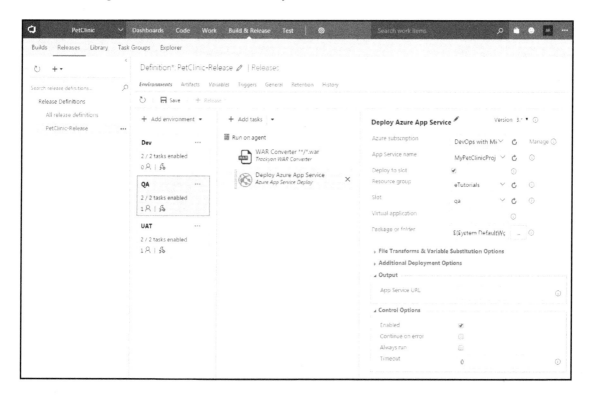

To configure the **UAT** environment, follow these steps:

1. Click on the **UAT** environment.
2. Go to the **Deploy Azure App Service** task in the release definition.
3. **Azure subscription** and **App Service name** are already configured, as we did that exercise earlier.
4. To deploy the WAR file into a specific slot, **dev** in this case, let's click on the **Deploy to Slot** checkbox.
5. It will ask for the **Resource Group**. Select the resource group in which Azure Web App is available.
6. In the **Slot** list, all the slots created for Azure Web Apps will be listed. Select the **uat/stage** slot.
7. Keep the rest of the details as they are and save the release definition:

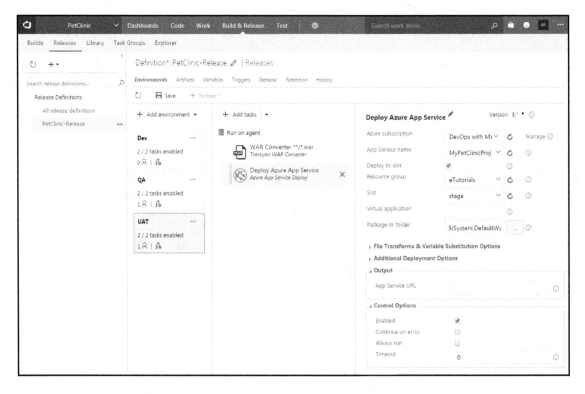

To deploy an application in the production slot or main Azure Web Apps, we don't need to select a slot. We just need to provide the Azure web application name, and it will deploy into the main web application in Azure:

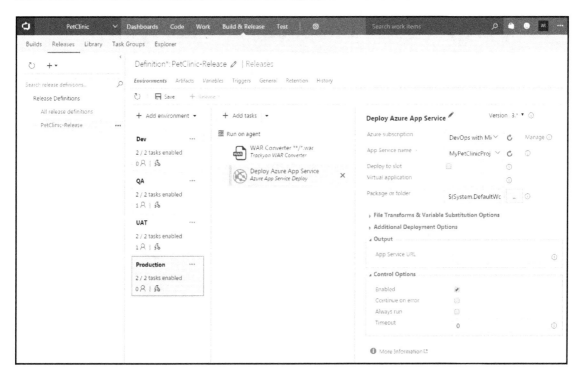

Save the release definition:

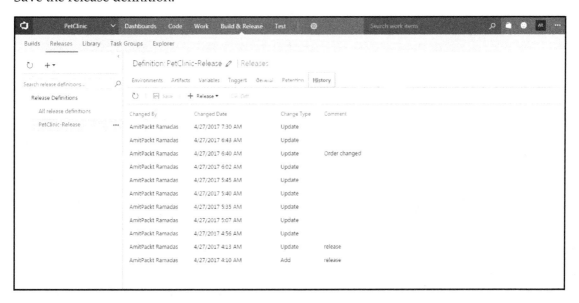

Click on the **Releases** link.

Pre-approval before application deployment

Here, we are exclusively executing the release definition just to check approvals and application deployment in different environments. So we are not executing the build definition for continuous integration.

In new release, a list box is available to select the build definition, so the artifact created by the execution of the build definition can be utilized in the deployment process.

Select the last build executed successfully from the list and click on **Create**:

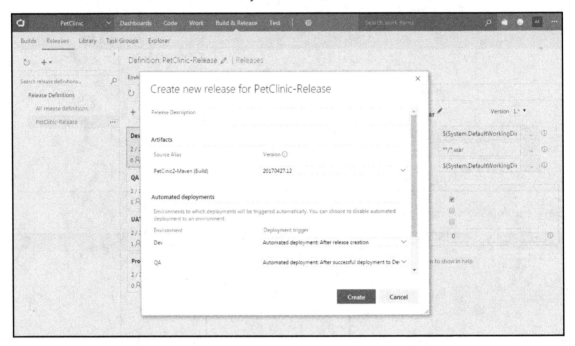

What should happen next?

Deployment, right? No!

We have set the approval process in the release definition execution, so until and unless the approver approves it, the execution of the release definition won't take place.

Look at the warning in the **Summary** section of the release definition execution. It says **A pre-deployment approval is pending for 'Dev' environment**.

As I have configured my own ID for this, links are available to approve or reject the build:

Let's click on the **Approve or Reject** link.

It will open a small dialog box. We need to provide a comment in it and click on **Approve** or **Reject**. We can assign multiple approvers with this mechanism, and we can also set whether we want to have approval from either approver.

In this case, we will click on **Approve**:

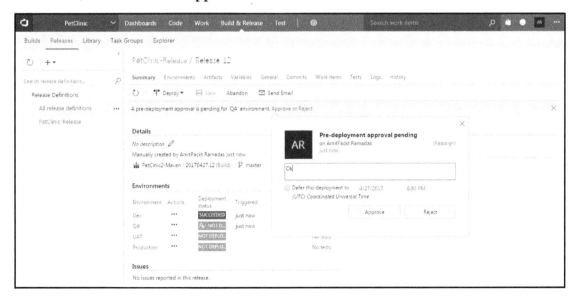

In **Logs**, now we can see that **Pre-deployment approval** is given and the rest of the processes are about to be executed for application deployment in the **Dev** slot:

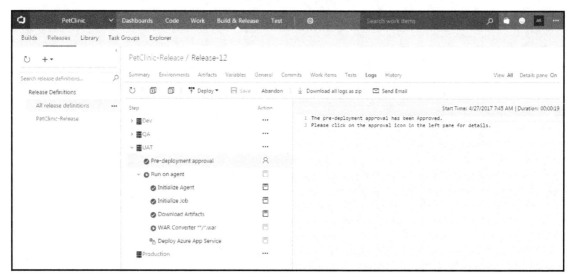

The artifact from the build definition will be downloaded so it can be converted to a ZIP file, and then we can deploy it into the **Dev** slot.

Once deployment to the **Dev** environment is successful, the execution process will wait for approval before it starts deployment into the **QA** slot.

We need to provide approval to get the execution going for the application deployment:

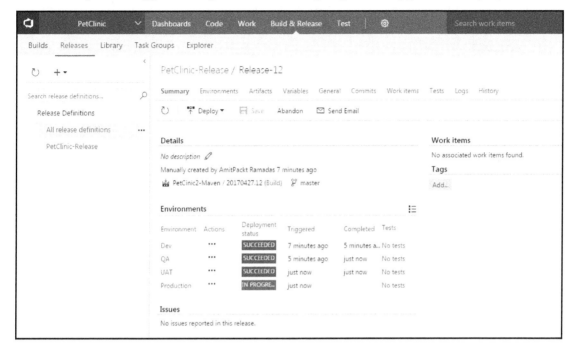

In the **Releases** section, we can see that there are four different environments, because we created those environments in our release definition.

We can see the current status of the release definition execution.

Deployment in the **Dev** slot of Azure web application is successful, while the next deployment is waiting for approval.

Give approvals for the **QA** slot deployment, and it will deploy a WAR file into the **QA** slot as well. We need to remember that the process is going to be the same, and nothing is going to change except some parameters during application deployment in the different Azure web application deployment slots.

We need to remember that every slot is a live web application, so if we want to see where the application is deployed and what else is going on behind the scene, then we can go to Kudu editor for each slot and verify the operations that have taken place for the deployment in each slot of Azure web application:

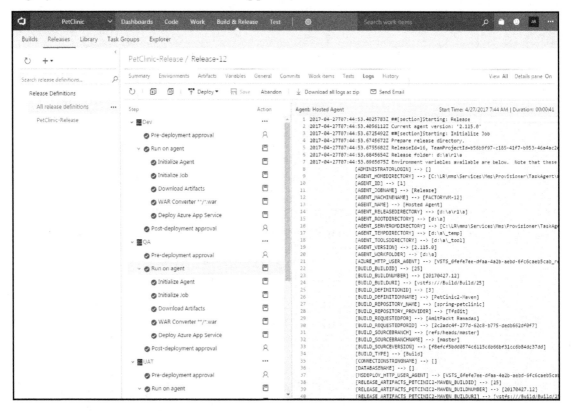

Similarly, deploy into the **UAT** or stage slot, and the **Production** slot too:

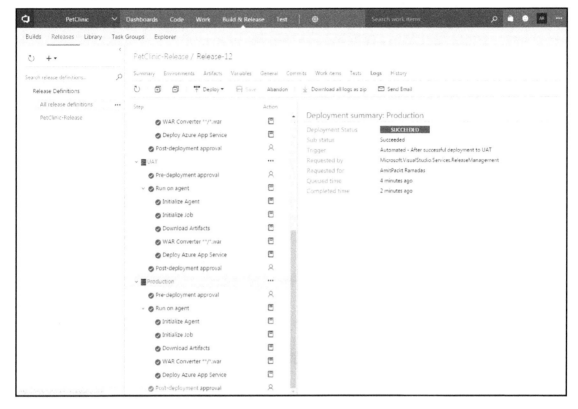

Now for self-exercise, commit some changes in the code of the application and observe how the build definition is executed, how it triggers the release definition after successful execution of the build job, and how an application is deployed on different slots. Once that is done, visit a specific URL of the deployment slot of an Azure web application and check whether application deployment in different environments is successful or not.

Summary

We are at the end of another milestone, and that is CD or continuous deployment of an application package into Azure Web Apps that can be hosted in ASE or non-ASE:

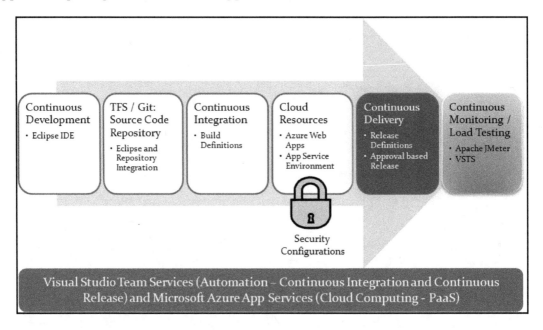

We covered the following things in detail:

- Creating a release definition to deploy a WAR file, an artifact, or an application package to Azure App Service
- Triggering a release definition execution based on successful build definition execution in VSTS
- Deploying a WAR file, an artifact, or an application package to Azure Web Apps deployment slots
- Converting a WAR file into a ZIP file using the Trackyon Advantage task so it can be distributed in the Azure Web Apps
- Creating or cloning multiple environments in the release definition to deploy Azure Web Apps to deployment slots
- Creating approval-based workflow for release management so the deployment process will start only after approval from designated stakeholders

So far so good.

We covered in detail the basic concepts related to DevOps, Eclipse, and TFS integration for a code repository, continuous integration using a TFS repository or Git repository, and VSTS, so any commit in code will result in build definition execution and trigger the release definition once the build definition has been executed successfully.

In a nutshell, we have covered continuous integration and CD or deployment using VSTS and Azure App Service hosted in ASE and non-ASE.

The next step is to maintain and manage the application hosted in ASE and non-ASE. We will also look into testing that can be performed in the different environments using Apache JMeter and VSTS.

Keep calm, the end is near!

7
Continuous Monitoring in Cloud Platform

The vision is really about empowering workers giving them all the information about what's going on so they can do a lot more than they've done in the past.

–Bill Gates

We have already completed the **Continuous Integration (CI)** and **Continuous Delivery (CD)** part of the vision for application deployment. In this chapter, we will cover another stepping stone in achieving end-to-end automation and that is continuous monitoring.

We will cover the importance of monitoring and the different ways to monitor and troubleshoot Azure Web Apps and **App Service Environment (ASE)** so we can ensure that applications remain problem free and highly available. The following topics will be covered in this chapter:

- Overview of continuous monitoring
- Azure Web Apps diagnose and monitoring
- Azure Application Insights for application monitoring
- Architecture of disaster recovery and high availability of Azure Web Apps
- Creating and configuring Traffic Manager with endpoints
- Performance testing using JMeter

Overview of continuous monitoring

CI and CD result in faster time-to-market. That being said, what if something goes wrong in this automated approach? Do we still need to do manual things or any automated or hybrid approach is available to monitor and manage this automation process?

Another question is what to monitor?

The following points can be some of the factors that needs monitoring:

- Static code analysis – code is not up to the quality gate defined
- Failure of the CI process
- Infrastructure or platform issues where an application needs to be deployed
- Application issues

If we observe properly, then it is all about notifications, infrastructure management, and application monitoring. We already configured notifications in VSTS for alerts and notifications in case of build or release failures. Let's see how we can monitor and manage Azure Web Apps or Azure App Service.

Continuous monitoring not only helps us identify the issue or find the main cause of issue, but it also helps to fix issues to keep operations smooth. Continuous monitoring is not only a part of production environment. It should not be. Why?

It is always better to detect errors in earlier phases or in non-production environments as we will have more time to fix, and there won't be any surprises in the production environment when the application goes live. It is always better to have monitoring in place for all the environments as we will have more experience, and most of the issues will be identified before the application goes into production and fixed.

Azure Web Apps troubleshooting and monitoring

Azure App Service / Azure Web Apps comes with **Diagnose and solve problems** to find out about the resource health and solutions to some common problems.

Let's dive deep into **Diagnose and solve problems** to get more details.

Diagnose and solve problems

Go to Azure **App Services** and select the Azure web application that we created earlier. Click on **Diagnose and solve problems**.

Another pane will be opened that will have the Health and Troubleshoot indicator and solution to some common problems.

We can see that the `MyPetClinicProj` Azure web application is available and running normally based on the status and the green indicator:

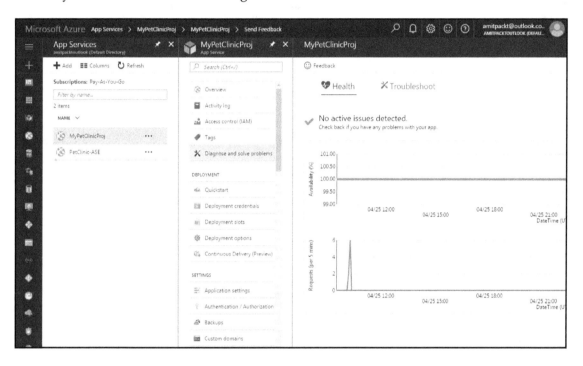

In my encounter with Azure Web Apps, I have faced the **HTTP 5xx** errors many times due to various reasons. It is also important to identify the root cause of an issue to fix it. However, there are some quick solution/suggestions given here.

Azure App Services – Resource health

We can get details on the health of a web application from **Diagnose and solve problems**:

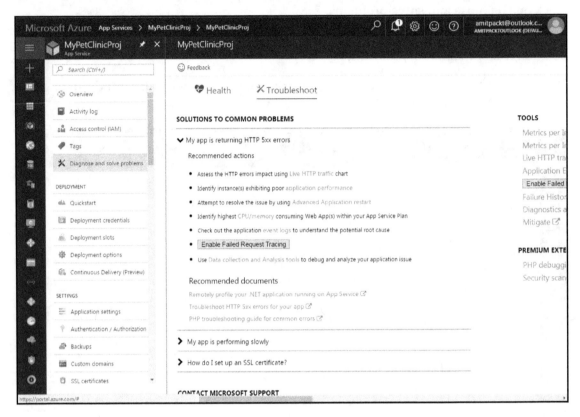

To get some more details on the availability of an application you can see the graph:

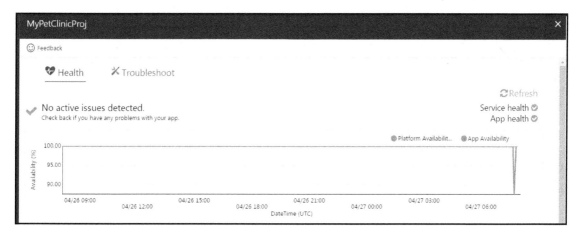

Azure App Services – HTTP live traffic

In solution to some common problems, we can assess live traffic to know whether existing resources can manage the current load or not.

If live traffic is normal then it may not be an issue and we should go a further step to troubleshoot the problem:

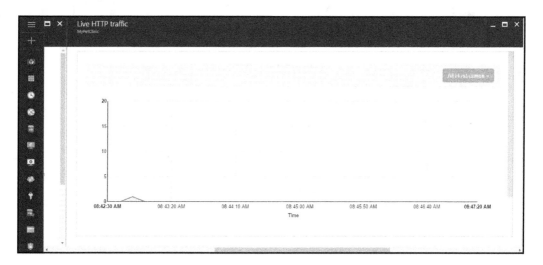

We can get HTTP live traffic based on one or all hostnames available in Azure App Services.

Azure App Services – Metrics per instance

We can also assess poor performances of instances available too.

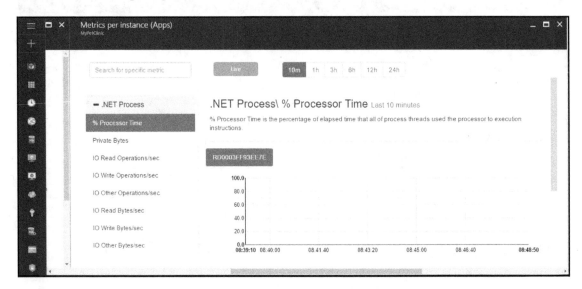

In **Site Metrics**, we can see the overall metrics values or instance-based metrics values to monitor. It shows the 2xx, 3xx, 4xx, Http server errors, and average response time:

Metrics per instances (Apps) also shows values of the CPU time and average memory utilization.

Apart from this, it also shows **Data In (MBytes)**, **Data Out (MBytes)**, **Local read bytes (MBytes)**, **Local written bytes (MBytes)**, **Network read bytes (MBytes)**, and **Network written bytes (MBytes)**:

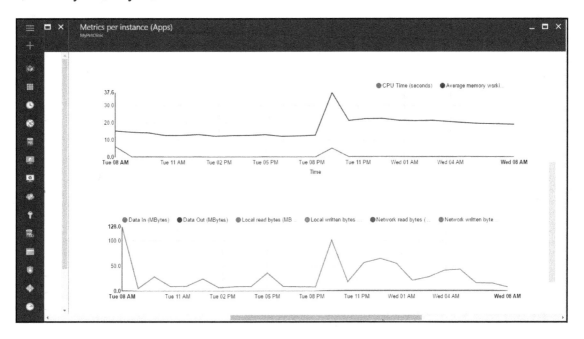

If all of these values are up to proper limits, then we can try to find other causes for failures, or else we can increase resources by scaling in or scaling out.

Azure App Services – Advanced Application restart

What if we have Azure Web Apps that have many instances, and we want to restart these instances one by one or with specific intervals after looking at some metrics of their performances?

We have one option to restart the Azure web application, but it will restart all the instances in one go. We can use **Advanced Application restart**.

We can decide **Restart Sleep timer** in between instances so the application doesn't go down:

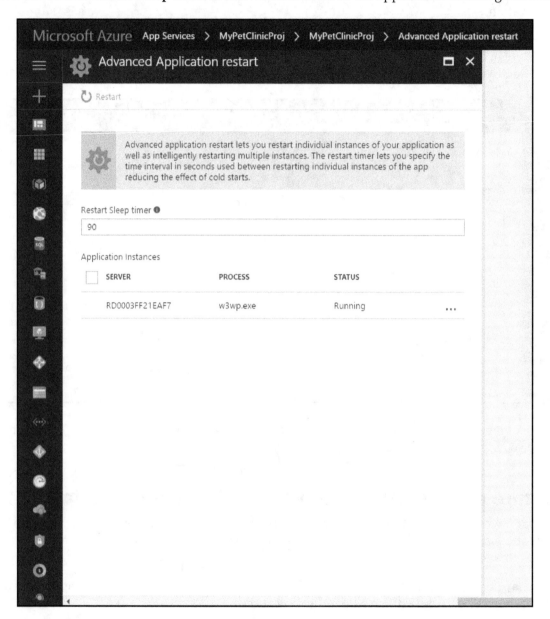

In our case, we have only one instance, so we can use either approach. Here we can select an instance and click on **Restart**.

It will ask for confirmation; click on **Yes**:

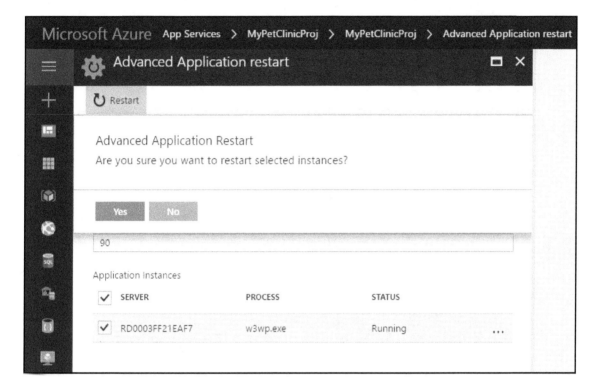

If we observe properly, then we see that it will only restart the `w3wp.exe` process and not the VM or instance:

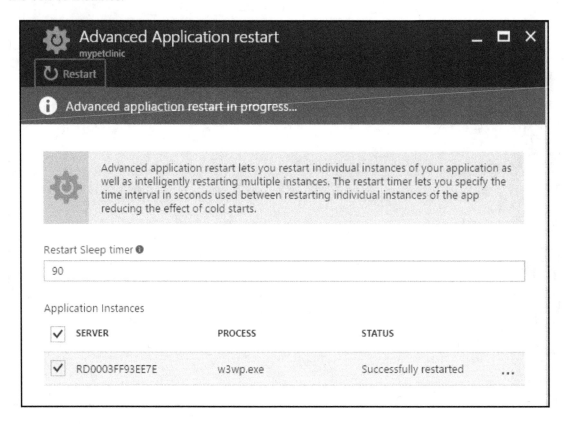

Once, instance is restarted successfully, we can access the Azure web application as usual.

Azure App Services – CPU and memory consumption

We can also get details regarding CPU and memory percentage to find the performance of the Azure web application and whether it is required to go for scaling operations:

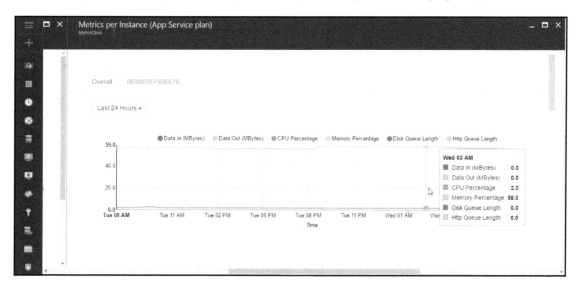

We already know that there is a main Azure web application, and other deployment slots are also available. We can get details of Azure Web Apps or sites in service plans too:

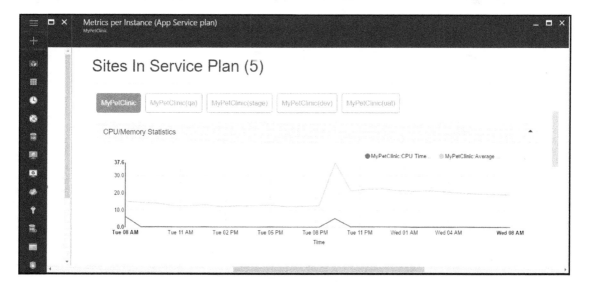

Here, we are looking at the details of the dev deployment slot of Azure Web Apps:

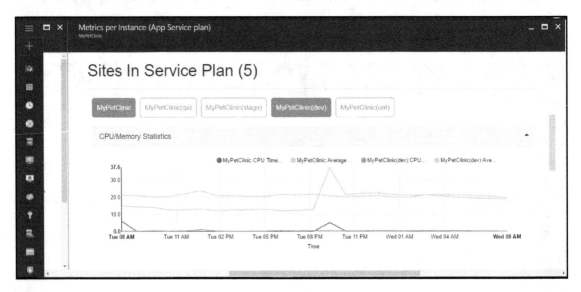

We can pick and choose the slots one at a time or select all of them to see CPU and memory utilization in ASP:

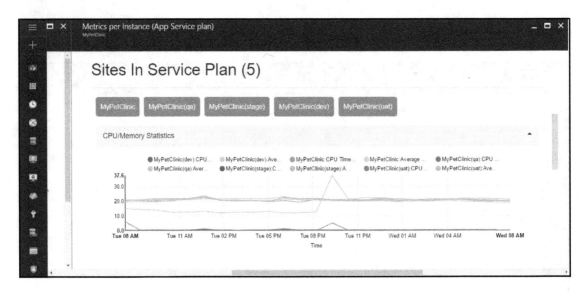

Similarly, we can verify **HTTP Statistics** for main Azure web application and deployment slots hosted in a specific ASP:

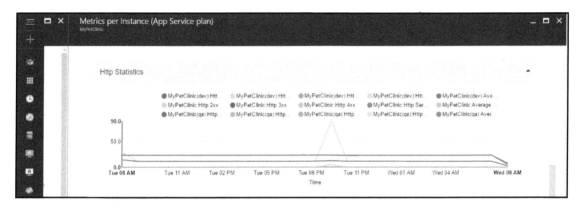

Similarly, we can verify **Network Statistics** for main Azure web application and deployment slots hosted in a specific ASP:

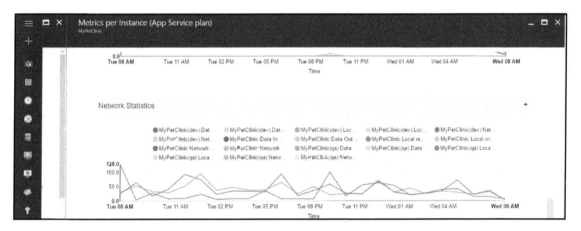

If we keep a cursor on a specific location of the chart, then we will get all the details of that specific point for main and other deployment slots:

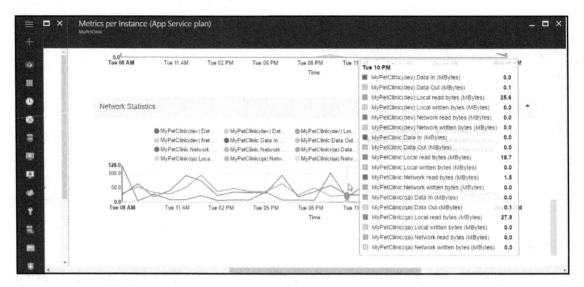

So we have seen the **Diagnose and solve problems** section until now. In the next section, we will look at details related to activity logs.

Azure App Services – Activity log

Activity log shows what actions have been performed in the Azure web application based on **Subscription**, **Resource group**, **Resource**, **Resource type**, **Operation**, **Timespan**, **Event category**, **Event severity**, and **Event initiated by**:

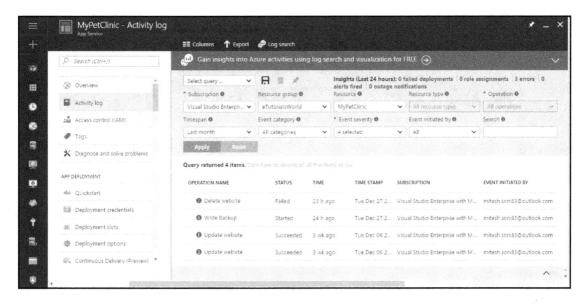

We can see different operations such as update, write, and delete operations.

In the next section, we will cover details on the Kudu editor in detail, which is very essential in terms of troubleshooting Azure App Services.

Kudu

Kudu is an engine behind different features in Azure Web Apps.

The GitHub URL for Kudu is `https://github.com/projectkudu/kudu`.

Go to Azure portal and then Azure **App Services**, select the Azure web application, go to the **DEVELOPMENT TOOLS** section, click on **Advanced Tools**, and click on **Go**.

Another way is to add `.scm` in the URL of the Azure web application.

Consider this example: `https://mypetclinic.azurewebsites.net` -> `https://mypetclinic.scm.azurewebsites.net`.

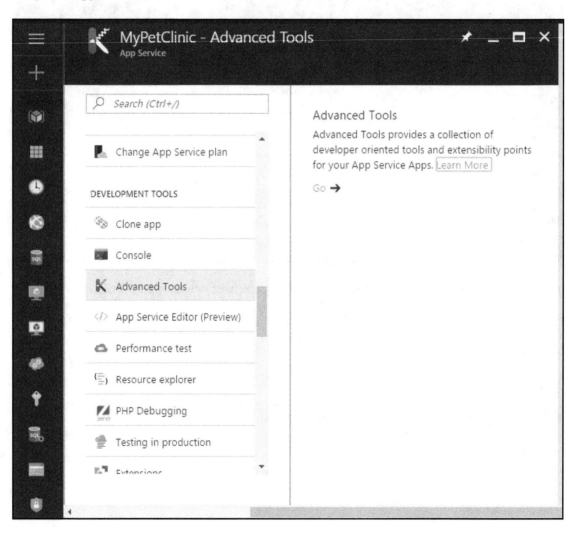

A Kudu editor will be opened, where we can see the folder structure of Azure web application, logs, and we can also perform some command-line operations and some troubleshooting as well:

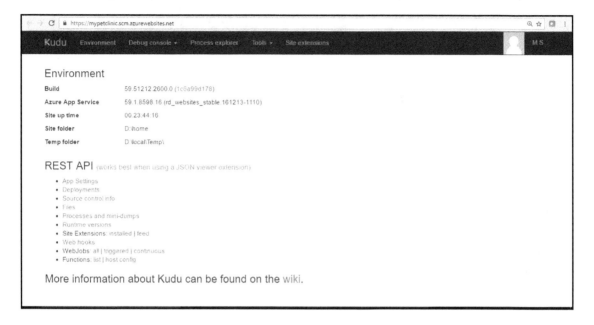

We can get all the environment- / system-related information by clicking on the menu item available in the Kudu editor:

Based on the system information, we can see that the Azure web application is hosted on a Windows instance.

Azure App Services – LogFiles

Click on the **Debug console** and select **CMD**.

Here we have `LogFiles` that will give detailed information on the Azure web application life cycle:

Click on `LogFiles` to see various kinds of log files stored here, and at the time of some issues we can utilize these log files for troubleshooting:

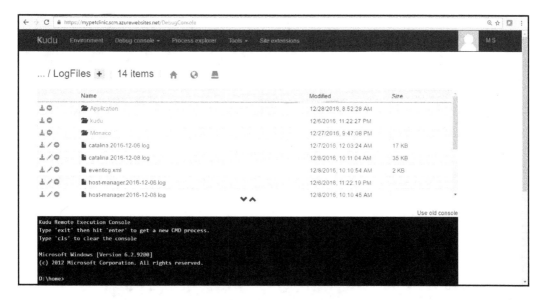

Just to see some log files, click on `eventlog.xml` and it will give us the process-related details:

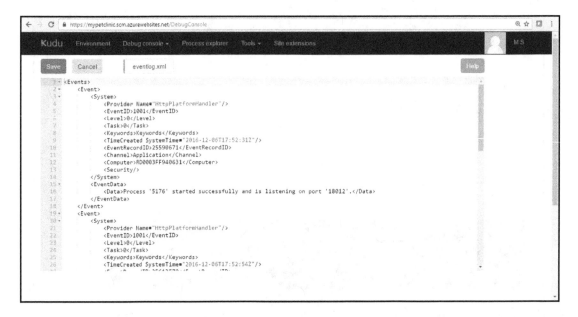

Click on **Debug console** and select **CMD**. Select the `site` folder. Here we can see many directories, out of which `wwwroot` is a significant directory:

Go to `wwwroot` and view the directory structure in it:

In the command window available, we can execute commands such as `ls` and `touch`.

Azure App Services (Kudu) – Process explorer

Click on **Process explorer** to get details on `w3wp.exe` and other properties:

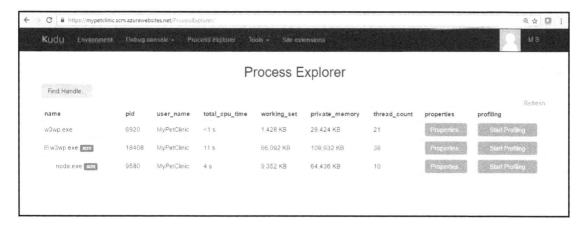

To get log stream based on the events, go to the Kudu editor, click on **Tools**, and then click on **Log stream**:

In the next subsection, we will see site extensions available in Kudu editor.

Azure App Services (Kudu) – Site extensions

Azure App Services provide a facility to use a set of tools for extensions. As of now, there is no site extension installed:

Click on **Gallery** and get more details on available site extensions:

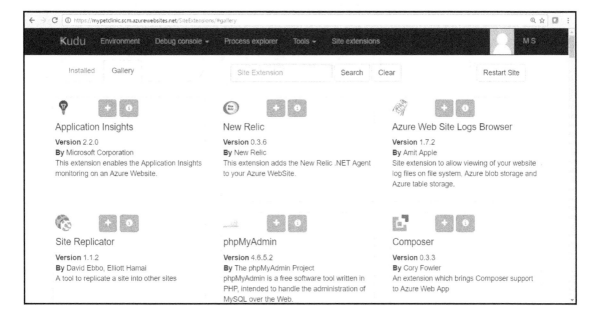

To describe how to install site extensions and utilize them is not in the scope of this book, and we are keeping it as a self-exercise.

Azure App Services (Kudu) – Autoheal

The **Autoheal** feature in Azure App Service helps us to observe, analyze, and mitigate issues if Azure App Service or Azure Web Apps is not giving performance as it should.

The **Observe** tab gives us average requests and average server errors in an existing state. If we get any issues here then we can set rules and define actions to mitigate them:

In the **Analyze** tab, we can get details related to **Diagnostics**, **Event Viewer**, **Metrics**, and **FREB Logs**.

Diagnostics settings for web applications allow us to collect and analyze the **Event Viewer** logs, take memory dumps of the process hosting your web application and analyze them for errors, collect and analyze the HTTP logs, collect and analyze the PHP error logs, analyze live PHP processes and generate a report for the process, thread and call stack information, and analyze live node processes and generate reports for the process, thread, and call stack information.

The **Event Viewer** tab contains information regarding all the events related to the Azure web application:

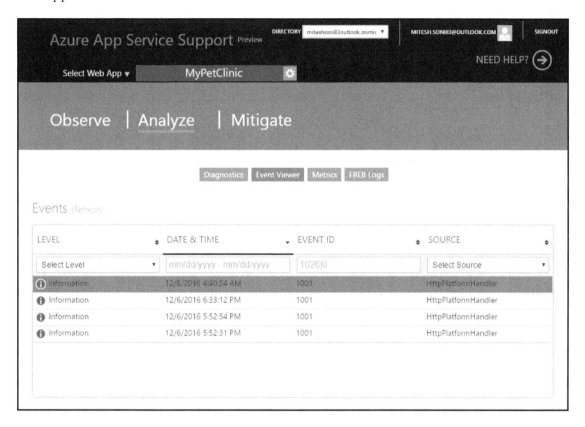

The **Metrics** tab contains details about **CPU/Memory Statistics**, **Http Statistics**, and **Network Statistics** based on the number of instances available to serve the Azure web application:

The following are **Http Statistics**:

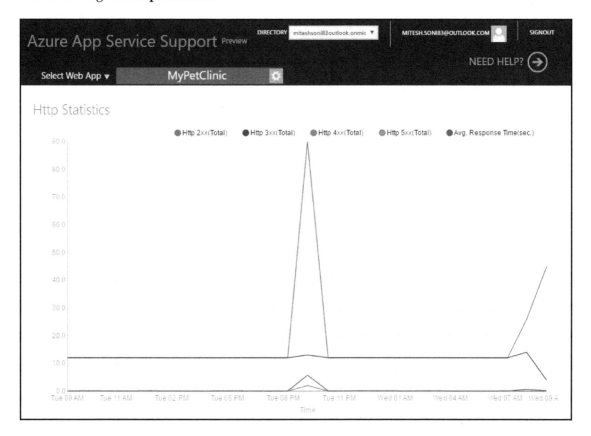

The following are **Network Statistics**:

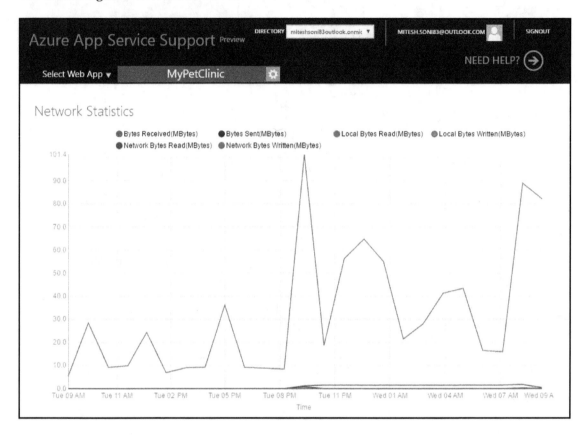

Now we are at the **Autoheal** junction.

By default, **Autoheal** is off for Azure web application. Switch it on:

Once we switch on **Autoheal**, we can configure **Max Requests**, **Status Code**, **Slow Requests**, and **Memory Private Set** related configurations and then set the action.

What if we want to recycle an application automatically once it serves a specific number of requests in a specific time interval?

We can add a rule in **Max Requests**:

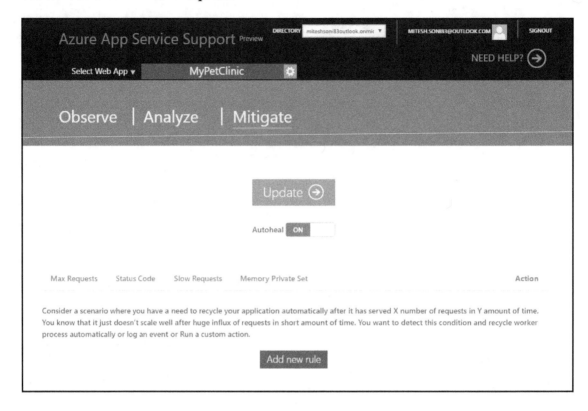

Provide details for **Number Of Requests** and **Interval (Seconds)** and click on the **Add** button:

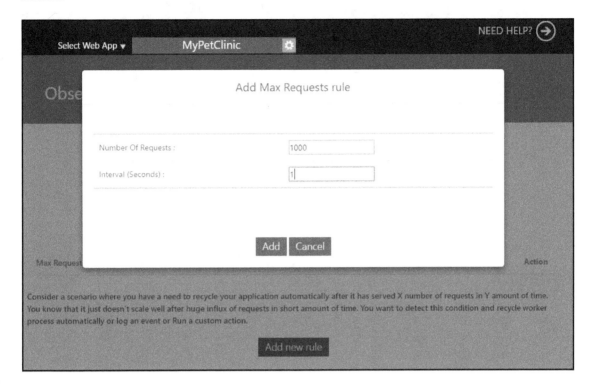

Click on the **Update** button to set rules for Azure web application:

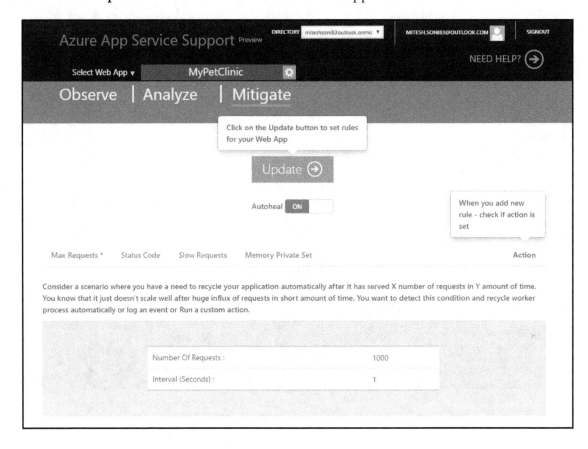

When we add a new rule, we need to set actions for it. We need to configure the actions to be performed when these following triggers are hit with **Action Execution Delay (Seconds)**. We can take the actions, namely **Recycle**, **Log Event**, and **Custom Action**:

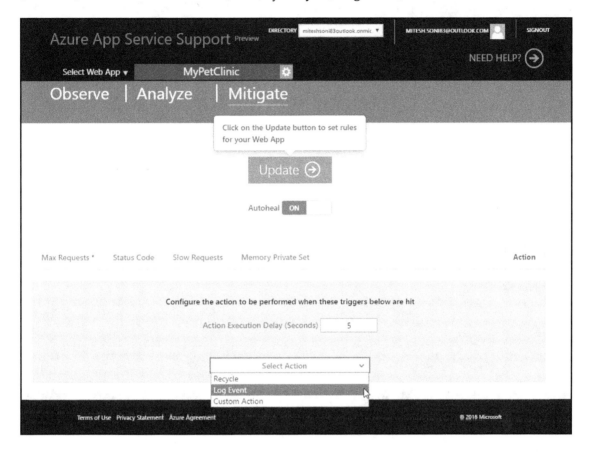

What if we would like to get notifications when the Azure web application starts throwing specific HTTP status codes, substatus code, or Win32 status codes?

We need to provide inputs such as **Number Of Requests, Status, SubStatus, Win32Status,** and **Interval (Seconds)**:

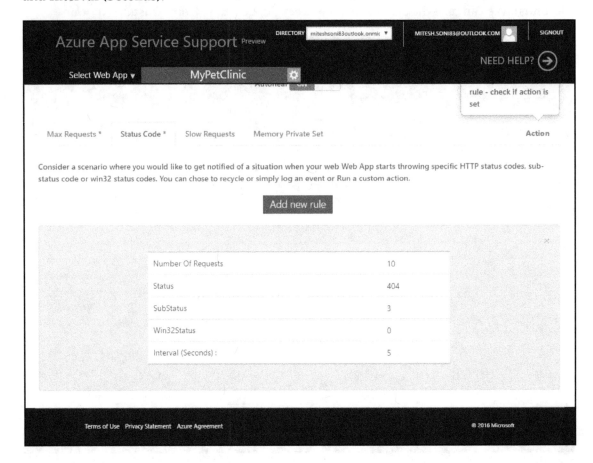

We can recycle, simply log an event, or run a custom action:

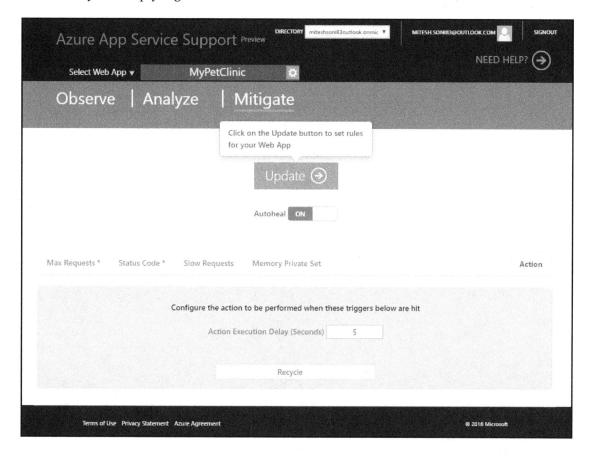

Once we set the action, click on **Update** to update the **Autoheal** settings in the Azure App Service **Support** portal:

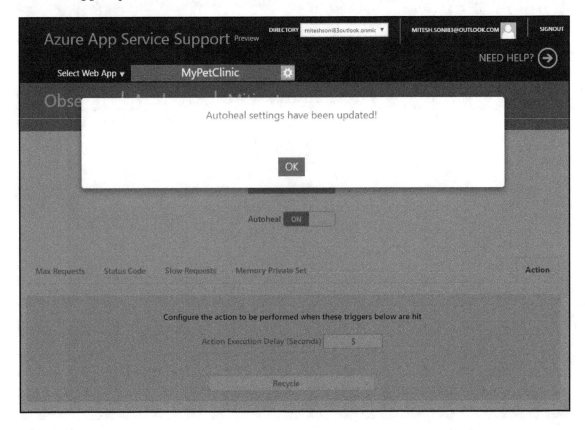

In the next section, we will cover Azure **Application Insights** for Azure App Service monitoring.

Azure Application Insights for application monitoring

In the Azure resource management portal, go to Azure **App Services**, select Azure web application, and go to the **MONITORING** section; click on **Application Insights**.

Application Insights helps us to identify and diagnose issues in Azure web applications. While we create Azure web application, we have the option to create **Application Insights** associated with Azure web application; in case we haven't done it, then we can create a new **Application Insights** resource too for our Azure web application:

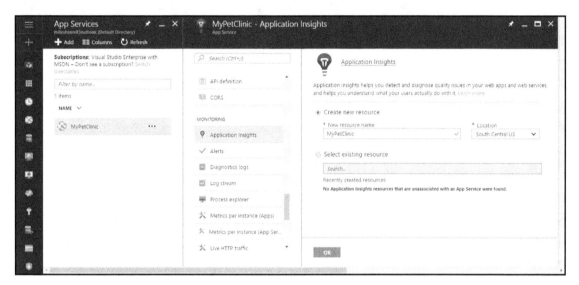

Once the **Application Insights** resource is created, we can access it from the Azure web application also. Let's try to check the availability of the Azure web application from different regions.

For more details, go to `https://docs.microsoft.com/en-us/azure/appl ication-insights/app-insights-overview`.

Azure web applications monitoring

We have seen different types of log files in Kudu editor. Let's see them in the Azure portal.

Diagnostics logs

To enable or disable **Diagnostic logs**, we need to go to Azure **App Services** in the Azure portal, click on the `MyPetClinic` Azure web application, and in the **MONITORING** section, click on **Diagnostic logs**:

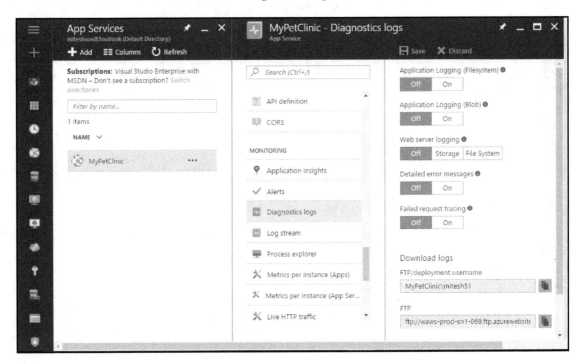

We can enable or disable different kinds of logs based on the need and environment:

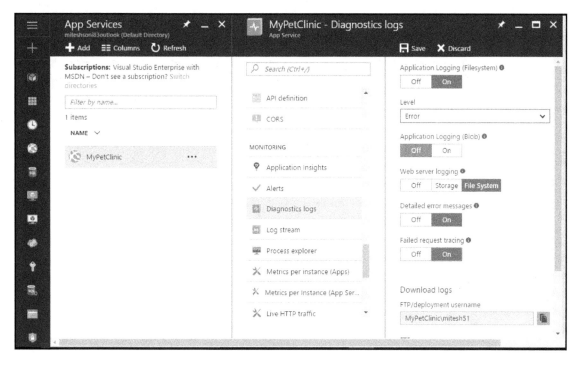

Once changes are done, click on the **Save** button.

Application events

We need to go to Azure **App Services** in the Azure portal, click on the `MyPetClinic` Azure web application, and in the **MONITORING** section, click on **Application events**:

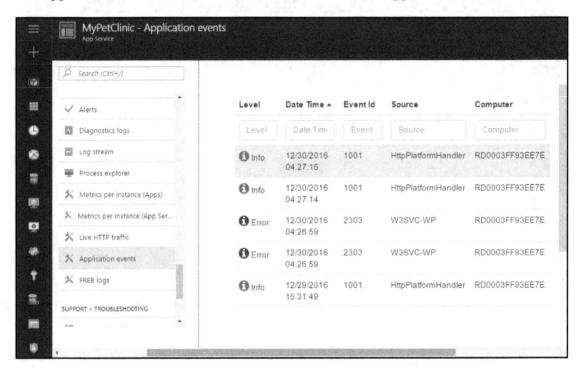

Application events provides details on information or errors that have occurred in the application life cycle.

FREB logs

FREB logs are useful when we want a detailed level of logs step by step. Most of the time, it will give details on which step Azure web application is finding issues for:

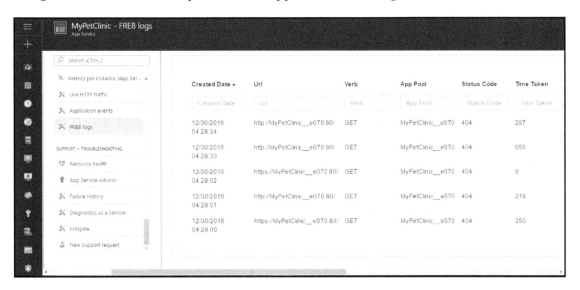

Scroll horizontally, and we'll find the name of the detailed log file as well. Click on it and we will get detailed step-by-step logs:

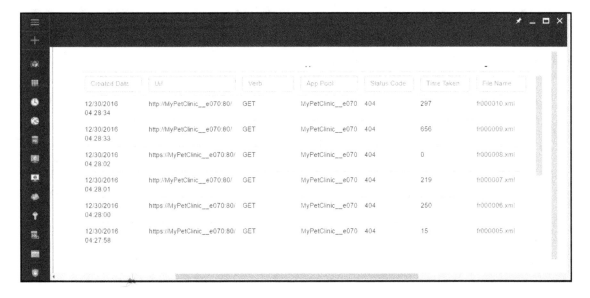

The log shows **Request Summary** with **Errors & Warnings** too:

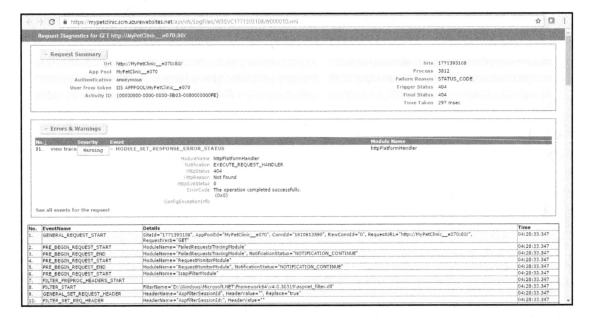

In the next section, we will see how to create a support request in Microsoft Azure portal.

Azure App Services support and troubleshooting

The Azure App Services **SUPPORT + TROUBLESHOOTING** section contains the **Resource health** option that we covered earlier in this chapter.

Resource health

Resource health shows the status of Azure web application and history also:

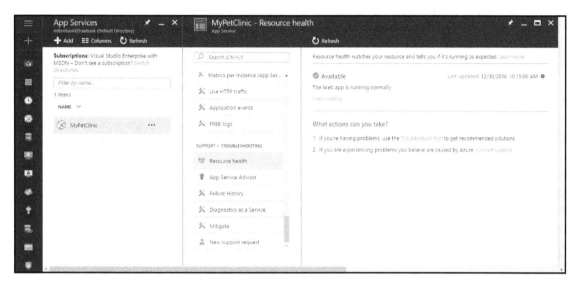

Failure History

SUPPORT + TROUBLESHOOTING also have **Failure History** that will tell us about **Availability** and **Request/Failures** of Azure web application:

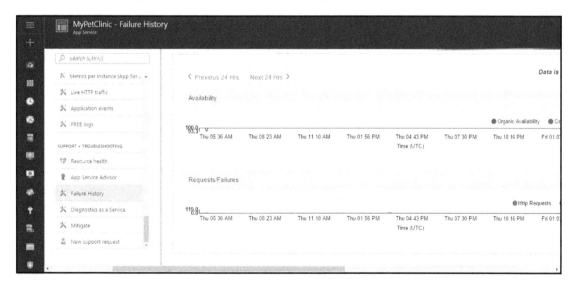

In the next subsection, we will create a new support request.

Support request

Often, we are in a situation where we don't know why Azure App Service is not running. There may be different reasons and even after advance restart, if it is not working then we may need to contact a Microsoft engineer for support. We can do it from Azure portal itself.

In **SUPPORT + TROUBLESHOOTING**, click on **New support request**.

In the **Basics** section, select **Issue type**, **Subscription**, **Service** (select **Web App (Windows)** in our case), **Resource** – Azure web application in which we are facing issues, and the support plan:

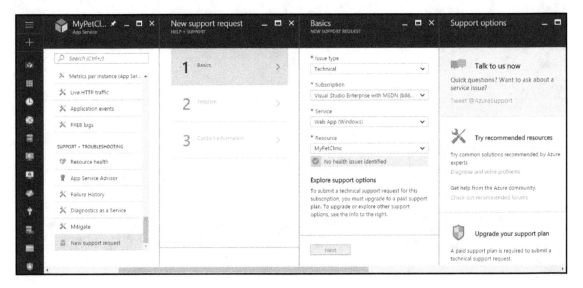

If support is not available, then we can upgrade the support plan to raise support request, then we can add details related to the problem and contact information:

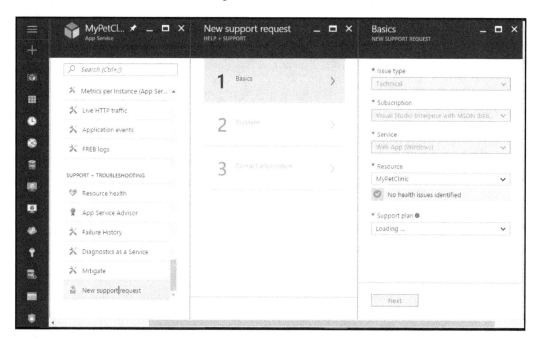

Once we raise a support request, based on the plan and problem, Microsoft representatives contact us and try to solve problems by suggesting solutions on mail or on call and by desktop sharing.

We have covered different ways to monitor and manage Azure web application so we can troubleshoot common problems and monitor Azure web application resources. In the next section, we will cover how to make Azure web applications highly available.

Architecture of disaster recovery and high availability of Azure web applications

Microsoft Azure traffic manager allows failover, performance, or weighted round robin methods to determine how a request can be satisfied using Azure App Services. Traffic manager applies the traffic routing method to each request and routing method decides how that request will be served and by which endpoint. Endpoints are nothing but Azure web application in our context. We have two Azure web applications so we can consider them as our endpoint.

In the **Resource Management** portal, the terms have been changed, as given here:

- The Load-balancing method is known as the Traffic-routing method now
- The Failover method is known as the Priority method
- The Round-robin method is known as the Weighted method
- The Performance method is known as the Performance method

To make Azure web application highly available, let's consider a scenario where our `PetClinic` application is deployed in a different ASP.

If an ASP is created in a different region, then even if the Azure web application hosted in another region goes down, we should be able to access the `PetClinic` application as it is also hosted in another region.

Let's create an ASP in a different region than the existing Azure web application's ASP.

 We need to make sure that both the ASPs have to be in the Standard pricing tier to achieve high availability.

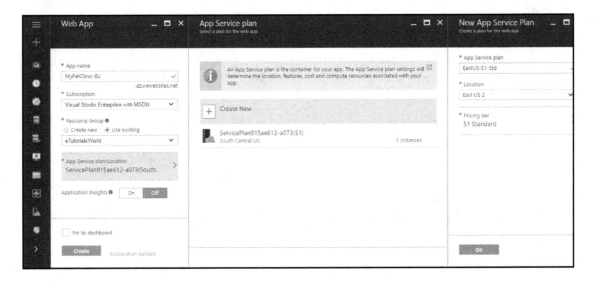

Once the ASP is created, create an Azure web application in the same ASP. Click on **Create**:

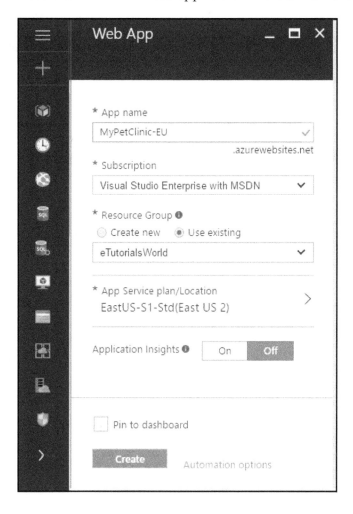

Deploy the `PetClinic` web application to the newly created Azure web application using VSTS:

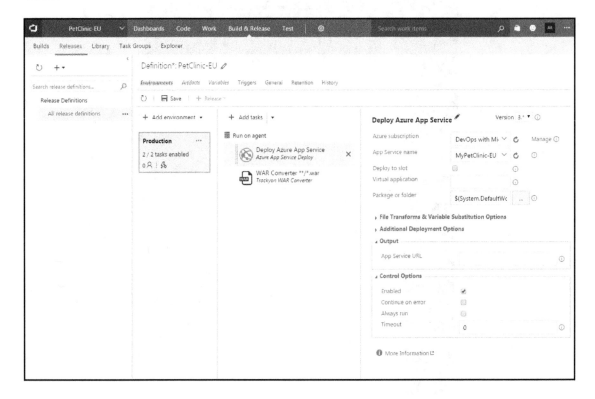

Check whether the application is deployed properly or not. This is our east US-based Azure web application:

Once we have the second Azure web application ready, we can create the traffic manager and configure endpoints.

Creating and configuring Traffic Manager with endpoints

Select **Traffic Manager profiles** from the left-hand side menu bar. Click on **+Add**. Enter **Name**, **Resource group**, and other details. Click on **Create**:

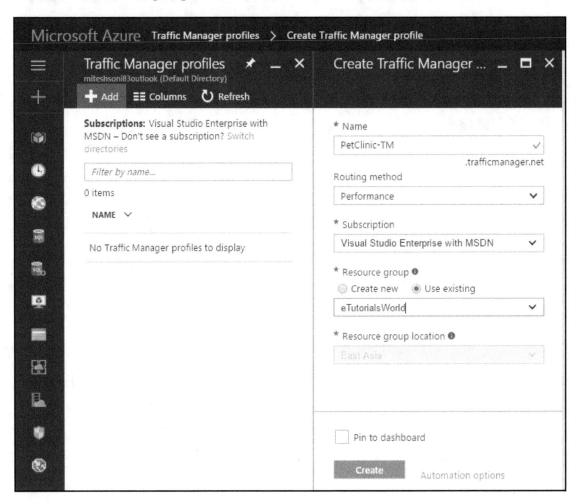

Once the traffic manager profile is created, verify the **Overview** section. The **Monitor status** is **Inactive**, the **Routing method** is **Performance**, and there are no endpoints in the given list. Hence our first task should be to create an endpoint that will serve the request:

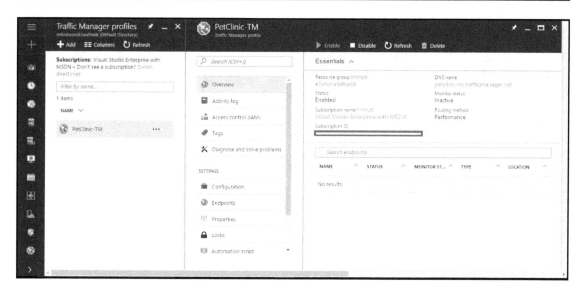

In **SETTINGS**, click on the **Endpoints**; it will open a pane. Click on **+Add** to add an endpoint. Select **Azure endpoint** as **Type**, enter the name of the endpoint, select **App Service** as **Target resource type** so we can select Azure web application as an endpoint:

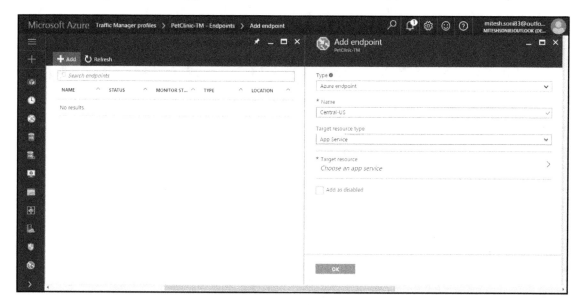

Click on **Target resource** and select the first Azure web application that we created:

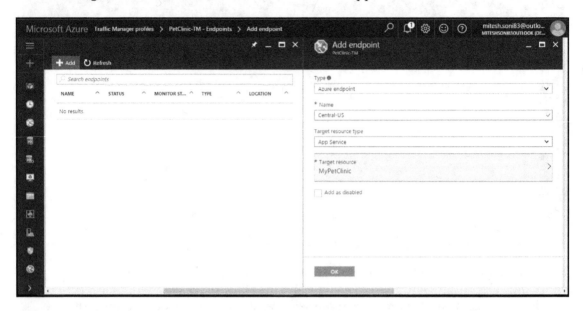

Similarly, add another endpoint for the second Azure web application:

Let's observe the status of **Monitor status** of the traffic manager profile and the status of the endpoints in the Azure portal.

Here, **Monitor status** is **CheckingEndPoints**:

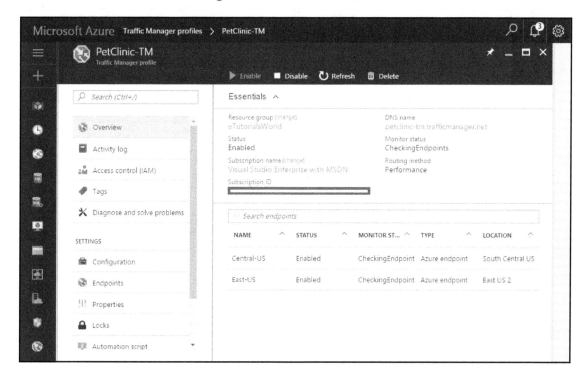

Once the status of the endpoint is verified, the **Monitor status** will be **Online** for the endpoint:

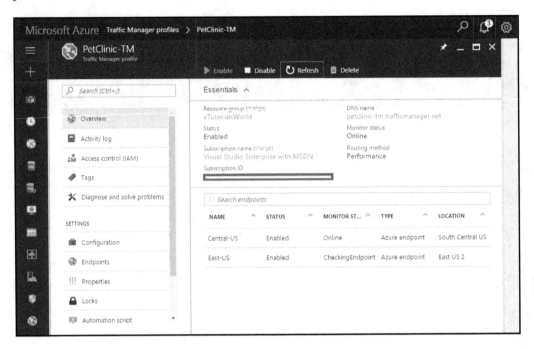

Visit the DNS name assigned to the traffic manager profile. As we have assigned the Azure web application as endpoints, it will be redirected to the PetClinic application:

Verify both the endpoints in the Azure portal. Both are online now:

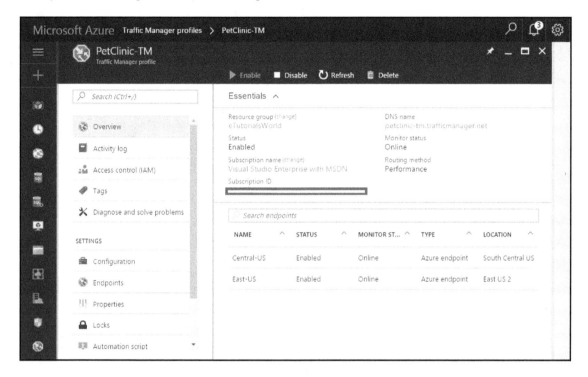

Now let's try to simulate failure by disabling the **East-US** endpoint and see whether requests are automatically redirected to another endpoint or not.

Go to the **East-US** endpoint and click on **Edit**:

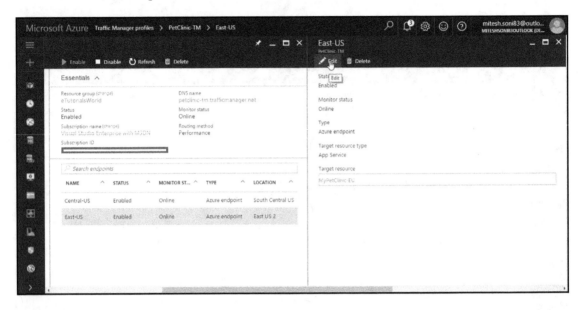

Disable the **East-US** endpoint and click on **Save**:

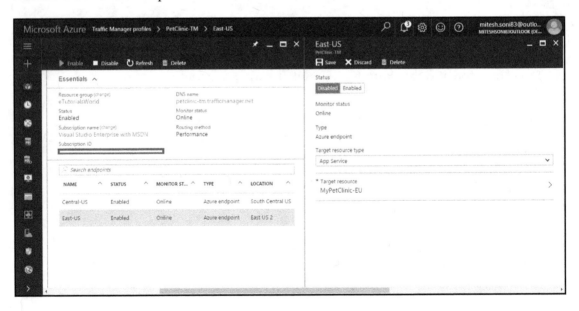

Verify the **Monitor status** of the endpoint that we disabled:

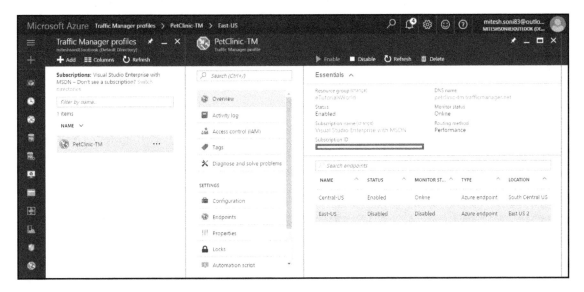

Now visit the traffic manager profile DNS again and check whether it is redirected to another endpoint or not. Spot the difference in the **HOME** page:

Try out other routing methods based on the need of an application as a self-exercise.

Load testing using a URL-based test and Apache JMeter

Once we have deployed our application in Azure App Services successfully, we can perform load testing on Azure App Service or Azure Web Apps. Let's see how we can use VSTS to perform testing.

URL-based test

In the top menu bar, click on **Test** and then click on **Load tests**. Let's create our first test in VSTS and execute it:

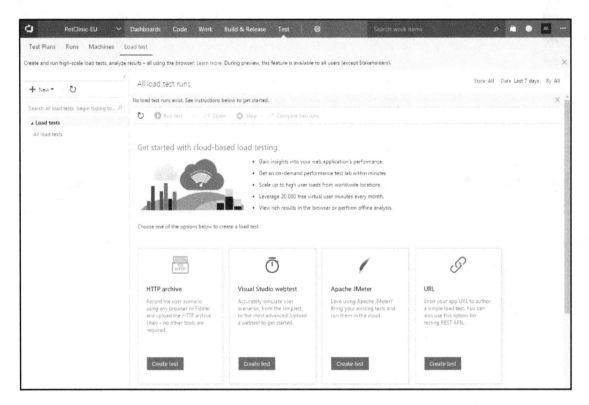

1. Click on **+New** and select **URL based test**:

2. Verify the **HTTP method** and **URL**:

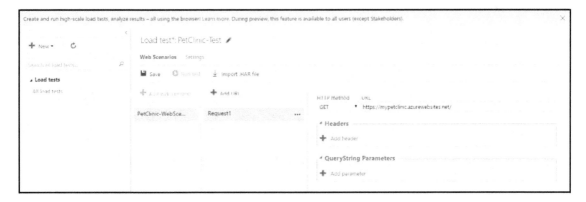

3. Click on **Settings** and provide inputs in different parameters based on need:

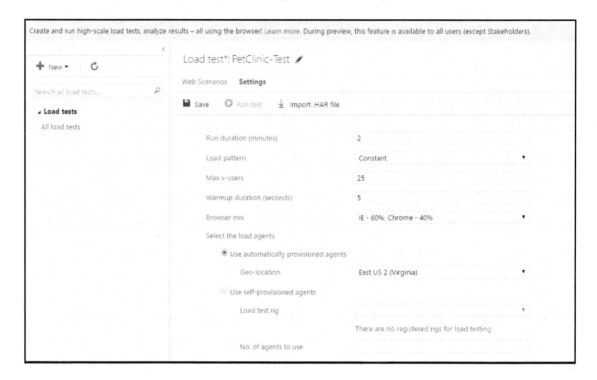

4. Click on **Save** and click on **Run test**:

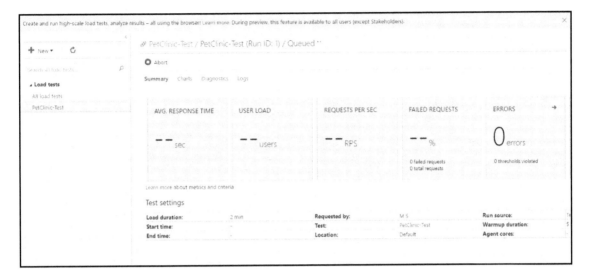

5. Load testing is in progress:

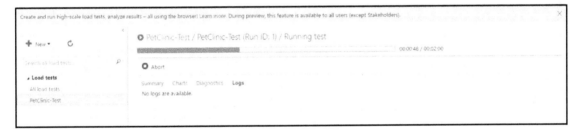

6. Verify the complete test data as and when it is available in the VSTS portal:

7. Verify the final summary of URL-based test execution in VSTS:

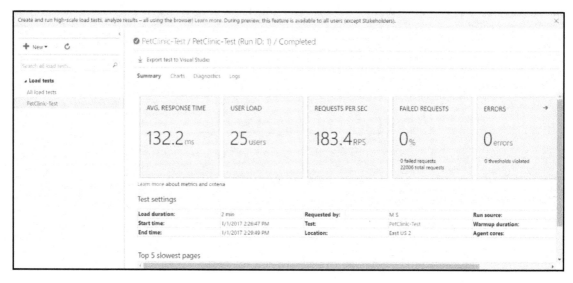

8. We will also get the **Performance** and **Throughput** charts after the test execution in VSTS:

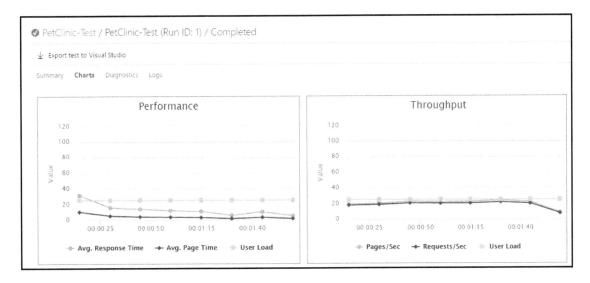

9. Verify **Tests** and **Errors** related details too:

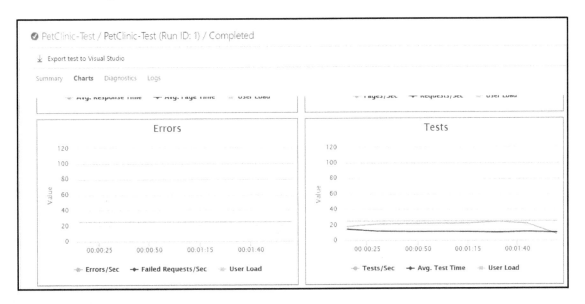

We have seen how the URL-based test can be performed on Azure web application. In the next section, we will cover how to use Apache JMeter for load testing.

Apache JMeter

In this chapter, we'll look into how to execute Apache JMeter testing. We will execute a load test on the `Petclinic` application deployed on Azure App Services.

 For more details on this topic, refer to `http://jmeter.apache.org/userm anual/`.

Download Apache JMeter from `http://jmeter.apache.org/`. Start it and create a **Thread Group** in Apache JMeter. Here, we mention number of users, ramp up period, and loop count:

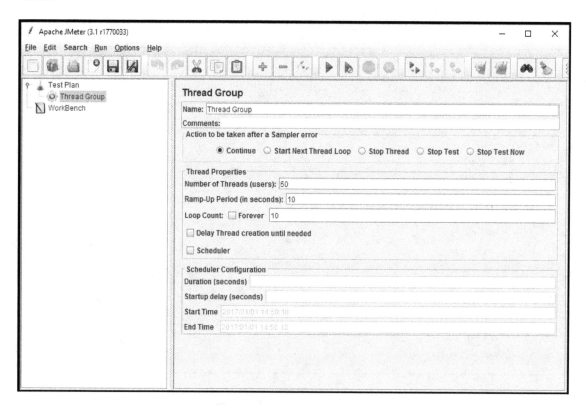

1. Right-click on the **Thread Group** and click on **Add**.
2. Select **Sampler**, and click on **HTTP Request**:

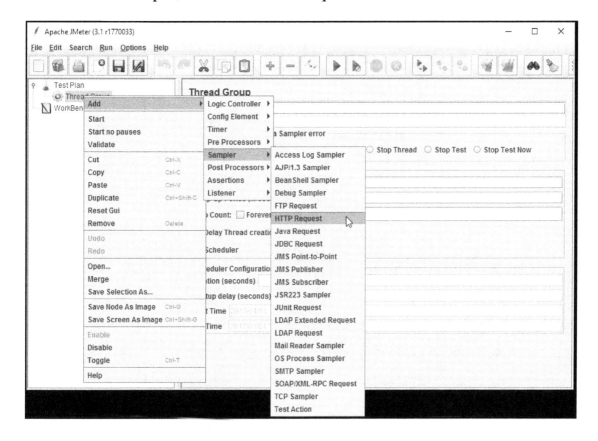

3. Provide the Azure web application URL in the server name and select HTTPS protocol:

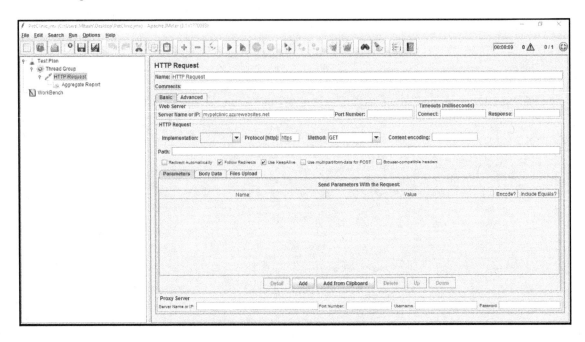

4. Execute the test and verify the result in Apache JMeter:

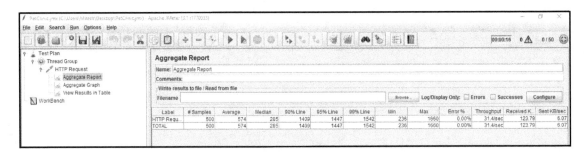

5. Add **Aggregate Graph** in the **HTTP Request**:

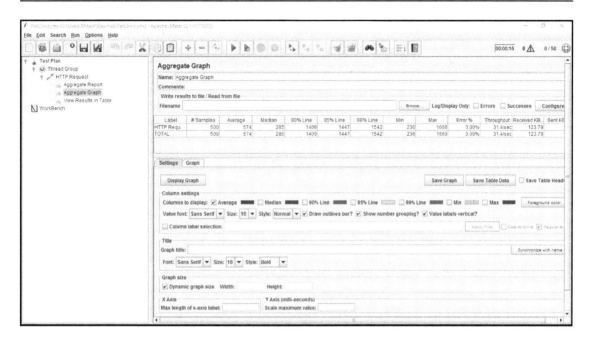

6. After the load test execution, verify the graph:

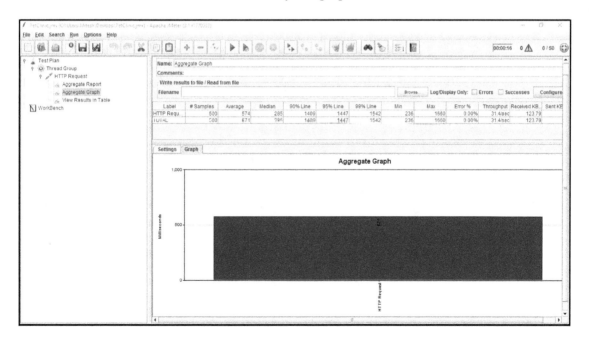

7. For more details, click on **View Results in Table:**

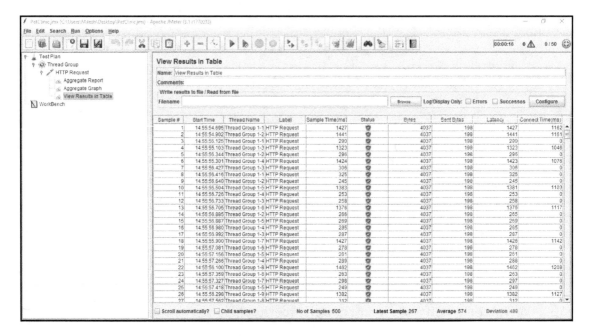

We can execute the Apache JMeter test in VSTS too. So, let's execute it:

1. Click on **+New** and select **Apache JMeter test:**

We will use the same JMX file that we have used earlier to load test the Azure web application.

2. Select **Load duration** and **Load location** as well. Click on **Run Test**:

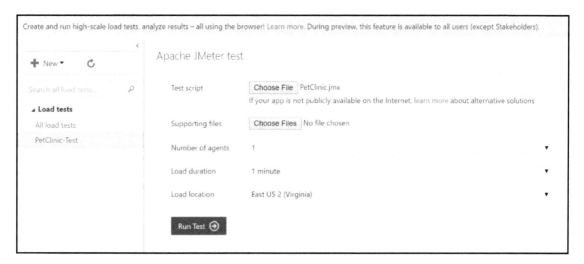

All listeners that we have used earlier might not be supported in VSTS, so we will remove all that are not relevant.

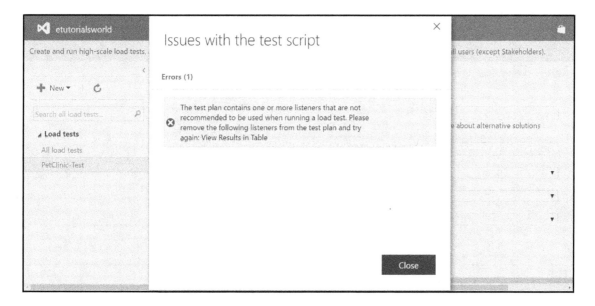

3. Execute the load test again:

4. Verify its execution status in VSTS:

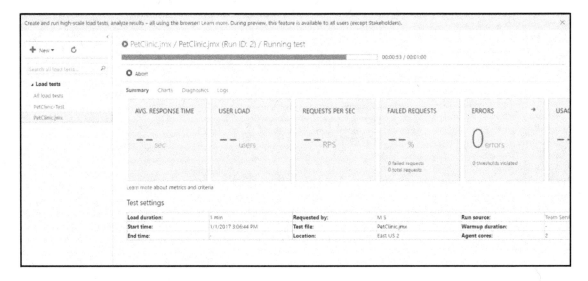

5. Go to the `MyPetClinic` Azure web application and click on **Overview** to get the metrics details. Observe the number of requests:

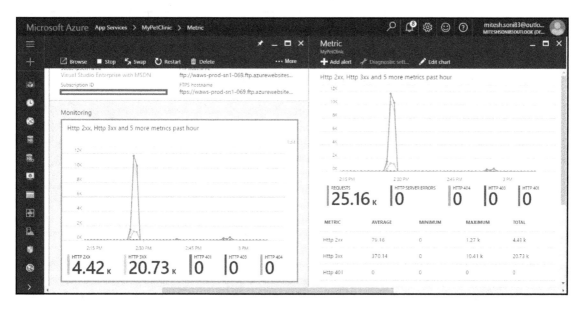

Now we are at the end of our journey. With monitoring, troubleshooting, and load testing, we are ending our journey.

Summary

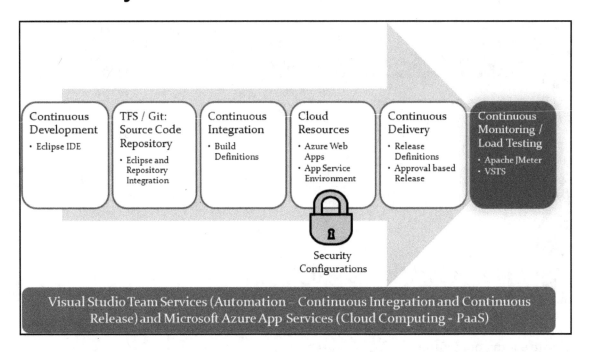

In this chapter, we covered basic Azure App Service monitoring, basic troubleshooting, Kudu editor, traffic manager for load balancing using Azure App Service endpoints, URL-based tests in VSTS, load testing with Apache JMeter, and executing Apache JMeter tests from VSTS.

So, in this book we covered continuous integration, continuous delivery, Microsoft Azure App Services (PaaS) to deploy our sample JEE-based application, basic monitoring and troubleshooting available in Azure, and load testing available in VSTS.

Every new beginning comes from some other beginning's end
- Seneca

Index

More from the Author

Here are some books authored/being authored by Mitesh Soni with Packt Publishing:

Jenkins Essentials

Continuous Integration – setting up the stage for a DevOps culture

DevOps for Web Development

Achieve the Continuous Integration and Continuous Delivery of your web applications with ease

DevOps Bootcamp

A fast-paced guide to implement DevOps with ease

www.ingramcontent.com/pod-product-compliance
Lightning Source LLC
LaVergne TN
LVHW081329050326
832903LV00024B/1081